RASTER GRAPHICS HANDBOOK

Second Edition

Conrac Division, Conrac Corporation

VNR VAN NOSTRAND REINHOLD COMPANY
——————————————————— New York

Copyright © 1985 by Van Nostrand Reinhold Company Inc.

Library of Congress Catalog Card Number: 84–11816
ISBN: 0–442–21608–4

Manufactured in the United States of America

Published by Van Nostrand Reinhold Company Inc.
135 West 50th Street
New York, New York 10020

Van Nostrand Reinhold Company Limited
Molly Millars Lane
Wokingham, Berkshire RG11 2PY, England

Van Nostrand Reinhold
480 Latrobe Street
Melbourne, Victoria 3000, Australia

Macmillan of Canada
Division of Gage Publishing Limited
164 Commander Boulevard
Agincourt, Ontario MIS 3C7, Canada

15 14 13 12 11 10 9 8 7 6 5 4 3

Library of Congress Cataloging in Publication Data

Main entry under title:

Raster graphics handbook.

    Includes index.
    1. Computer graphics. I. Conrac Corporation.
Conrac Division.
T385.R37 1984   001.64′43   84–11816
ISBN 0–442–21608–4

Preface

Within months after publication, the first edition of the *Raster Graphics Handbook* became a collector's item. Over 50,000 copies were printed and distributed. Yet the demand for a unique text that brought together the disparate worlds of analog television and digital computers has continued to grow with the proliferation of computer-driven CRT displays and digital broadcast-TV equipment.

This second edition of the *Raster Graphics Handbook* answers that need. It is also an appropriate time to look back and examine why the engineering staff at the Conrac Division, Conrac Corporation, chose to author the original text.

History does not provide us with the names of the individuals who first tried to create line-type graphics on a raster-scan color CRT. We can assume, however, that if any of the early experiments were performed on home-television receivers, the results were disappointing. Mass-produced TV sets deliver a remarkable level of technology, but the competitive consumer marketplace also dictates that so long as viewer satisfaction is not seriously affected, corners must be cut— literally. The quality of a broadcast-TV image is defined, therefore, at the center of the screen. From a TV director's viewpoint, there are actually advantages to be gained from the fact that the image becomes less sharp and defined as the eye moves away from the center of interest.

Most computer-graphics applications, by comparison, require uniform quality across the entire screen, and from one display device to the next. In the case of business graphics, for example, the title of a chart is likely to be at the top of the screen or in the upper left corner. Colors must be true, moreover, from one edge of the screen to the other. And bar or pie charts would become confusing or meaningless if subjected to non-linearities that would be all-but-invisible to a person watching a speech or a soap opera.

Fortunately, however, at least one company, Conrac, was already producing raster-scan color monitors that could meet the new requirements—but for a different set of reasons. Conrac products played a pivotal role, therefore, in the transition from stroke-writing monochrome CRT's to raster-scan color monitors.

For almost two decades, Conrac monitors had been the arbiters, the platinum meter stick, for the television broadcast industry. Nearly every major studio in the country was, and still is, equipped with Conrac monitors to assure consistent broadcast quality. Any question or dispute over color rendition, camera work, or the quality of the television signal itself is generally settled by reference to a Conrac monitor.

As computer graphics emerged from the engineering laboratory and became a commercial force, Conrac found, to its initial surprise, that over half of its monitor production was going to this new, demanding application. The company also discovered that it was talking to a new class of system designers and users with little or no background in television or CRT technology. Its established broadcast-industry base was being simultaneously transformed by an infusion of equally foreign digital devices for storing pictures and creating special effects. The analog and digital worlds were coming together from both sides, with Conrac at the center. Clearly there was a need for communication, for a translation of terms and concepts. The *Raster Graphics Handbook* was Conrac's response.

If anything, the demand for better communication and understanding has increased sharply during the intervening years. Computer graphics is on its way to becoming a dominant force not only in computer technology, but in our culture and our view of the world. The second edition of the *Handbook* comes, then, at a propitious moment.

Edmund Van Deusen
Editorial Consultant

Laguna Beach
California

Contents

1
Purpose and Scope
of the Handbook

Two separate technologies have converged to make "raster graphics" the dominant visual image of the 1980s—in business, science, industry, education, and the home.

Alphanumeric raster-scan CRT displays already form the principal communication link between computer users and their hardware/software systems. As computer installations expand into the millions, worldwide, there is an accelerating trend toward the use of monochrome and full-color graphic images to enhance the information transfer at this vital "video" interface.

Accelerating changes are also occurring in the television industry. Computer-generated captions, graphics, and special effects have already transformed the appearance of newscasts and commercials. Computer processing is now altering the form of the television signal itself. TV cameras and receivers are analog devices, but the quality of the raster display can be significantly improved (or restored) by digital techniques. Computer-controlled, "all-digital" broadcast studios and teleproduction facilities will soon be a practical reality.

A SYNERGISTIC INTERCHANGE

Both technologies, computer and television, have benefited from each other's accomplishments. The basic display device for computer-generated raster graphics is the CRT monitor—a non-broadcast version of the standard TV receiver. Decades of mass production experience have refined the receiver CRT and raster-scan circuits to a high level of reliability and cost effectiveness. Adaptation to computer graphics has required only incremental improvements. (In the case of

1

lower-performance "alphagraphic" applications, the CRT package may be actually downgraded to provide further savings in material and assembly costs.)

Until the past few years, however, the full potential of raster graphics has been beyond the reach of computer-system designers. All of the major benefits offered by the raster-scan technique—photographic detail, cinematic animation, an unlimited range of colors—require the support of systems with large-scale, random-access memories and, in the case of animation, high-speed computational capabilities devoted exclusively to the display task. Only a few specialized applications, such as medical instrumentation and flight simulation, could justify the hardware investment.

Technical competition within the computer industry has released graphics-system designers from these restrictions. Large-scale integration has dropped the price of digital memory by a factor of a hundred to one. Hardware function generators are available to perform the highly repetitive tasks which characterize most display programs. Control and timing functions can be accomplished by versatile, low-cost microprocessors. The result, predictably, has been a surge of development interest in raster graphics, helping to make computer graphics the fastest growing segment within an expanding computer industry.

Television system designers have been equally quick to take advantage of the technical advances in computer hardware. Earlier digital processing had been performed "on the fly," with only a few lines of raster data stored in memory. The new, lower-cost memory modules now allow complete frames to be captured—economically—and manipulated under computer control. Weather maps have become animated, teachers are able to add their own notations to instructional materials shown on closed-circuit monitors, and advertising agencies can rearrange the visual elements within a commercial until exactly the desired effect has been achieved.

Most important, the gap between television and computer-based graphics hardware has become almost non-existent. Interfacing can be accomplished with off-the-shelf conversion modules. This means that all of television's new digital (and analog) "black boxes" can be readily adapted to computer graphics, expanding its potential in ways which are just being explored.

CONRAC'S ROLE

A major purpose of the Conrac Raster Graphics Handbook is to facilitate this continuing, synergistic interchange between the television and computer technologies. The Conrac Division of Conrac Corporation has, in fact, served as a catalyst and technical leader in both fields for a number of years. Conrac supplied graphics-display units for one of the earliest computer-controlled utility systems. For over a quarter of a century Conrac has also been the country's leading supplier of high-performance television monitors.

Raster graphics combines the company's two historical strengths. Yet the monitor is only part of a total graphics system. The scope of this Handbook reflects this fact. The text draws on the knowledge and background of the Conrac engineering staff as these resources apply to the entire field of raster graphics, independent of Conrac's specific products.

The principal emphasis is on the design of computer-based systems. Where applicable, television design concepts, equipment, and standards are incorporated into the discussion. When possible, a unifying terminology has been used, drawing from both disciplines. The authors have also felt free to include ideas and equipment descriptions from other fields which seem, on the surface, far removed from raster graphics. Included in this category would be circuit concepts and hardware developed for video games, cable-television networks, and facsimile systems.

The Handbook presumes a familiarity with computer technology, and is addressed to individuals who are actively engaged in the design of raster graphics systems. The goal is to present the broadest possible overview of the current state-of-the-art in this rapidly evolving technology and, at the same time, point the way toward developments which will influence the design of graphics systems in the foreseeable future.

The text is also organized so that it can serve as a valuable checklist for readers who are evaluating the capabilities of systems now being offered. The entry cost into raster graphics can range from a few hundred to over a half-million dollars. Clearly, there are economic tradeoffs which may or may not limit the future potential of the selected system. There are, too, a variety of performance features which may have little value technically, but are necessary in terms of subjective "appeal." Technology aside, the human factor remains an important variable, perhaps the most important variable, in every raster-graphics equation.

"RASTER GRAPHICS"

The emergence of a higher-performance, more cost-effective raster-scan CRT display has required a redefinition of terms. "Computer graphics" had its start with X-Y plotters. The technology was soon extended to include vectorgraphic (line-drawing) CRT systems based on refresh-vector hardware and, at a later date, direct-view storage tubes followed by higher performance refresh-vector systems.

Only the endpoint coordinates of the lines needed to be stored, so memory requirements were held to a minimum. Refresh-vector writing speeds made it possible to "animate" the display and to create interactive systems which allowed the operator to control the display in "real time" through such input devices as lightpens, joysticks, and digitizer tablets. Again, however, only the endpoints needed to be recalculated with each refresh cycle, minimizing the need for high-speed computational capabilities (see Chapter 2, Display Principles).

Meanwhile, a separate "image processing" technology had been following its own evolutionary path. Instead of dealing with lines and points, randomly positioned anywhere on the display surface, image processing was based on a rectangular array of picture elements or "pixels." Digital information defining the state of each pixel was stored in a random-access (or rotating) memory and used to generate a television-type, raster-scan CRT display—in monochrome or full color.

The source of the pixel data might be a computer, as in the case of a CAT (computer-aided tomography) scanning system. Or the source data could be the digitized output of a TV camera mounted on a satellite, or of a spot scanner in a photo-analysis laboratory. In every case, new information or insights could be gained by using computer techniques to alter contrast or color, or to perform more sophisticated procedures such as correlations, convolutions, and digital filtering of the pixel data. The image processing systems required large amounts of memory, enough to store up to several bytes of data for each of hundreds of thousands of pixels. But the displays were relatively static and, considering the nature of the applications, there was little pressure for high-speed alterations in the displayed images. A delay of seconds, or even minutes, was entirely acceptable.

The division between vectorgraphic "computer graphics" and raster-scan "image processing" has now been bridged by the new raster display technology. Low-cost memories have made it economically feasible to assemble high-resolution, fine-detail raster images that all but eliminate the objectionable stairstepping of vectorgraphic lines when displayed on a raster-CRT screen. Microprocessor-based system architectures have also made it possible to alter selected display elements at full animation rates. The result is "raster graphics"—combining the full-color, pixel-by-pixel control potentials of image processing and the line-drawing capabilities of vectorgraphics in a single display system.

Raster graphics encompasses, in effect, virtually every type of computer-generated or computer-processed display: alphagraphic, vectorgraphic, and continuous-tone imagery. The only type of raster scan display excepted from this definition would be purely alpha-numeric systems with fixed character spaces and a limited choice of character fonts.

A specific raster graphics system may be optimized for imaging or vector-oriented graphics. Often as not, however, both capabilities are incorporated into the system design. Line-drawing software, for exam-ple, may be employed to generate a pixel-data image of an object in the system's display memory. The displayed color or intensity of the pixels may then be defined—or redefined—by image-processing hardware, such as programmable lookup tables. Or conversely, a system designed primarily for image processing may use a graphics "overlay" to add captions and/or to "key" the processing procedures to specific display areas on the CRT screen. Figure 1-1 illustrates this cascading and com-bining of graphics and image-processing functions.

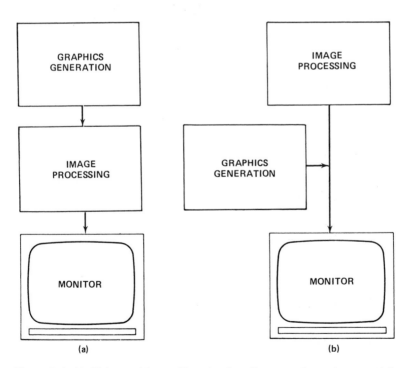

Figure 1-1. Multiple graphics and imaging functions—performed sequentially (a) or combined on monitor screen (b).

Cascading and combining can also be applied to multiple display sources—both analog and digital. Television system designers have, in fact, developed a variety of sophisticated techniques for this purpose. The output of the graphics generator shown in Figure 1-2 could be superimposed on a "live" or recorded video picture, for example, or video images may be inserted into selected areas, such as outlined letters, within a graphics display. (The term "video" will be limited in this Handbook to the raster-scan output of a video camera, disk, tape recorder, or similar analog source.)

The same principles, in many cases the same equipment, can be applied to computer-based raster graphics systems to increase their scope and versatility. Business charts from previous financial periods could be recorded, for example, on videotape and combined on the monitor screen with current-period displays generated by the graphics system. Frequently used graphic overlays and formats could be added in analog form at the monitor input rather than digitally regenerated in display memory each time they are needed. Background patterns or images could also serve as a visual analog of background music—relieving tedium and helping to maintain the operator's attention.

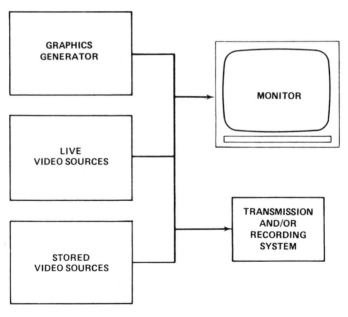

Figure 1-2. Television switching/mixing system with multiple display-signal sources.

THE GRAPHICS SYSTEM

There is not, and may never be, a strict definition of the functions and hardware that constitute a "graphics system." Too much depends on the relative importance of the graphics-generation process, compared to the overall purposes served by the computer installation.

At one extreme is the "standalone" graphics system shown in Figure 1-3. Nearly all of the system's computing capabilities and most of its memory resources are dedicated, we can assume, to the display task. A number of commercially available systems oriented to a specific application, such as image processing or computer-aided design, fall in this category.

At the other extreme is the configuration illustrated by Figure 1-4. Nearly all of the graphics-generation functions must be performed, in this case, by a host computer's hardware and software. The "graphics system" is reduced to a monitor and display-generation circuits are incorporated into the host interface. The graphics output of a process-control computer could be implemented in this form, for example, if the images are limited to relatively simple flow charts with alphanumeric notations indicating the state of process variables.

The majority of raster graphics systems fall midway between these two extremes. As noted above, standalone graphics systems with sufficient computing power to perform the extensive "modeling" and "viewing" functions are generally limited to a specific application. The generation of a raster graphics display can, at the same time, impose a severe burden on a host computer's processor and memory resources. The answer has been to "offload" the host computer by transferring a part or all of the repetitive graphics functions to a separate graphics subsystem with its own processor hardware and graphics software.

One option is to add a graphics capability to the functions of a

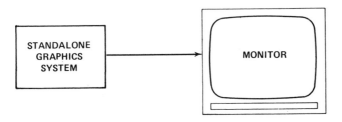

Figure 1-3. Standalone graphics systems with dedicated minicomputer or microprocessor.

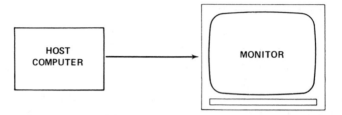

Figure 1-4. Direct interface between host computer and monitor.

microprocessor-based intelligent CRT terminal, as illustrated in Figure 1-5. The resulting "graphics terminal" is usually limited to alphagraphic or, at most, vectorgraphic displays. This is more than adequate, however, for a number of applications, such as the generation of business, process control, or educational graphics. Interaction with the system may be through the standard terminal keyboard or through such added accessories as lightpens and digitizer tablets.

Another approach (Figure 1-6) is to concentrate display-generation functions into a "graphics controller"—physically separated from both the host computer and the CRT monitor. The monitor may be, in fact, only one of several display or recording devices controlled by the graphics subsystem. The host computer may also be only one of several data sources for the graphics controller. Display information may be supplied, for example, by mass storage devices or data communication links connected directly to the controller. In general, however, the host computer retains control over the graphics-generation process, including the operation of the graphics controller and its accessories.

We will be using the graphics-controller configuration as our descriptive model in the following chapters. But the raster graphics

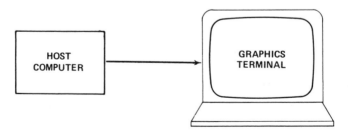

Figure 1-5. Intelligent terminal with "graphics" capabilities.

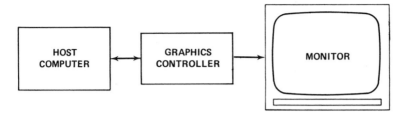

Figure 1-6. Programmable interface between host computer and monitor.

"system" will not be limited to the controller-monitor package which characterizes a number of commercially available systems. Instead, the system definition will encompass *all* of the functional resources, including those of the host computer, which contribute to the generation

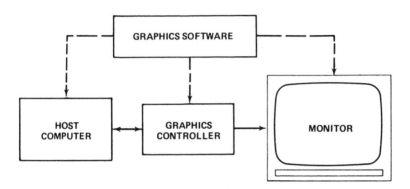

Figure 1-7. Distribution of graphics-system software functions.

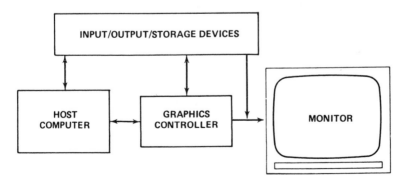

Figure 1-8. Graphics-system I/O and data-storage resources.

of a raster graphics display. Graphics system software could include, therefore, program modules executed by the host computer, by the graphics controller and by programmable hardware in the display monitory itself (Figure 1–7). The same would be true of accessories and peripherals which may be physically connected to the host computer, graphics controller, or the monitor input (Figure 1–8). As long as they contribute to the graphics-generation functions, they will be considered a part of the graphics system.

From all of this it can be seen that the purpose of this Handbook is not to define an *optimum* raster graphics system, but to emphasize the wide range of options and alternatives available to the systems designer—starting, in the next chapter, with the basic question of whether CRT-based raster graphics is, in itself, the best solution to the specific display problem.

2
Display Principles
and Technologies

Two questions must be considered before any decision is made regarding the design or purchase of a raster-scan CRT system. First, is a CRT the most appropriate display device? Second, and equally important, is the raster-scan technique the best way to present information on the CRT screen?

The CRT has been creating luminous images for approximately a hundred years. It was, in fact, the first electronic vacuum tube, predating the term "electronics" by a half-century. During the greater part of this period, particularly during the past thirty years, there has been an intensive search for an electronic-display device that could replace the CRT—or more precisely, a device that would overcome the major shortcomings of the CRT in its present form. The CRT is bulky, with a very high ratio of depth to display area, is relatively fragile, poses high-voltage and radiation hazards, and is among the least efficient of all display methods in terms of energy consumption.

Despite these faults, the CRT has maintained its position as one of the most versatile, cost-effective devices available to the display system designer. Considerably more than half of all the electronic displays now in service (including television receivers) are CRT's. The ratio is shrinking with the introduction of simpler, lower cost devices for such new high-volume applications as digital instrumentation and consumer electronics (e.g., wristwatches and pocket calculators). Within the range of graphics applications covered by this Handbook, however, the CRT remains dominant. Alternative methods may provide a narrow advantage in specific cases, but only the CRT is a potential candidate for *every* application.

e.g., Flat Screen displays (LED, Plasma)

11

DISPLAY CLASSIFICATIONS

Electronic graphic displays can be divided into three descriptive groups—projection, off-screen, and direct-view—and further categorized by the specific technology used to produce a visual image. Figure 2-1 summarizes the principal types of displays now available, both commercial and experimental.

Projection-type displays fall into two categories, depending on whether or not the source of projected light is also the image source. By definition, the image seen by the viewer consists of light that has been projected onto and reflected off a display surface. By implication, there is an optical system to direct the light to the reflective surface.

Conventional and special-purpose CRT's are the most common devices used in the combined light-and-image category. Luminous images created on the CRT screen are projected directly onto the display surface. A variety of optical systems can be utilized (Reference 2).

Display devices in the second category are often called "light valves." A light source, typically incandescent or gas discharge, is projected through a non-emitter display (see below). By diffusing, diffracting, or absorbing a portion of the projected light, the light valve creates an image on the display surface in the same manner as a photographic slide or motion-picture frame. Again, however, CRT-type electron beams serve as the image-forming mechanism in the principal commercial systems of this type.

Off-screen displays are beyond the scope of this Handbook, but they, too, can be divided into two categories. Coherent types use laser technology to form holographic three-dimensional images. Non-coherent off-screen displays are typified by "heads up" or helmet-mounted systems for fighter pilots. An optical system focuses the image at infinity in the pilot's line of sight. The image source may be a miniature CRT.

Direct-view displays are the broadest category and of the greatest interest to the designer of a graphics system. By definition, the viewer sees an image directly on or near the display surface. Figure 2-2 summarizes the current status of the principal direct-view display techniques. Referring back to Figure 2-1, there are two basic types. "Emitter" display techniques generate the light seen by the viewer. "Non-emitter" display techniques do not generate light directly, but modulate either ambient light or light from a supplemental source.

Strictly speaking, the CRT is an emitter in the same category with the cathodoluminescent displays in Figure 2-1. It creates an image by directing an electron beam from a cathode (negatively charged) source

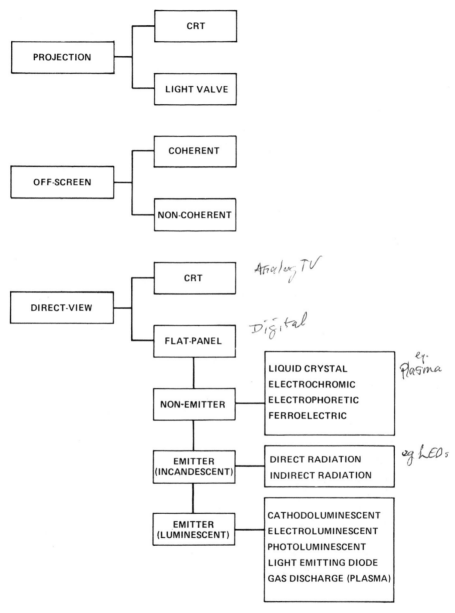

Figure 2–1. Display technologies, commercial and experimental. (Source: Reference 1)

DIRECT-VIEW DISPLAY APPLICATIONS

	ALPHAGRAPHIC	VECTORGRAPHIC	PHOTOGRAPHIC
COMMERCIAL	CRT INCANDESCENT LIGHT-EMITTING DIODE LIQUID CRYSTAL GAS DISCHARGE CATHODOLUMINESCENT	CRT GAS DISCHARGE	CRT
EXPERIMENTAL	ELECTROLUMINESCENT ELECTROCHROMIC ELECTROPHORETIC FERROELECTRIC	ELECTROLUMINESCENT LIGHT-EMITTING DIODE LIQUID CHRYSTAL	ELECTROLUMINESCENT LIGHT-EMITTING DIODE LIQUID CRYSTAL GAS DISCHARGE

Figure 2-2. Status of direct-view display technologies. (Source: Reference 1)

to a luminescent phosphor surface. But in Figures 2-1 and 2-2 it is listed separately because its physical form is so distincly different.

As a general rule, the depth of a CRT is equal to or greater than the diagonal distance across its display surface. This form factor can be reduced by half with only a minor degradation in the display quality, or to a fourth or less by the flat-CRT development efforts that are now reaching the commercial stage.

By contrast, all other direct-view display techniques are inherently "flat," with a depth-to-diagonal ratio of well under a fourth. Individually, many of them also have a number of other distinguishing features, such as ruggedness, low power consumption, and low potential cost. As a group, however, they are identified as flat-panel displays to emphasize the single, most obvious characteristic which differentiates them from the CRT.

DISPLAY REQUIREMENTS

The function of an electronic graphic display is to communicate information to the human brain by creating patterns of light which can be sensed and interpreted by the human eye-brain visual system. Display requirements—and display comparisons—are dictated, therefore, by both machine and human considerations. What type and volume of information must be communicated? What is the required rate of data transfer? How fast can the viewer assimilate the information—without confusion or error? To what extent does the display technique take advantage of the observer's visual capabilities? Even more important, how effectively does the display exploit the *limitations* of the eye-brain linkage?

There are a number of other considerations—on both sides of the interface—which may be secondary to the communication task yet, often as not, may dictate the choice of a particular display technology or device. The system designer must take into account, for example, the physical form of the display, including such factors as the display-area size of available devices and the depth of the device package as a function of the display area. The choices may also be limited by safety or power-supply constraints, as in the case of portable or battery-operated equipment. Economic evaluations must encompass not only the display device itself, but also the cost of the electronic circuitry required to drive the display.

The technical and economic characteristics of a display are subject to engineering analysis. Human factors influencing the design of a display system are not so easily defined. It is not enough simply to communicate information. A display must also "look good," by whatever standard is likely to be applied by the intended viewer. This phrase translates, in turn, into such difficult-to-define considerations as aesthetic taste, cultural conditioning, intelligence, attentiveness and patience.

It is the looking-good criterion that has limited the development of many of the CRT-alternatives listed in Figures 2-1 and 2-2, partly because the CRT, especially the television-type raster-scan CRT, has had decades to establish what is, in effect, a universal standard of acceptance. But even the designers of CRT display systems must incorporate human intangibles into their decision-making processes. In terms of economic tradeoffs, for example, what is the cost of an eyestrain headache? And to what extent should designers cater to the subjective demand for color in applications where a monochrome display would be more than adequate?

Legibility

The first requirement of a visual display device is that the displayed information must be *seen*—easily, accurately, without ambiguity—under the conditions of use. This quality can be summarized as "legibility." A great deal of human-factors research has been conducted on this subject, with speed-of-recognition and error-rate as the principal measurement parameters. The situation is complicated by the fact that prior training, environmental distractions, and cumulative fatigue can directly influence the results—independent of the quality of the display.

It is clear, however, that three major factors—contrast, luminance, and size of the graphic elements—contribute to the legibility of a display. In order to provide the maximum amount of information within a display of a given size, it is an advantage to keep the size of the graphic elements (e.g., line width, character height) to a theoretical minimum established primarily by the viewing distance. But the *legible* minimum is directly affected by contrast and luminance. With a given graphic-element size, legibility can be significantly enhanced by increasing either or both of these variables.

The human eye (or more precisely, the eye-brain system) is a differential-input device. It is designed to gain information by interpreting the differences detected in color values and luminance levels. Hence, the importance of contrasting colors and luminance contrast, which can be defined generally as the difference between the color or luminance that represents information and the corresponding values for the "background" or non-information areas of the display surface.

The ability to discern luminance differences is the more primitive attribute, and is far more important than color detection in terms of information acquisition and interpretation. More than three-fourths of the light-sensing cells in the human eye are color-blind; at low luminance levels, the eye can see only shades of gray; the bandwidth of a "full color" television color signal averages less than a third of that of the luminance signal. Color is, in effect, a bonus display quality—a valuable enhancement, but only after the more fundamental legibility requirements of adequate luminance and luminance contrast have been fully met.

Luminance

Increased luminance contributes to display legibility by increasing the acuity of the eye—the ability to separate fine detail such as individual dots or lines on the display surface. An "average observer" under average lighting conditions has an angular acuity of approximately one minute of arc, or 0.000046 of the viewing distance times 2π. For a typical viewing distance of 18 inches, this means that the lower separable limit for dot diameters or line widths is on the order of 0.005 inch (O.13 mm). Above-average luminance levels can reduce this dimension by nearly half, but lower luminance levels have an even more significant effect. At very low levels, the minimum separable display-element size may increase to several minutes of arc.

Such precision may seem irrelevant for most display applications. Increased visual acuity directly enhances, however, the "crispness" of the boundary lines that define, for example, an alphanumeric character. This, in turn, increases the legibility of each character or graphic element, but only if adequate contrast between image and background is also maintained. If the luminance levels of both are increased simultaneously (as occurs when ambient light is reflected off the entire display surface), legibility will actually go down.

This paradox is partially the result of a second characteristic of the human eye. Increased levels of luminance may increase the acuity of the eye, but they reduce the all-important ability to discern a luminance difference. The minimum discernable luminance difference is, over a broad range, a fixed percentage of the average luminance level. The higher the average luminance, therefore, the less sensitive the eye is to absolute luminous differences.

Contrast

This relationship between luminance level and the ability to perceive a luminance difference explains why the contrast of a display is normally expressed as a ratio. The absolute luminance values of image and background are, within reasonable limits, not nearly as important as their *relative* luminance values. In fact, the contrast ratio of a display device is probably the most important single characteristic contributing to the legibility of a display and its "looking good" appearance.

Unfortunately, the contrast ratio is also one of the most difficult display parameters to define in a meaningful way, and this difficulty is compounded when an attempt is made to compare different display technologies or even different devices within the same technology. In theory, the contrast ratio of a display device can be simply calculated as follows:

$$\text{Contrast Ratio} = \frac{\text{Maximum Luminance}}{\text{Minimum Luminance}}$$

It is then a matter of personal preference whether the value is expressed as a ratio (e.g., 7:1), a numerical value (7.0), or a percentage (700%).

The effective maximum and minimum luminance values may not, however, be easily obtained. Many manufacturers of display devices publish only the "intrinsic" contrast ratios of their displays—without taking into account the effect of reflected ambient light. The environmental conditions in which the displays may be used are too variable to anticipate. This leaves it up to the display-system designer or user to predict (or suffer with) the "extrinsic" contrast ratio, which can be significantly lower. Reflected ambient light (Figure 2–3) increases both the numerator and denominator of the maximum/minimum contrast-ratio calculation. This can sharply reduce the effective contrast, with corresponding reductions in legibility and gray-scale range. If reflected ambient light has a luminance equal to half the maximum image luminance, for example, an intrinsic contrast ratio of 10:1 is reduced to an extrinsic ratio of only 2.5:1 (10 + 5 divided by 1 + 5).

The extrinsic contrast ratio can be calculated, of course, for any known ambient condition. But this statement presumes that the display-system designer knows the reflective and diffusing qualities of the display surface (and any internal visible surfaces). Such information is rarely provided by the published literature for a display device and may require specific tests by either the manufacturer or the potential user.

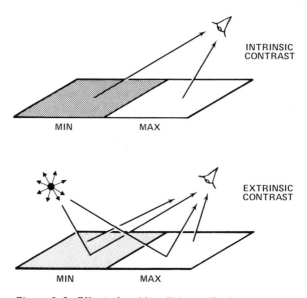

Figure 2–3. Effect of ambient light on display contrast.

To complicate matters further, a number of other contrast-calculation conventions have been established, some of which result in values identified as "contrast" rather than "contrast ratio." The two terms may even be used interchangeably in the same written material. It is advisable, therefore, to determine the ways in which contrasts or contrast ratios have been calculated before using them for comparison. The following, for example, may be encountered:

$$\text{Contrast} = \frac{\text{Background} - \text{Image}}{\text{Background}}$$

$$\text{Contrast Ratio} = \frac{\text{Background} + \text{Image}}{\text{Background}}$$

The first formula may be positive or negative, depending on whether the display image is black-on-white or white-on-black. It can also be smaller or greater than unity. The second assumes that the background luminance contributes to the image luminance, even in the absence of reflected ambient light.

If the display consists of discrete discernable elements, the contrast specifications may also differentiate between display-element "on" and "off" conditions, with separate contrast ratios for each state.

Another way to specify contrast is to state the "shades of gray" which the device can display. As noted earlier, the minimum discernable luminance difference is a function of the luminance level with 3% as a rule-of-thumb value based on a variety of test conditions. The shades-of-gray convention uses a much coarser measure of 1.41 (the square root of 2), or 141% for each gray-scale step. Figure 2–4 translates the resulting shades-of-gray values into equivalent contrast ratios.

All of the contrast considerations discussed up to this point have related to the display itself, including the effect of reflected ambient light on the display contrast. There is, however, a secondary ambient-light effect which must be taken into account. Light reflected off the surroundings or projected directly into the viewer's eyes can alter the luminance-adapation level of the eyes, and this, too, can affect the legibility of the display.

The "surround contrast" is defined as the ratio between the luminance level of the surroundings and the background luminance of the display (Figure 2–5). The ideal surround-contrast ratio is 1:1. If the surrounding luminance is markedly lower than that of the display background, the effect on legibility is relatively minor, although

Shades of Gray	Minimum Contrast Ratio
1	1
2	1.4
3	2.0
4	2.8
5	4.0
6	5.7
7	8.0
8	11.3
9	16.0
10	22.6
11	32.0
12	45.3

Figure 2-4. Shades-of-gray values converted to contrast ratios.

eyestrain may result. But as the surround-contrast ratio increases toward 10:1, which can easily happen in an outdoor environment, the display-contrast ratio must be at least doubled to maintain an adequate level of viewing comfort and legibility.

Luminosity Measurements

Light is a narrow band of electromagnetic frequencies with wavelengths ranging from approximately 400 to 700 nanometers. We call the radiations "light" because our brains register a sensation when electromagnetic energy at these wavelengths impinge on the retina of the human eye. Light measurements are inseparable, therefore, from the physiological and psychological aspects of human sight. Three

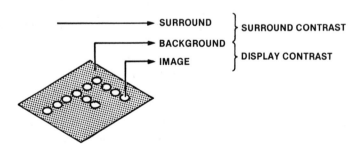

Figure 2-5. Relationship between surround and display contrast ratios.

related but separate terms are used to describe this complex relationship:

Radiance is a measure of the rate of energy flow from an electromagnetic source. It can be measured with physical instruments, and is normally expressed in power units—joules per second or watts.

Luminance is a psycho-physical measure of *perceived* radiant power under carefully controlled and defined conditions. Luminosity measurements take advantage of the fact that the human eye-brain system can identify two equal levels of radiation with considerable accuracy—when compared side by side or in rapid sequence. The luminosity measurement system starts, therefore, with observations of a standard radiation source by a large number of individuals and proceeds through a series of comparisons to arrive at luminance values for non-standard sources. Electronic instruments are then calibrated to match the human observations. The unit for luminous power is the lumen.

Brightness is a purely psycho-physiological attribute—the subjective response to electromagnetic energy that occurs when the eye-brain system has adapted to a particular radiation level. The adaptation includes the rapid contraction or expansion of the eye pupil and a slower shift in the equilibrium point of the radiation-initiated chemical reactions within the eye. Adaptation also includes, we must assume, alterations in the sensory-input logic networks of the brain. All of these changes combine to allow us to see under widely varying conditions—but at the cost of extremely poor judgment as to the absolute value of the radiant energy we are observing. A lighted match, for example, has a constant radiance and intrinsic luminance. Yet the flame which appears bright in a darkened room is almost invisible in the sunlight. Conversely, if the two eyes are separately exposed to luminance levels which differ by a factor of a thousand to one, the brain will within minutes "sense" equal brightness in both fields of vision.

Brightness is what we see when we look at—and judge—a graphics display. It is impossible, however, to measure the sensation. We must rely, instead, on an artifically contrived system of luminosity measurements to give us a first-order approximation of how two displays will compare under identical conditions, or how the same device will appear when observed under different conditions.

Two factors add to the complexity of luminosity evaluations. One is the long history of light measurements, which has resulted in a proliferation of terms and arbitrarily defined units. A lumen is a lumen, just as twelve inches equal a foot, and there is little value in asking "why?" The second source of complexity is the fact that the eye not only responds to electromagnetic radiation, but also differentiates between radiation wavelengths to produce a range of sensations called "color."

Totally aside from the uncertainties of the brightness factor, it is the wavelength-dependent color response that makes it impossible to establish a simple relationship between radiant power (e.g., the watts of power required to drive a display device) and luminosity. If we think of the lumen as a unit of luminance power that will produce a particular level of eye-brain response, we can start, at least, to define the lumen by stating that one watt of radiant power will produce a visual sensation to approximately 680 lumens; but this is true only if the light has a yellow-green color. Any departure from this center-of-the-spectrum wavelength results in a sharp drop in the sensory response. Because the lumen is based on a fixed level of sensory response, the lowered sensitivity of the eye to longer and shorter electromagnetic wavelengths means that the number of lumens per watt of radiant power also drops precipitously.

Figure 2–6 shows the logarithmic nature of this relationship between color and eye response. The eye's sensitivity to radiation at red or blue wavelengths is only a small fraction of its sensitivity to yellow or green light. This does not mean, however, that a lumen of red light, for example, is any different than a lumen of green light in terms of sensory response. The two are equal. Only the amount of radiant power required to produce the sensory response is different. To be explicit, it may take a hundred times more electrical power to generate a red display element of the same luminance (sensory response) as an equivalent green display element.

The two curves in Figure 2–7 translate the color-response relationship into a linear "luminosity function" which must be applied whenever radiant power is converted to luminous power—with each wavelength in the source spectrum calculated separately. The upper curve applies to average daylight conditions and is simply a restatement of the Figure 2–6 values. The lower curve is for low-luminance conditions and shows that the sensitivity of the eye shifts toward the blue end of the spectrum when the eye is adapted to "night vision." The relative luminance of displayed colors may change, therefore, when a display device is moved from the laboratory to a darkened control room. The blues will appear relatively brighter; the reds may turn to a dark gray. Similar effects occur outdoors at twilight. The transition is gradual, reaching a full night-vision level when the surrounding luminance drops below O.01 to 0.005 nit.

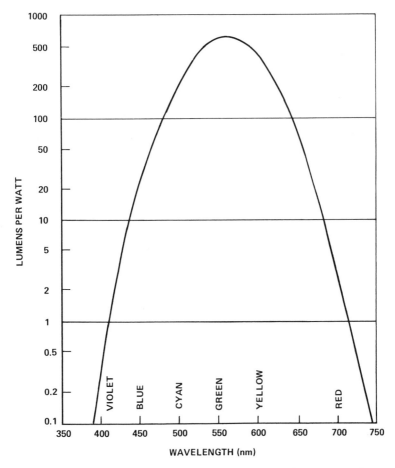

Figure 2-6. Eye response to radiant power as a function of wavelength. Curve represents a recalculation of the power conversion factor for each nanometer change in the wavelength.

The terms and units used in luminosity measurements are summarized in Figure 2-8. Most display applications involve luminous surfaces, making "luminance" and its derivative, luminance contrast, the most important luminosity characteristics of a display. The term "intensity" (or candlepower) is reserved for point sources and may have application when the display consists of discrete luminous elements such as light-emitting diodes or incandescent lights.

Nearly all of the terms are defined in terms of a unit solid angle or

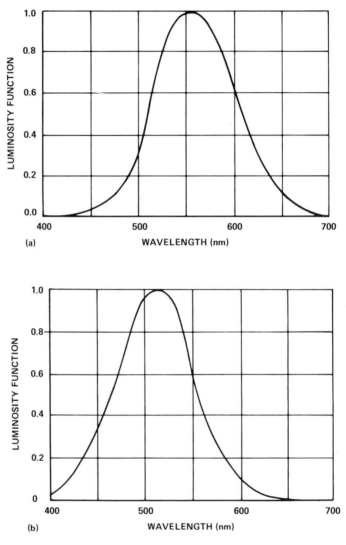

Figure 2-7. Luminosity-function values for normal (a) and night (b) vision.

"steradian." Figure 2-9 shows that a steradian consists of the solid angle that subtends an r^2 area (of any shape) on the surface of a sphere with a radius of r. There are 4π or approximately 12.5 such steradian-subtending areas on the surface of a sphere.

A candela is defined as the intensity of a point source that generates

Electrical Analog	Luminosity Term	Luminosity Unit
Power (rate of energy flow)	Luminous flux	Lumen = 1/680 watt/ luminosity function
Power-source output	Intensity (point source)	Candela = lumen/steradian
	Luminance (surface)	Nit = lumen/steradian/meter^2 = candela/meter^2
Delivered power	Illuminance	Lux = candela x steradian/meter^2 = lumen/meter^2
Power-transfer efficiency	Transmittance	Transmittance factor = 0.0 to 1.0
	Reflectance	Reflectance factor = 0.0 to 1.0

Note: All areas measurements are based on the "apparent area" of the luminous or illuminated surface.

Figure 2-8. Terms and units used in luminosity measurements.

one lumen per steradian. It follows, then, that the total luminous power produced by a candela point source in all directions is 4π lumens. The same intensity source, if positioned directly above a surface, would radiate through a hemisphere, producing 2π lumens of available luminous power.

In the case of most luminous display surfaces, however, the emitted or reflected light stems from multiple point sources *within* the surface. Luminance is defined, therefore, as intensity per unit of luminous surface, with candela/meter^2 (or "nit") as the international unit of measurement. The intensity of the in-the-surface point sources is never the same in all directions, so a full luminance statement must always in-

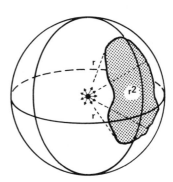

Figure 2-9. One steradian, or "unit solid angle."

clude a direction vector, normally expressed as an angle away from the perpendicular. The varying intensity also means that the available luminous power from a surface is rarely equal to that generated by an equivalent point source. In fact, as explained below, the maximum luminous power from a perfectly diffusing surface is only half that of a point source above the surface (π lumens per candela per unit area instead of 2π lumens per candela).

The lumen-per-steradian notations included in the definitions for both intensity and luminance lead directly to the familiar inverse-square law. As shown in Figure 2–10, the solid angle subtended by an illuminated surface decreases by the square of the distance away from the illuminating light source. If the light source generates four lumens per steradian and the surface itself subtends exactly one steradian, only a single lumen would illuminate the surface when the solid angle is reduced to 0.25 steradian by doubling the distance. The same effect occurs when a luminous display is viewed from an increasing distance. The solid angle subtended by the pupil of the eye is decreased by the square of the distance, reducing the number of lumens entering the eye by the same proportion.

Several other factors have to be incorporated into the luminosity calculations, especially as they relate to display surfaces. The degree of diffusion of reflected or emitted light varies widely, as illustrated in Figure 2–11. The effective luminance may be very dependent, therefore, on the reflection or viewing angle. In addition, all illumination and luminance calculations are based on the "apparent area" of the surface, which varies as the cosine of this angle (Figures 2–12a and 2–12b). The further away from the perpendicular to the surface, the smaller the apparent area.

As a convenience, designers may choose to treat the display surface as if it were Lambertian or "perfectly diffusing." The phosphor surface of a CRT screen is, in fact, close to this ideal. Figure 2–13 shows how the directional intensity of such a luminous surface varies as the cosine of the viewing angle. As noted in the previous paragraph, the apparent area also varies as the cosine of this angle. The result is a constant value for the intensity per unit apparent area—which happens to be the definition for luminance. A perfectly diffusing surface has, therefore, a constant luminance, independent of the viewing angle.

One other fact of interest can be derived from Figure 2–13. The luminous intensity of a perfectly diffusing surface varies from a maximum value at the perpendicular to zero when the viewing direction is parallel to the surface. Shortcircuiting the calculus, we can say that the average intensity is half the maximum, which reduces the total lu-

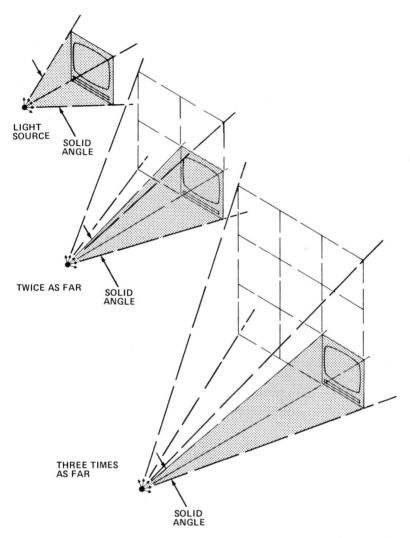

Figure 2-10. Inverse-square law. The illuminated (or observed) surface remains constant, but the subtended solid angle (measured in steradians) decreases by the square of the distance.

minous power passing through a hemisphere on the surface to π lumens per candela instead of the 2π lumens per candela that would be generated by a point source directly above the surface and radiating light equally in all directions.

REFLECTED LIGHT

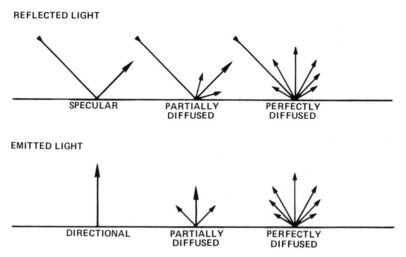

EMITTED LIGHT

Figure 2–11. Types of display-surface reflections and emissions.

A variety of luminance and illumination terms are now in use. Figures 2–14a and 2–14b convert these to the international standard of nits to facilitate the comparison of display techniques and the calculation of extrinsic luminance-contrast ratios. Factors of $1/\pi$ enter frequently into the conversion values because of the tendency to treat all surfaces as perfectly diffusing with a constant luminance expressed as

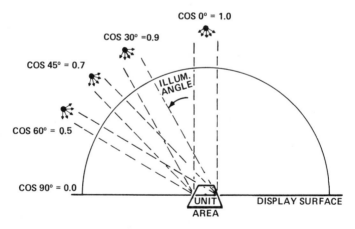

Figure 2–12a. "Apparent area" of an illuminated display surface as a function of the illumination angle.

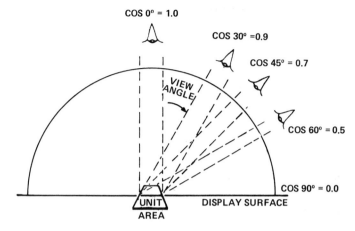

Figure 2–12b. "Apparent area" of a luminous display surface (reflective or emissive) as a function of the viewing angle.

lumens per unit area. Luminance expressed as candelas per unit area assumes the more general case and results in measurement units that represent π times as many lumens per unit area.

Color and Color Contrast

The perception of color is purely psycho-physiological. It may be stating the obvious, but electromagnetic radiations have no quality that even remotely resembles "color." In fact, there is no assurance that the wavelengths identified as "blue" generate the same eye-brain

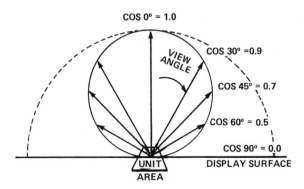

Figure 2–13. Directional intensity of a perfectly diffusing surface. Luminance is independent of viewing angle.

Luminance Unit	Nits
Skot*	0.00032
Apostilb	0.3183
Blondel	0.3183
Meter-lambert*	0.3183
Candela/m^2	1.0
Troland	1.273**
Millilambert*	3.183
Footlambert*	3.426
Candela/ft^2	10.764
Candela/in^2	1,550.
Centimeter-lambert*	3,183.
Lambert*	3,183.
Candela/cm^2	10,000.
Stilb	10,000.

*Conversion factor is accurate only for a perfectly diffusing source or reflective surface.

**Divide by the square of the eye-pupil diameter in mm.

Figure 2–14a. Conversion table for luminance units.

Illuminance Unit	Nits*
Nox	0.00032
Lux	0.3183
Milliphot	3.183
Footcandle	3.426
Phot	3,183.

*Multiply by reflectance factor to obtain reflected luminance. Accurate only for a perfectly diffusing reflective surface.

Figure 2–14b. Conversion table for reflected luminance.

sensations for any two individuals. We can communicate in terms of color, however, because all of us have learned to associate a particular color sensation with a specified color name.

The best guess at this time is that there are three types of color-sensing cones in the central portion of the human retina. One type is designed to absorb green-light wavelengths near the peak of the luminosity-function curve and to convert the energy through chemical processes into nerve-cell signals. The other two types of cones "sense" blue and red wavelengths, respectively. In either case, when all three types of cones are sensing approximately equal radiance levels of all three wavelength bands, the brain interprets the combination as white. (Note that it is the relative *radiance* levels that count, not the luminance levels. The lumens of red and blue will always be very low, compared to the lumens of green, when sensing white light. Equal luminances of all three colors would be perceived as purple or magenta.)

A true white light consists of equal radiance levels across the entire visible-wavelength band. If the light is diffracted by a prism, as shown in Figure 2-15a, the result is a rainbow of colors, from violet to deep red. Exactly the same sensation of white light can be produced, however, by a properly balanced blend of any *three* colors—so long as a mixture of two can not be used to reproduce the third. The three "primaries" that form the theoretical basis of color vision—red, green, and blue—may have been naturally selected because they are widely separated on the spectrum and can be blended into the broadest range of intermediate colors (Figure 2-15b).

The continuously variable blending capabilities of the eye mean that even two colors can combine into white (Figure 2-15c). But now the choice is more restricted. The two colors must be "complements" of each other, which means that one color must be the hue that remains when the other is subtracted from white. In effect, we are simply putting back together colors which we have, by our complementary definition, taken apart.

The complements of red, green, and blue are cyan, magenta, and yellow. Cyan is white minus red. It is just as true, however, to say the red is white minus cyan, which makes red the complement of cyan. The convention of referring to red, green, and blue (RGB) as primary colors and to the others as complementary colors is, we can theorize, a direct outcome of the color-sensing process of the eye-brain system. The sensitivities of the three types of color-sensing cones center on these three electromagnetic wavelengths. The other three colors are artifacts, created by the eye-brain system. In fact, one of the complementary colors, magenta, does not even appear in the rainbow spectrum. We sense shades of magenta by calculating the ratio between the electromagnetic radiations at both ends of the spectrum.

The primacy of the primaries explains why light-emitting "additive" color displays use the RGB colors (Figure 2-16a). We want at least a part of the display to contain these shades in a pure, undiluted state. For the same reason, we are more comfortable with non-emitting

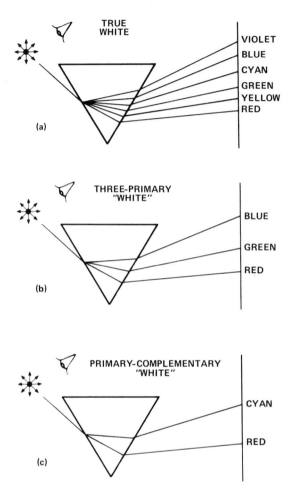

Figure 2–15. Three types of light perceived by the human eye-brain system as "white."

"subtractive" displays that use the complementary colors. Such displays, which would include photographic slides and hardcopy prints, create colors by extracting a part of the spectrum and allowing only the balance of the white viewing light to reach the eye. A magenta dye, for example, extracts the green component of the white light (Figure 2–16b), while a yellow dye extracts the blue. If both dyes operate simultaneously, the result is a pure reproduction of the remaining eye-brain primary: red.

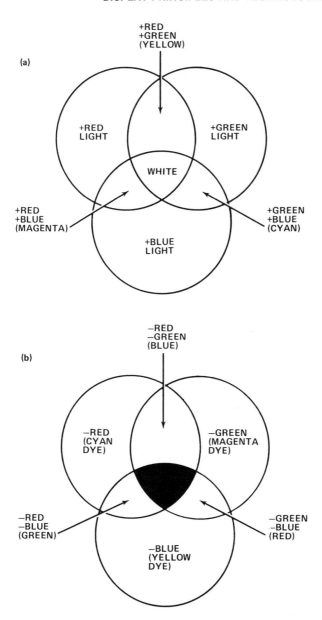

Figure 2–16. Additive color mixing (a) applies to emitter-type displays. Subtractive mixing (b) applies to non-emitter displays, photographic reproductions, and printing inks.

As in the case of luminosity measurements, a variety of terms and measurement units have been developed for the description of color. In one form or another, however, all of them deal with three characteristics which together define a color with precision:

Intensity is the luminous power of the colored light reaching the eye. We have previously reserved this word for point sources of light, with luminance (or intensity per unit area) as the more accurate term for display surfaces. But color-description conventions have settled on either intensity or "brightness," which is even less accurate because the sensation of brightness is so subjectively dependent on the viewing environment and prior conditioning of the eye-brain system. The most direct, objective way to quantify color intensity would be to use the international unit for luminance, the nit.

Hue is the "color" of the color as subjectively perceived by the eye-brain system. It could represent a narrow band of the visible spectrum or just as likely, a variety of wavelengths from throughout the spectrum which together give a visual sensation equal to the narrowband color. An alternate, more objective and measurable term is "dominant wavelength," which implies that there are probably other colors in the color we are seeing, but it can be physically duplicated by a color with a single wavelength value. A non-spectrum magenta color is defined by the wavelength of its visible-spectrum complementary color with a "c" after the wavelength value. (See Appendix III.)

Saturation is the degree to which the hue of a color subjectively appears to be undiluted by its complementary color to form white, gray, or black. If there is no trace of apparent white in the color, it is described as fully saturated. If the color and its complement are present in proportion, the result is black, gray, or white depending on the intensity, and the saturation is said to be zero. The objective term for saturation is "purity."

Of the three characteristics, saturation is the most difficult to describe and, define, except in numerical terms. It is, in effect, a measure of the relative intensities of the hues present—but not individually sensed—in a particular color. If we simplify the problem by assigning values to just the three primary colors (out of the millions of hues we can theoretically perceive), it should be possible to construct a three-dimensional descriptive system that takes into account all three of the color characteristics: hue, intensity, and saturation (HIS). A variety of schemes have been developed to accomplish this task. The most useful and widely used is the convention established by the Commission Internationale de L'Eclairage (CIE). The CIE system reduces the three-dimensional primary-color "space" to a two-dimensional chart on which any color can be precisely positioned and defined in terms of hue, saturation and relative luminance or intensity.

A description of the CIE system is included in the Appendix, along with a number of diagrams which can serve as reference sources. The most distinguishing characteristic of the CIE color-representation method is that all three of its "primary colors" are hypothetical—chosen so that a number of important true-color relationships can be read directly off the diagram. The x axis of the diagram, for example, is the "alychne," a term used to denote the location of theoretical colors with zero luminance. Increasing y-axis values provide, therefore, a direct indication of relative luminance. (In television terminology, the "Y" component of a color-encoded video signal contains all of the luminance or black-and-white information.) As we might expect from our earlier depiction of the luminosity function, green colors have the highest y values, reds lie at an intermediate level, and blues are close to the baseline.

The CIE diagram assumes that all of the colors have been generated by equal-radiance sources—which puts "white" near the center of the triangular area. The actual luminance of individual colors generated by a display will, as a consequence, reflect both their y values and their relative radiance levels. Together, the two luminance factors establish the "color contrast" between, for example, the background and image portions of a display.

All of the rules applying to luminance contrast can be extended to color contrast, including the fact that legibility is enhanced with increased color contrast and ambient light will tend to degrade the contrast, with further losses in legibility if the surround contrast is excessive. In the case of color contrast, however, the *color* of the ambient and surround light sources can have a further effect, altering the hues of the displayed colors and changing their relationships. The same would be true of any colors introduced by a filter added as an accessory to a display to reduce the effects of ambient light (see Chapter 9).

This brings us to the subject of "contrasting colors, " as opposed to color contrast. One of the CIE diagrams in the Appendix depicts the ability of observers to detect color differences as a function of the positions of the colors on the diagram. Earlier it was stated that color is a bonus display quality, compared to the more basic requirements of adequate luminance and luminance contrast. Color can add to the realism of a pictorial image, and hold attention by increasing the subjective appeal of a display. But coding techniques based on contrasting colors have practical value in almost every application.

A monochrome display communicates information through the

shape and position of the display elements. Contrasting colors allow differences between the elements (e.g., importance, "density," or "distance") to be defined even though the shapes are identical and are in near proximity to each other on the display surface.

Gray-scale differences could be used, of course, for the same purpose. But the eye has a limited ability to judge absolute luminance or intensity values, and this reduces the useful number of gray-scale "codes" to three or four. By comparison, a dozen or more color codes can be incorporated into a display program. The observer may not remember their exact significance, but there will never by any misjudgment of one color for another (assuming that the limitations of color-blind individuals are taken into account).

The customary way to code and manipulate colors is in terms of their RGB values. A case can be made that human perception and response to colors is equally or even more strongly influenced by HIS values (the standard television color signal is coded in HIS terms). A number of graphics systems have been designed, therefore, to give the programmer or operator direct control over the hue, intensity, and saturation of a display element's color without any concern or knowledge of the RGB values required to achieve a particular effect. Graphics software described in Chapter 4 gives the programmer a choice of RGB or HIS color definitions, and the basic block diagram of an HIS-based system is given in Chapter 7.

Display Resolution

The "resolution" of a display provides a first-approximation measure of the amount and variety of information that can be presented on the display surface. Resolution also helps to determine the aesthetic appearance of a display, independent of the displayed information.

There are a variety of technical definitions for display resolution. The term may refer, for instance, to either the "density" or the total number of addressable display elements. The elements themselves may be defined as dots, lines, image-background transitions (with two transitions for each dot or line), or hypothetical grid intersections. If the display is viewed at a distance, the resolving powers of both the display and the human eye must be taken into account. It is also necessary to differentiate between the resolution of the "system" and the intrinsic capabilities of its components. In the case of a television system, for example, the resolving power of the camera is generally much higher than the information content or bandwidth of the video signal. The best that a monitor can do is to preserve the resolution of the signal it receives.

Similar considerations apply to computer-based display systems. Source-data and display-device resolutions are independent variables. The subject of resolution will be raised repeatedly, therefore, throughout the balance of this Handbook. For now, however, we can concentrate on the physical display, and use as our resolution measurement the total number of separately addressable display elements under the control of the system software or operator.

Expressed in this manner, resolution becomes a power factor, with exponential increases in the potential amount of displayed information as the number of display elements increases linearly. Assuming that the display elements are binary (on or off, visible or invisible), the number of distinctly different patterns that can be created by a 5-element display is 2^5 or 32. A threefold increase in resolution expands the number of patterns to 2^{15}, or 32,778. (The equivalent figures for an eight-color coded display would be 8^5 and 8^{15}.)

The exponential nature of the resolution relationship means that as the number of elements reaches into the hundreds or thousands, further increases in resolution start to become meaningless in terms of the gross number of patterns or images which can be formed. The benefits of increased resolution shift, instead, toward enhanced legibility and finer detail (number of readable characters, density of vectorgraphic lines, subtle graduations in color or gray-scale intensity).

For reasons that relate primarily to display addressing (see below), resolution has been a major hurdle for the various technologies attempting to compete with the CRT. Most of them have been progressing, therefore, through a series of limited-resolution steps, starting with simple 7-segment, "double-hung window" characters such as the example shown to the left in Figure 2–17. The higher-resolution 14-segment character to the right increases the number of potential patterns by a factor of 2^7, allowing a full set of alphanumeric characters to be displayed. The added resolution also permits the selection of "fail-safe" patterns which require that at least two segments be faulty

Figure 2–17. Two types of characters with 7-segment (left) and 14-segment display resolutions.

(mistakenly on or off) before one character can be confused for another.

The next steps in the progression toward increased resolution would be dot-matrix patterns. A 5-by-5 matrix (25 elements) represents a lower resolution limit for alphanumeric information. The 5-by-7 pattern shown on the left in Figure 2–18 provides increased legibility and has become the industry standard. Additional "columns" (vertical lines) and "rows" (horizontal lines) add to the appearance of the characters, but only marginally to their readability.

Alternative technologies do not begin to compete with the full potentials of the CRT until they reach the level of the larger-scale array illustrated in Figure 2–19. The transition can be accomplished by "filling-in," in effect, the spaces between the characters of a dot-matrix display. There may be, however, a step-function increase in addressing complexity. Instead of forming images within well-defined character spaces, the display must be capable of creating graphic designs that extend across the display surface.

Any increase in array resolution will generally require a corresponding decrease in the size of the individual display elements—assuming that the boundaries of the display surface remain fixed. The allowable area for each display element in a 512-by-512 array is only a fourth as large as the per-element area in a 256-by-256 array. This puts a severe limit on the maximum resolution which can be achieved when the display elements consist of discrete components (e.g., light-emitting diodes) or take the form of two opposing electrodes (e.g., gas-discharge devices).

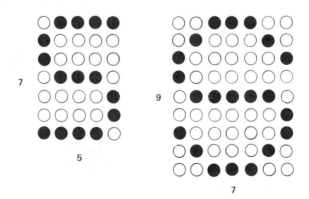

Figure 2–18. Dot-matrix patterns. Right-hand pattern has 80% higher resolution than standard 5-by-7 dot matrix.

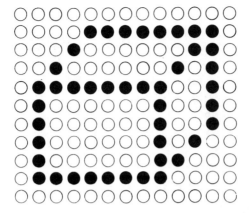

Figure 2–19. Display-element array. Resolution may be limited by the size of the individual display elements.

Nearly every CRT alternative suffers from this limitation—leading to such "heroic" measures as the fabrication of monolithic arrays on semiconductor substrates. Meanwhile, only the monochrome CRT enjoys the distinction of being theoretically free of any spatial limitations on resolution. The display surface is a continuum, without any break or division. There are, in fact, *no* distinguishable display elements. Resolution must be defined, therefore, in terms of *potential* display elements—addressable locations where images may be selectively positioned and displayed.

Two distinctly different techniques can be used to define and locate images on a CRT display surface. Both use an imaginary grid of coordinate lines. In one case, however, the lines serve as boundaries for an array of picture-element (pixel) *areas,* each of which can be "coded" in a different color or gray-scale intensity (Figure 2–20). In the second case, the grid lines form an array of *intersection points,* each of which can serve as the coordinate address for the center of a dot, the endpoint of a line, or the locus of a curve (Figure 2–21).

The two types are exemplified by the raster-scan and "stroke-writing" CRT systems described later in this chapter. A raster-scan pixel occupies a finite area defined by the timing interval between signal transitions and the physical spacing of the raster lines. The number of pixels (resolution) of a raster-scan CRT monitor is limited, therefore, by the spot size, the bandwidth of the display signal, and the number of raster lines that the monitor can scan during each refresh cycle.

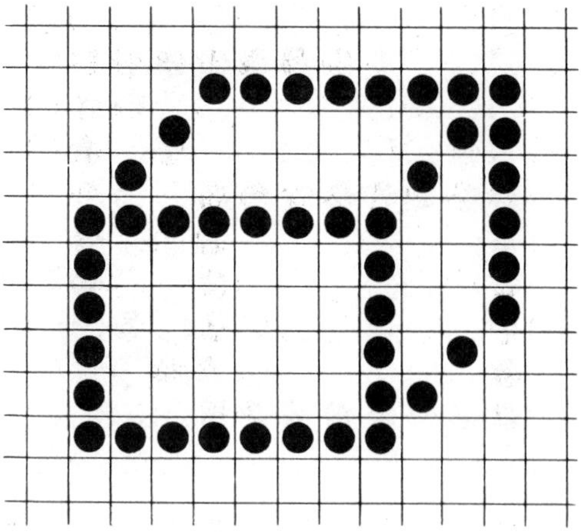

Figure 2-20. Picture-element (pixel) array. Each pixel occupies an area bounded by a set of hypothetical grid lines.

There are no equivalent limitations on the potential resolution of a stroke-writing system. A point has no dimension, so there is no theoretical limit on the number of hypothetical intersecion points which can be arrayed on the surface of a CRT screen. Stroke-writing resolution is determined primarily by the precision of the display data (e.g., 11-bit coordinate values create a hypothetical 2,048-line grid with

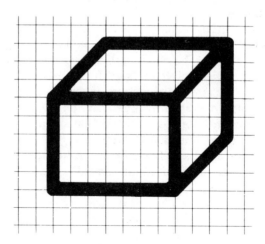

Figure 2-21. Coordinate-address array. Graphic elements are defined and positioned by a hypothetical array of intersection points.

over 4 million intersection points). Display resolution can be increased by simply increasing the precision of the data—up to and beyond the point where the eye can detect the difference and it becomes academic whether the monitor is actually positioning the information as precisely as the data would indicate.

Element Time Sharing

Display elements must be "accessed" in order to create an image. They must also be reaccessed each time the image is to be changed. The method used to control the display is influenced, therefore, by both the number of elements which must be accessed and the level of "animation" required by the display application.

The most direct way to access and control an array of display elements is to connect a separate signal source to each element on the display surface, as shown in Figure 2–22. But a practical limit is quickly reached—even in the case of simple segmented-character displays. A display consisting of ten 7-segment characters, for example, would require 70 driver circuits plus 70 signal inputs and a common, for a total of 71 hardwire connections. The same display in the form of ten 5-by-7 dot-matrix characters would require 350 driver circuits and at least 351 signal leads. Such a system would be impractical for most graphic-display applications (except, perhaps, for a large outdoor incan-

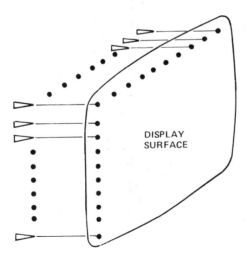

Figure 2–22. Direct accessing. A separate signal input is required for each display element. (Source: Reference 1)

descent-light display). Alternative methods must be found, therefore, for reducing both the signal-source circuitry and the number of physical connections.

One way to reduce the display-driver costs would be to time-share or "multiplex" the display elements, connecting them randomly or sequentially to a limited number of signal sources through an external switching system. If the display elements are bistable—remaining on or off, visible or invisible, until reaccessed—the only factors limiting the number of multiplexed display elements would be the switching rate and the image-change requirements. In most cases, however, the display elements are volatile, producing visible images for only brief time intervals after they have been accessed. Such displays can still be multiplexed, however, by taking advantage of the relatively slow rate at which the eye responds to changes in the luminance level. If the system returns to each display element and "refreshes" its output at sufficiently frequent intervals (independent of whether the status of the element is to be changed), a constant, flicker-free image will be perceived by the eye-brain system.

Figure 2–23 indicates that the minimum refresh rate or "critical

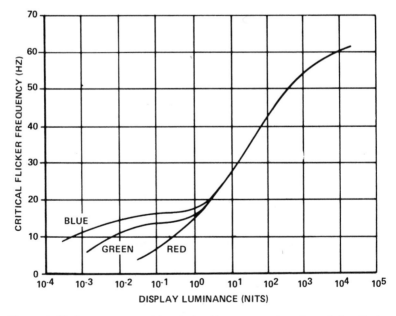

Figure 2–23. Minimum repetition (refresh) rate as a function of the display luminance.

flicker frequency" (CFF) is a function of the luminance level. The higher the luminance, the faster the eye responds to changes in the light level—requiring a higher refresh rate to avoid objectionable flicker. Conversely, with each increase in the refresh rate, a higher luminance level can be tolerated. At 60 Hz, for example, the luminance level can be ten times the allowable luminance at 50 Hz. (At extremely low levels, the color of the light affects the flicker threshold. Not apparent from Figure 2-23 is an anomaly—an increase in the perceived luminance that occurs at approximately 10 Hz, the alpha-rhythm frequency of the brain.)

The CFF puts an effective limit on the number of display elements which can time-share a single signal source. The reciprocal of the number of display elements is termed the "duty factor." The duty factor for a 1,000-element display, for example, is 0.001, and represents the fraction of the refresh time interval (one thousandth of a sixtieth of a second or 16.6 microseconds for a 60-Hz refresh rate) during which each element is connected to the signal source. The display element must be able to create a recognizable image within this time limit. In some cases, it is the speed of response that limits the duty factor and number of elements. In other cases, it is the minimum amount of power that must be delivered to produce a visible image.

If the response time of the display elements is on the order of milliseconds, a relatively small number of elements can be time-shared by a single source. If the response time is measured in fractions of a microsecond, a much larger number of elements can be multiplexed and the principal limitation becomes the minimum power input required per element.

The eye averages and also integrates luminance over time, which helps to account for the flicker-free phenomenon and the fact that even a refresh rate above the CFF may produce an occasional "blink" in the perceived display output. A display element that decays slowly (either intrinsically or, for example, because "memory" has been added in the form of capacitance) may appear more luminous than the duty-factor calculation would predict. But for reasons not clearly understood, the perceived luminance can also be enhanced by extremely brief flashes of light. Within limits, the eye apparently responds to both the rise and fall rates of the light output as well as to the absolute level of the luminance signal.

Addressing Techniques

Time-sharing can reduce the cost of the support electronics, but it does not, in itself, alter the number of physical connections. These, too, must be "shared" by the display elements if the number of connections is to be reduced. One way to achieve this objective is to divide the display elements into groups and "levels" with each element assigned to at least two groups in separate levels. Individual elements can then be uniquely accessed by addressing two or more group-input leads.

"Matrix addressing" is an implementation of this principle. The display elements in Figure 2–24 have been organized into two levels with nine vertical-column and seven horizontal-row groups, reducing the number of signal-input leads to the *sum* of the rows and columns (16) rather than their *product* (63). Individual display elements are accessed by applying a signal-source voltage to a column input connector, for example, while selected row connectors are switched to ground.

An equivalent two-level matrix addressing scheme can be applied to segmented-character displays by providing a separate "column" input signal for each character and linking together the equivalent segments in each character to form display-element "rows." The effect on the 10-character segmented display described in the previous section would be to reduce the total number of hardwire connections from 71 to 17.

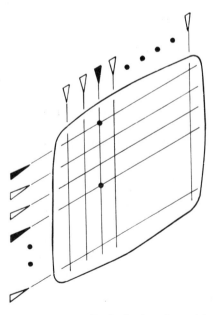

Figure 2–24. Matrix addressing. Each display element has a unique vertical-column and horizontal-row address. (Source: Reference 1)

In both cases, only a single group of elements—a row or a column—can be accessed during a given time interval. Random or sequential multiplexing is therefore an inherent requirement of the matrix-addressing technique. The most common method is to "strobe" either the columns or rows while "data" signals are applied to the other set of signal leads. The strobe rate becomes the governing parameter, then, in determining the duty factor for individual display elements. Assuming a column strobe of the matrix in Figure 2–24, the duty factor becomes 0.11 (one-ninth of the refresh interval) rather than the 0.016 which would apply if the 63 elements were individually multiplexed. Stated another way, there has been a sevenfold increase in the amount of power delivered to each display element by using the matrix-addressing technique—as well as a significant reduction in the number of connections.

Matrix addressing is not, however, without its faults. In theory only the display elements at the intersections of the selected address lines are switched on by the display-signal voltage. But all of the other dozens or hundreds of display elements form sneak-current paths which can reduce the voltage gradient across the selected elements. Of even greater concern is the fact that the non-selected elements may be partly turned on by the sneak currents, lowering the display contrast at the same time the luminance from the selected elements is reduced. Both of these effects would be minimized, of course, if the elements were either unipolar (i.e., diodes) or demonstrated an intrinsic non-linear threshold or hysteresis response to the applied voltage. Light-emitting-diode, cathodoluminescent, and gas-discharge devices have these features to a sufficient degree so that no external circuitry is required to reduce the effect of sneak currents. But liquid-crystal and other display technologies often require an "active" switch at each element (Figure 2–25) to provide a measure of non-linearity.

Both the advantages and disadvantages of matrix addressing increase with each additional matrixing level. The "grid addressing" system shown in Figure 2–26 can be viewed as a three-level matrix which requires only 12 signal leads to select any one of 64 display elements (compared to 16 leads for a conventional two-level matrix or 65 leads for a direct-accessing system). It is only applicable, however, to cathodoluminescent, gas-discharge, and other displays that have mobile charge carriers that can be controlled by the selective charging of the grids.

For a maximum reduction in the number of signal leads, we must look to "scan addressing" and the CRT, which is again in a class by itself. Only three signal connections (Figure 2–27) are required for a

COLUMN ADDRESS LINES

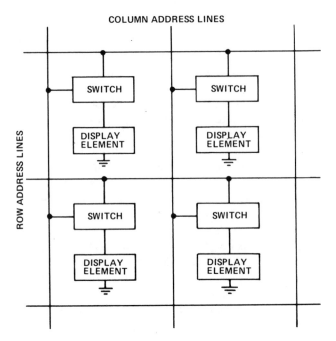

Figure 2–25. "Active" switches may be required to inhibit sneak currents through non-selected display elements.

monochrome CRT. Yet thousands, even millions of display-element locations can be accessed.

In a sense, the monochrome CRT represents the ultimate expression of the multiplexing technique. Only one signal-source input is time-

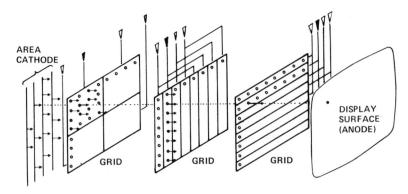

Figure 2–26. Grid addressing. Grids control flow of electrons from cathode to display-surface anode. (Source: Reference 1)

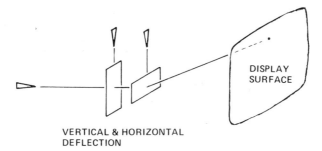

VERTICAL & HORIZONTAL
DEFLECTION

Figure 2–27. Scan addressing. Accessing of individual points on the display surface can be either random or in a fixed (e.g., raster) pattern. (Source: Reference 1)

shared by all of the display-element locations on the CRT screen. The other two inputs serve a scan-addressing function, directing the electron beam either randomly or in a sequential raster pattern. Color CRT's with three electron beams require five signal inputs to accomplish the same objective, but this is still a minuscule figure, compared to the number of addressing lines required by any other type of display device.

CONVENTIONAL CRT'S

Figure 2–28 shows the basic components of a conventional CRT. A heated cathode emits a continuous stream of electrons. These are formed into a beam by an aperture in a control grid surrounding the cathode. The electrons are then accelerated by one or more positive-potential grids and focused to a point at the display surface by an electrostatic or magnetic "lens."

The focused beam is turned toward the top, bottom, or sides of the CRT screen by a deflection mechanism which again can be electrostatic or magnetic. After deflection, the electrons travel in a straight line toward the faceplate in a uniform field created by a high positive potential on a conductive surface that covers the inside of the CRT "bottle." The front surface is coated with a thin layer of phosphor particles. When the electrons strike the phosphor particles, a fraction of the kinetic energy is absorbed, "exciting" electrons in the phosphor molecules to a higher energy state. A photon of visible light is emitted as each excited electron falls back to its natural energy state. The duration or "persistence" of the photon emission may last for milliseconds or microseconds, depending on the type of phosphor (Figure 2–29).

This brief description applies to all conventional CRT's. But few

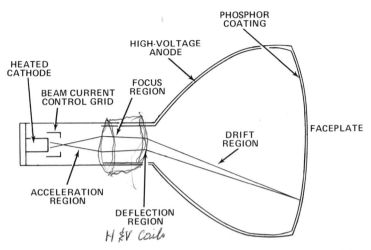

Figure 2-28. Basic design of a conventional CRT. Focus and deflection mechanisms can be electrostatic or magnetic.

CRT's are "conventional." Instead, there are dozens of different construction and performance variables that can be combined to meet a particular set of application requirements. The most important factors affecting the cost and performance of raster-scan CRT monitors are described in Chapter 9, Monitor Evaluation and Selection. The balance of the present chapter will examine the differences that distinguish raster-scan CRT's from other types of CRT's which have been historically important in the development of computer-based graphics systems.

The first "graphics" CRT was a modified oscilloscope—a direct ancestor of today's high-performance refresh-vector systems. The amount of data which could be displayed during each refresh cycle was severely limited, however, and this led to a variety of techniques for "storing" vectorgraphic lines and displaying them, as a second step, on a conventional raster-scan monitor.

The so-called "scan-converter" systems increased the volume of information which could be displayed, but due to the nature of the storage surface (e.g., a wire grid), resolution was less than satisfactory. Storage *and* resolution had to wait until the development of the "direct-view" storage tube described below. Meanwhile, scan-coverter technology has continued to evolve, resulting in systems of the type depicted in Figures 2-30 and 2-31. Semiconductor fabrication techniques have increased the resolution of the storage surface to

PHOSPHOR	COMPOSITION	PEAK WAVELENGTH NANOMETERS	COLOR	DECAY TO 10%	APPLICATIONS
P1	Zn_2SiO_4:Mn	525	YG	24mS	OSCILLOSCOPES; RADAR
P2	ZnS:CU	543	YG	35-100μS	OSCILLOSCOPES
P4	ZnS:Ag ZnS-CdS:Ag	460/560	W	25/60μS	TELEVISION
P7	ZnS:Ag ZnS-CdS:Cu	440/560	B/YG(W)	40-60μS/.3S	OSCILLOSCOPES; RADAR
P11	ZnS:Ag	460	B	25-80μS	PHOTO RECORDING
P16	$Ca_2Mg_2Si_2O_7$:Ce	385	UV	.12μS	FLYING SPOT SCANNERS; PHOTO RECORDING
P20	ZnS-CdS:Ag	560	YG	.05-2mS	HIGH-EFFICIENCY PHOSPHOR
P22-B	ZnS:Ag	440	B	22μS	COLOR TV
P22-G	ZnS-CdS:Ag	535	YG	60μS	COLOR TV
P22-R	Y_2O_2S:Eu	625	R	1mS	COLOR TV
P22-G $_{LP}$	Zn_2SiO_4:Mn::As	525	YG	150mS	LONG-PERSISTENCE PHOSPHOR; COLOR GRAPHICS
P31	ZnS:CU	522	G	40μS	HIGH-EFFICIENCY PHOSPHOR; OSCILLOSCOPES
P39	Zn_2SiO_4:Mn::As	525	YG	150mS	LONG-PERSISTENCE, LOW-FRAME-RATE DISPLAYS
P42	ZnS:Cu Zn_2SiO_4:Mn::As	520	YG	10mS	INTEGRATING PHOSPHOR; LOW-FRAME-RATE, HIGH-BRIGHTNESS DISPLAYS
P43	Gd_2O_2S:Tb	544	YG	1mS	VISUAL DISPLAYS
P44	La_2O_2S:Tb	540	YG	1mS	VISUAL DISPLAYS
P45	Y_2O_2S:Tb	420/540	W	2mS	VISUAL DISPLAYS
P49	Zn_2SiO_4:Mn YVO_4:Eu	525/615	YG/RO	30/1.2mS	PENETRATION-COLOR DISPLAYS

Figure 2–29. Characteristics of phosphors used in typical CRT applications. (Source: Reference 1)

4,096-by-4,096 display elements, allowing selected areas to be panned, scrolled, or continuously "zoomed" up in size without dropping below the resolution limit of the raster-scan monitor used as the display device.

Storage-Tube CRT's

A storage-tube CRT preserves an image for extended periods of time by incorporating several unusual features into the conventional CRT design. Figure 2–32 illustrates a commercially available storage-tube configuration. Several "flood guns" continuously bombard the phosphor surface with electrons. An anode coating on the face of the CRT is kept at a relatively low positive potential, on the order of + 200 V. The effect of the low-level electron bombardment is to keep the

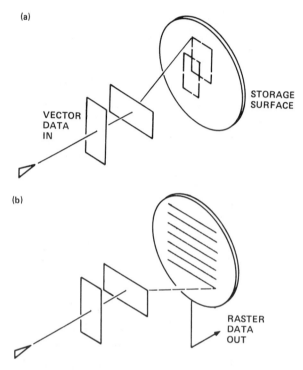

(a)

VECTOR
DATA
IN

STORAGE
SURFACE

(b)

RASTER
DATA
OUT

Figure 2–30. Two-step scan-converter system. Electron beam "writes" on image memory plane (a). The same beam then traces a raster (b) to refresh a conventional raster-scan monitor. (Source: Princeton Electronic Products, Inc.)

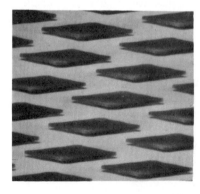

Figure 2–31. Microphotograph of image memory plane. Over 4 million siliconoxide microcapacitor elements are deposited on one-inch target disk (Source: Princeton Electronic Products, Inc.)

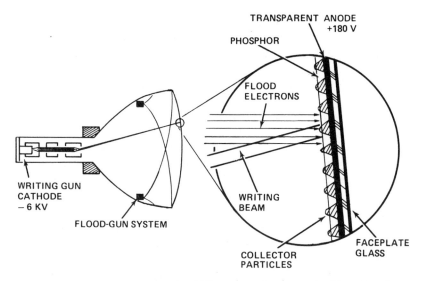

Figure 2-32. A typical storage-tube CRT construction. Image is either stored or refreshed, depending on the electron energy of the writing beam. (Source: Tektronix, Inc.)

phosphor surface at a neutral, zero-volt potential—equal to that of the flood guns.

By contrast, the writing-gun cathode has a negative potential of several thousand volts. When the electron beam from the writing gun strikes the phosphor surface, a secondary emission of electrons occurs, positively charging the phosphor particles in the immediate vicinity. Flood electrons are attracted to the positive-potential pattern created by the secondary emission, resulting in a continuously regenerated display image.

The secondary electrons and any excess flood electrons are "collected" by raised conductive particles embedded in the phosphor coating. Whenever any part of the display is to be deleted or changed, the entire stored image is erased by increasing the positive anode voltage, causing the flood electrons to "flash" the entire display surface. The anode voltage is then returned to its operating level so that a new image can be "written."

The stored image can be combined with a volatile image by reducing the writing-beam energy to a "writethrough" level, below the stored-charge threshold value. By refreshing the volatile image at a flicker-free rate, a movable cursor, for example, can be displayed on the surface along with the static stored image. The writethrough energy level can also be used to generate a hard copy output signal by sensing the faceplate collector current while the entire surface is raster scanned. The collector current remains at a constant level except when the writethrough beam crosses over lines in the stored image.

In principle, the stored or refreshed images could be (and often are) written in both random-scan and raster-scan patterns. But the deflection and modulation circuits are optimized for random "stroke-writing." Images are created by scanning straight-line vectors between randomly selected points on the display screen (Figure 2–33). Circles and arcs can be simulated by a succession of short vectors. Characters are traced as a series of vector strokes. Dot patterns are created by "stroking" a series of zero-length vectors.

The storage-tube image is, in this instance, a relatively low-contrast green. Other storage-tube designs have been developed, however, to display multiple colors and intermediate gray-scale values. They have also been designed with extremely long bistable characteristics that extend the "persistence" of the stored image for hours or even days.

The storage-tube CRT is a relatively complex structure, but the cost of the tube is balanced by savings in the support electronics. There is no constraint in the amount of time required to trace an image. The amount of data that must be stored for quick-access "refresh" is reduced to a minimum. The bandwidth of signal-processing circuits can be very modest. Yet given time, extremely complex images can be created, such as the one shown in Figure 2–34. In fact, a 25-inch storage tube can be used to display more than 15,000 typewriter-size characters—far beyond the capacity of any other type of electronic-display device.

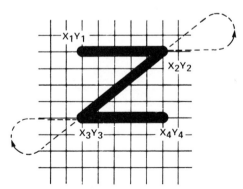

Figure 2–33. Stroke-writing sequence. Endpoint coordinates locate vectors on hypothetical grid.

Figure 2–34. High-density display "written" on storage-tube surface. (Source: Tektronix, Inc.)

Refreshed-Vector Monitors

As in the case of storage-tube displays, refreshed-vector monitors are optimized for drawing straight lines. The major difference is that the refreshed-vector CRT does not have any image storage capability. The traced lines are volatile, requiring the entire display to be retraced at a rate above the flicker threshold of the human eye.

The necessity for refresh limits the amount of information which can be presented. But high-speed analog circuits and deflection techniques have been developed to produce very fast writing rates. Over 150,000 short vectors, for instance, can be traced within 1/60 of a second. Long vectors are drawn at rates up to an inch per microsecond.

The retrace-time limitation of the refreshed-vector CRT is balanced by two major advantages over the storage tube. Since a completely new image is traced with each refresh cycle, the display can be easily animated and the operator can interact with the display in real time. As illustrated in Figure 2–35, a lightpen can be used to "drag" a portion of the image from one position on the display screen to another. Moreover, selected segments can be instantly erased without affecting the balance of the display, and key feature can be blinked or intensified to draw the operator's attention.

The second advantage of the refreshed-vector CRT is that it can be designed to produce images in color. One way to achieve this result is to modify a standard three-gun color tube for high-speed stroke writing. By adjusting the output of the three primary-color electron guns, individual vectors can be drawn in an unlimited number of different colors. Color can also be added to the display by using a "beam penetration" tube with two or more phosphor layers superimposed on the CRT screen. At low electron-beam energy levels, the electrons penetrate only the inner layer, typically a red phosphor. With increased energy levels, the beam penetrates to the outer layer, normally a green phosphor. The higher perceived luminance of the green light masks the

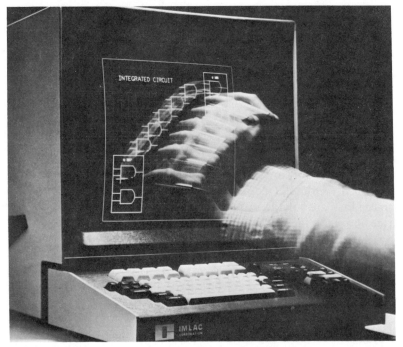

Figure 2–35. "Dragging" a display element across a refresh-vector screen. (Source: IMLAC Corporation)

output of the red-phosphor background. An intermediate energy level will produce a yellow color (Figure 2–36).

There are a number of variations on the beam-penetration technique. One method is to coat phosphor particles with one or more "onion-skin" layers of different-colored phosphors. Another alternative is to mix two or more phosphors which have distinctly different response curves; at low electron-beam energy levels, only the more sensitive phosphor emits light; at higher energy levels, a mixed light output is produced.

Raster-Scan Monitors

Raster-scan monitors lack the "random access" flexibility of the storage-tube and refreshed-vector stroke writers. Raster-scan deflection circuits are designed, instead, to trace a fixed pattern of parallel lines on the screen (Figure 2–37). Images are created by modulating the electron beam—changing the intensity or color at precisely timed intervals as the raster lines are scanned from left to right, top to bottom.

The scanned lines are volatile, which means that the complete raster pattern must be redrawn at a repetition rate above the flicker level of

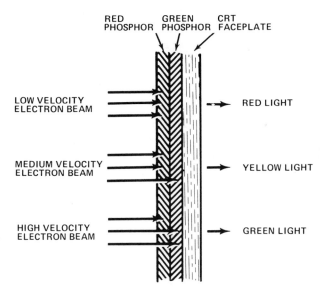

Figure 2–36. Phosphor layers on surface of three-color "beam penetration" CRT. Acceleration of electron beam determines color output.

Figure 2–37. Raster-scan pattern. Raster lines are "written" from left to right, top to bottom, with each refresh cycle.

the human eye. But unlike the refreshed-vector display, a raster-scan monitor is not restricted to the number of lines or dots which can be stroked within a limited refresh interval. The raster pattern addresses *every* pixel location on the CRT screen with every refresh cycle, allowing it to portray not only lines and dots, but also solid or continuously varying areas of color or gray-scale intensity.

Pixel-by-pixel addressing—at the full refresh rate—is the most important single factor contributing to the versatility of raster-scan displays. Alphagraphic, vectorgraphic, and photographic images, static or animated, can be combined on a single display surface. Add in the full-color capabilities of CRT's developed for commercial raster-scan television receivers, and it is understandable why raster scanning has become the dominant display technique for computer-based graphics systems.

There is, however, a price for this versatility. Pixel-by-pixel raster scanning also imposes severe economic and performance constraints on the design of a graphics display system. In one form or another, data for every pixel on the screen (Figure 2–38) must be stored in memory and accessed during each refresh cycle. If the image is to be displayed in color or in a range of gray-scale intensities, several bits of information for each of hundreds of thousands of pixels must be stored in a bit-map memory and converted into display-signal modula-

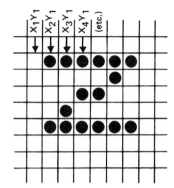

Figure 2-38. Pixel-by-pixel raster scanning. Display data must be supplied for each pixel, whether or not an image is to be displayed at that location.

tions within the time limits established by the scanning process. Lower-cost semiconductor memories have made this economically feasible. Alternate mapping methods, described in Chapter 7, can also be used to decrease the amount of stored information and further reduce the memory costs. But a series of other technical requirements and limitations are not so easily resolved.

To "animate" a line, for example, may require the recalculation of dozens or even hundreds of pixel values. By comparison, a line displayed on a refreshed-vector screen can be moved by simply recalculating its endpoint coordinates.

Pixel-by-pixel, raster-scan addressing also increases the amount of information that must be transferred from display memory to monitor. Interface and monitor circuits must be capable of processing broadband signals to avoid loss of data. Despite the wider bandwidth signal paths, however, displayed raster-scan information appears "coarser" and less detailed. Diagonal lines and boundaries are "stairstepped" instead of smooth and straight like the lines displayed by a refreshed-vector or storage-tube monitor.

Figure 2-39 shows this stairstepping and the beneficial effect that increased resolution has on the appearance of the lines. But increasing the resolution with more raster lines and more pixels per line only compounds the other raster-scan problems. Doubling the resolution has the effect of quadrupling the number of pixel values which must be calculated, stored in memory, and transferred to the monitor screen. A 512-by-512 pixel array, for example, has 262,144 addressable pixel locations. A 1024-by-1024 array has 1,048,576 pixel locations. The system must have not only a larger, faster display memory, but also a wider monitor-interface bandwidth, a faster-scanning monitor, and in

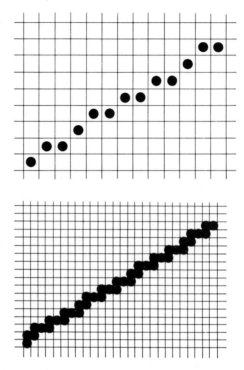

Figure 2–39. Effect of increased raster resolution on appearance of diagonal vectors, assuming a constant electron-beam spot diameter.

the case of color displays, a more precise convergence of the monitor's three electron beams.

System Resolution

By raster-scan standards, a 512-by-512 pixel array represents a "medium" resolution level. A 1024-by-1024 array would be a "high" resolution display and close to the upper limit of the present state of the art. Yet stroke-writers start at the 1024-resolution level and extend up to 2048 or 4096 "addressable" display locations along the X and Y axes.

A direct comparison between the two types of displays is not, however, entirely valid. The endpoint coordinates of a stroke-written vector apply to a hypothetical X-Y grid on the display surface. The resolution of the display *system* can be doubled by simply adding another bit to the binary-coded words used to store the coordinate data. The actual increase in resolution might be imperceptible on the monitor screen but could be of value when the same coordinate information is used to create an integrated-circuit mask or to produce a part on a numerically controlled machine tool. The added precision could also be of value when sections of the display are "zoomed" up to provide a more detailed look at the image data.

By contrast, the resolution of a raster-scan display is only half hypothetical. Vertical resolution is physically fixed by the number of raster lines traced by the CRT's electron beam. Horizontal resolution is more abstract. Strictly speaking, it is defined by the number of pixel values communicated to the monitor while each raster line is scanned. Again, however, depending on the electron-beam spot size, the monitor performance, and the bandwidth characteristics of the interface circuits, the theoretical horizontal detail may or may not be perceptible to the human eye.

It is important to keep these variables in mind as we examine, in the following chapters, the functions to be performed by a raster graphics system, the design parameters of a graphics controller and monitor interface, and the selection criteria for a raster-scan monitor.

There is, in effect, a succession of factors affecting the resolution of a display system (Figure 2-40). A graphics-oriented, raster-scan display system will typically start with coordinate data that is identical to that of a refreshed-vector or storage-tube system. It may be

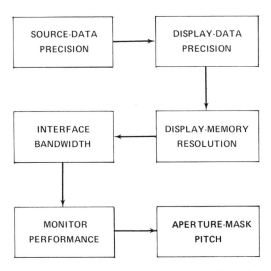

Figure 2-40. Factors contributing to "system" resolution.

valuable, for all the reasons given earlier, to specify a higher level of coordinate precision than that represented by the "resolving power" of the display device. After the coordinate data has been mapped into display-memory pixel values, however, the maximum resolution of the image is fixed. A wider-bandwidth interface or a higher-performance monitor can preserve the resolution of the data stored in the display memory, but not improve on it. Finally, there is the perceived resolution of the displayed image, which can be directly affected by such variables as the electron-beam diameter, the precision of convergence control circuits, and the spacing or "pitch" of the phosphor patterns used to generate a color display.

3
Functions and Tasks

The end product of a raster graphics system is a raster-scan display on a CRT screen. Or is it? As shown in Figure 3-1, the CRT monitor could also serve as the starting point. In an interactive system, decisions by the operator serve to close the loop. The total system takes a circular form, without beginning or end.

Of course, not every graphics installation follows this pattern. The term "interactive" is generally restricted to systems which allow the operator to manipulate the image on the screen in real time, using physical devices such as keyboards, digitizer tablets, or lightpens. But the purpose of any graphics display is to communicate information—to a person. If the recipient acts on the basis of this information, and if the actions affect the process which generated the information, a

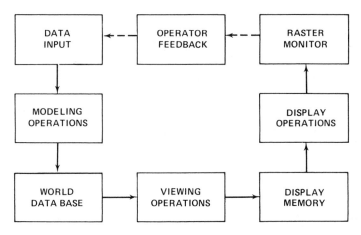

Figure 3-1. Processing functions, interactive raster graphics system.

feedback will occur and the system is, in the broadest sense, interactive.

The "operator," by this definition, could be a sales manager, reassigning sales territories based on the latest performance figures; or a doctor, deciding on a course of treatment; or a power-plant supervisor, responding to emergency conditions displayed on a control-room screen.

We will be using the interactive term in the narrower sense throughout this Handbook. But it is important to keep the broader view in mind, even if the raster graphics display is "for information only." In nearly every case, actions will result, and it is imperative that the display be as accurate, easy to understand, and informative as possible.

The present chapter describes the functions and tasks required to convert numerical source information into a display on a raster-scan CRT monitor. Figure 3–1 summarizes the processing sequence—independent of any specific hardware configurations or supporting software. The same requirements apply, whether the "graphics system" is a stand-alone unit, or its functions are distributed between a host computer and a separate graphics controller with its own microprocessor software.

A WORLD VIEW

Several terms and concepts need to be examined before we describe the functional requirements of a raster graphics system.

One of the first tasks for a raster graphics system designer or application programmer, for example, is to define the "world" which will be depicted—in whole or in part—on the monitor screen (see Figure 3–2). Within this world the application program or operator can place any number of "objects." An object might be a simple bar-chart rectangle, representing last-year's profits. Or the object could define the complex three-dimensional form and dimensions of a car body. Or it could be a weather-map outline of the United States.

The objects are described—in world dimensions—by a limited variety of "primitive" elements, such as dots, lines, areas enclosed by polygons, or solid forms such as cubes and cones. In most cases, descriptive text is also treated as a primitive. Dimensional notations, for example, can become a part of the object they help to describe.

The variety and type of primitives are established by the software system. Software also allows for a specified set of "attributes" which define the appearance of each primitive when it is shown on the monitor screen. The attributes of a primitive line could include its

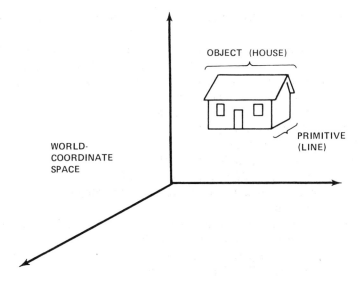

Figure 3-2. Primitives and objects in a world-coordinate space.

weight, gray-scale intensity, color, or whether it is to be shown in a dotted, dashed, or solid form.

MODELING VS. VIEWING

The world concept creates a distinct division in the operations which must be performed during the processing of source information into a raster graphics display.

The initial definition of the world—and the objects within that world—is called "modeling," and may be compared to the activities of a model shop. Forms are shaped and positioned, based on the available information, within a world environment.

The next task is to establish a "view" of the world. Viewing operations determine the actual appearance of the objects when their images are depicted on the monitor screen, and can be compared to the decisions made by a photographer who is free to position his camera at different angles and distances, select different focal-length lenses, and control the direction and level of illumination. The photographer can also select the parts of a negative to be enlarged, change the angle of projection, and use special filters or papers to obtain a particular contrast, pattern, or color reproduction. Viewing operations can dramatically change the perceived images of objects shown on the monitor screen. But the modeled objects in the world environment remain unchanged.

The distinction between modeling and viewing is reflected in the types of software written for computer graphics. Modeling operations are very dependent on the application. The data-processing steps required to produce business-chart objects would be very different from those used in the design of an integrated-circuit mask. Once the objects have been defined, however, similar viewing-operation software would be helpful in both applications.

Stated another way, model-shop tools and skills would differ widely, depending on the type of models to be built. But the same camera and darkroom equipment could be used to create a photographic record of the completed models.

Because modeling operations are so application oriented, most "graphics-software" packages emphasize the viewing operations which can or must be performed. In the extreme case, all of the modeling must be accomplished by the application program, using such primitive elements as dots, lines, and polygon areas. Graphics-software packages that reach beyond this limitation are, as we might expect, generally oriented to specific applications. Business-graphics packages, for example, would normally provide standard routines for generating graphs or bar charts. Computer-aided design packages might include provisions for generating standard electronic, mechanical engineering, or architectural symbols.

In one important sense, however, every interactive-graphics soft-

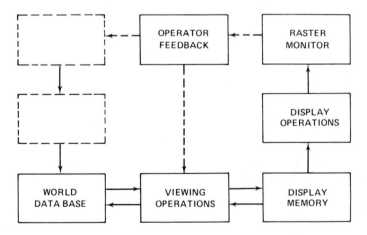

Figure 3-3. Direct operator interaction with viewing operations.

ware package has a potential modeling capability. Returning to Figure 3-1, we can see that any data-input feedback by the operator, based on the results of the viewing operations, could have the effect of "re-modeling" the world model.

But the operator will seldom want to make drastic, irrevocable changes until he is certain that the alterations are desirable. Most systems, therefore, give both the operator and the application programmer short-circuit control over the viewing operations (Figure 3-3), including the ability to change the viewed image of objects without altering their original form as world objects.

SEGMENTATION

The operator or programmer may want to change, for example, the relative position of displayed objects or the form of an individual object. It would be both time consuming and confusing, however, if each primitive in each object had to be manipulated separately. The solution is "segmentation." Individual primitives are grouped together into segments (Figure 3-4), each of which can be manipulated as a unit.

A segment could include all of the primitives which define a single object or several different objects—or similar primitives in different

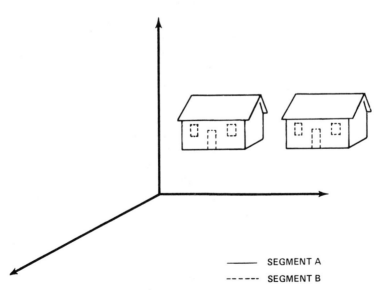

———— SEGMENT A

------ SEGMENT B

Figure 3-4. Segmentation of primitives and/or objects.

objects could form a single segment, allowing all of the elements to be changed simultaneously.

The primitives in a segment may be shifted to another location on the monitor screen, expanded, reduced, or rotated to a new orientation—or completely new segments, with their own primitives and attributes, may be temporarily created, while others are deleted. All of this can be accomplished without jeopardizing the earlier modeling operations.

The final step, when the operator is completely satisfied with the changes, is to change the world objects to match the viewed objects—either by inputting new information or, as shown in Figure 3–3, by reversing the flow of information through the viewing operations.

TWO VS. THREE DIMENSIONS

A raster graphics monitor screen is a "view surface." It has only two dimensions: width and height.

A great deal of research has been directed toward the development of a CRT display that can be *perceived* as three dimensional. Figure 3–5 illustrates one method. The viewer observes the monitor screen "through" a 20-inch mirrored-plastic disc, oscillating between convex and concave in response to a 30 Hz "woofer" signal. With only a 4-mm movement at the center of the mirror, the 15-inch monitor screen appears to move a distance of 12 inches, forward and backward, establishing the limits of a trapezoidal virtual-image "space." Images on the screen are timed to coincide with the mirror's movement, creating a three-dimensional display that can be viewed from the front or side. Up to 12 low-resolution rasters can be scanned during the mirror cycle. Each raster image represents, therefore, a one-inch cross section of the three-dimensional objects "sculpted" by the graphics program.

Meanwhile, conventional graphics systems are categorized as "two-dimensional" or "three-dimensional" depending solely on the sophistication of the system software. The two categories could be compared to photocopying machines and cameras. Both can be used to reproduce two-dimensional copies of images. But the two-dimensional camera output can also recreate three-dimensional scenes—in the mind of the viewer—by providing such visual clues as the relative size of objects at different distances, the distortions caused by the view perspective, and the obscuring of background details by foreground forms.

Both modeling and viewing operations are impacted by the difference. The two-dimensional world is a plane; a three-dimensional

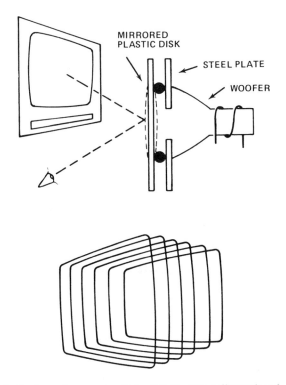

Figure 3-5. System for generating "true" three-dimensional views of computer-graphics images. Viewer sees a series of spatially separated raster planes. (Source: Genisco Computers)

world is a space. If modeled objects are inherently three-dimensional, the most a two-dimensional system can define is the data on a single plane within the three-dimensional space. But there is an even greater impact on the viewing operations—just as the image manipulations which can be accomplished with a photocopying machine are relatively limited compared to the variety of effects which can be implemented with a mobile camera.

Figure 3-6 illustrates the difference, taking just image rotation as an example. The only variables in two-dimensional rotation are the turning point and angle. Three-dimensional rotation capabilities would have to include, in the simplest case, rotation centered on any one of the three coordinate axes. Progressive system-software sophistication would include rotation centered on any line parallel to one of these axes, and finally, rotation centered on any vector in space.

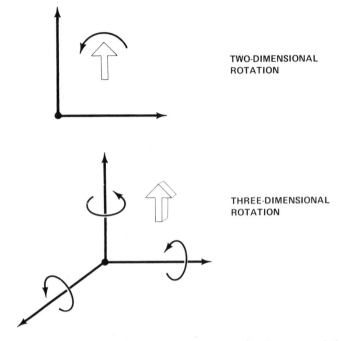

Figure 3-6. Rotation of objects within a two-dimensional plane and three-dimensional space.

COORDINATE TRANSFORMATIONS

Coordinates are the "language" of a graphics system, and in many respects, a graphics system could be viewed as a "coordinate processor."

Unfortunately, coordinate conventions are far from standardized. Coordinate transformations are likely to be a repeated requirement, therefore, throughout both the modeling and viewing operations. The only compensation is that nearly all of the coordinate systems are Cartesian, with right angles between adjoining axes.

The coordinate schemes encountered within a graphics system may have infinite, semi-infinite, or limited magnitudes. These choices are illustrated in Figure 3-7 for two-dimensional coordinates.

Coordinate systems can also be hybrid, with positive-only dimensions along one axis, but both positive and negative dimensions along the other. It would be an advantage, for example, to locate the origin of positive-coordinate character masks at the lower left corner of each

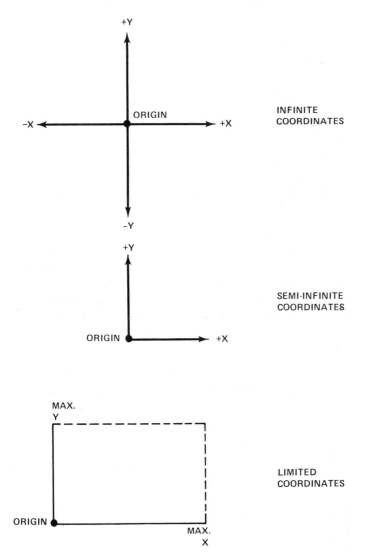

Figure 3-7. A choice of coordinate systems, even within the category of two-dimensional Cartesian rectangular coordinates.

character space on a positive-coordinate display surface. But this can be accomplished (Figure 3–8a) only if the lowercase *g, p* and *y* descenders have negative mask values along the Y-axis.

Such masks are based on "relative" rather than "absolute" coor-

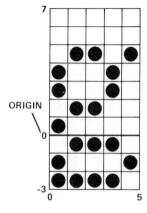

Figure 3–8a. Character mask with negative Y-axis coordinate values.

dinate values, and the same principle can be applied not only to frequently used, hardware-generated alphanumeric and graphic characters but also to modeled or viewed objects. Figure 3–8b shows how an object defined by relative coordinates can be moved from one location to another by simply changing the coordinates of the origin. Implicit in this technique, however, is the use of both positive and

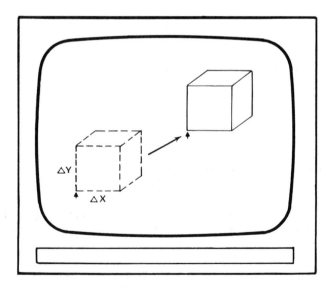

Figure 3–8b. Object defined by relative coordinate values. Image can be translated from one position to another by simply changing the coordinates of the origin.

negative coordinate values in what is normally an all-positive coordinate environment.

A number of the coordinate inconsistencies can be traced to earlier conventions in disciplines which are now, for the first time, interacting at the graphics-system level. For example, the historical coordinate system for plane geometry (and most scientific applications) is based on a horizontal X-axis, increasing positively to the right. The Y-axis is vertical, increasing positively in an upward direction, as shown in Figure 3–9a. But the early developers of television systems settled on a raster pattern that starts in the upper left corner of the screen. The X-axis is still horizontal, increasing positively to the right. Yet the raster is assembled from top to bottom, like the lines of type on this page, producing a Y-axis dimension that increases positively in the downward direction (Figure 3–9b).

The designer of a raster display memory must decide, therefore, whether to establish an addressing scheme based on the coordinates of the source information, which will probably be conventional X-Y, or on the order in which the information is presented to the CRT monitor during each refresh cycle.

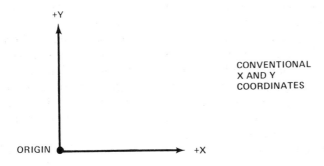

Figure 3–9a. Conventional two-dimensional X-Y coordinate system.

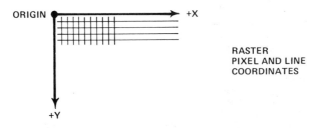

Figure 3–9b. Optional X-Y system based on raster-scan pattern.

The raster lines and pixels create a coordinate system, similar to the hypothetical coordinate grid which is used to locate the endpoints of lines drawn by a refresh-vector or storage-tube system. But each raster pixel occupies an area on the screen surface—not a dimensionless coordinate intersection. Raster coordinates are defined, therefore, by hypothetical lines *between* the physical raster lines and pixel columns. The convention is to identify a raster line, pixel column, or individual pixel by the immediately preceding coordinate line or lines. For example, the X-Y coordinates of the single pixel in Figure 3–10 would be (104, 24). The vertical column of pixels would have an X-axis value of 106.

The importance of this convention can be appreciated by considering the ambiguity that would occur if the column of pixels represented the border of a shaded area and the coordinate line passed through the center of each pixel. The shaded area could, in this case, extend either a half-pixel beyond the coordinate line or be a half-pixel short, depending on whether the pixels are taken as the boundary of the shaded area or the background. The between-the-pixel scheme resolves this problem but creates another inconsistency in the realm of two-dimensional coordinate systems.

Three-dimensional coordinate systems can be even more inconsistent. Geometric (land-measurement) theory had its start with surveying and map making. X-and Y-axes represented vectors on a flat land surface. A third dimension, Z, represented elevations above the surface, with increasing values in an upward direction. This has become the conventional method for representing three-dimensional space.

Two-dimensional views of this world space present us with several problems. If we look at the space horizontally from the front, in the same way that we view a monitor screen, we would have a horizontal X-axis and a vertical Z-axis.

We could, of course, obtain a conventional X-Y view by looking at

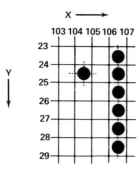

Figure 3–10. Raster-scan pixels occupy areas bounded by coordinate lines.

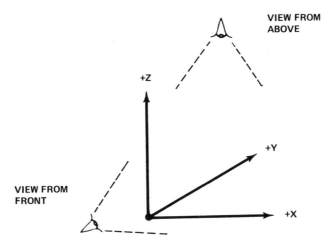

Figure 3-11. Conventional X-Y-Z three-dimensional coordinate system.

the space from the top (Figure 3-11), or by rotating the space around the X-axis (Figure 3-12a). Either way, however, the Z-axis would be pointing toward our eyes or "camera." The maximum positive Z dimension would be the distance between our viewpoint and the origin of the coordinate system.

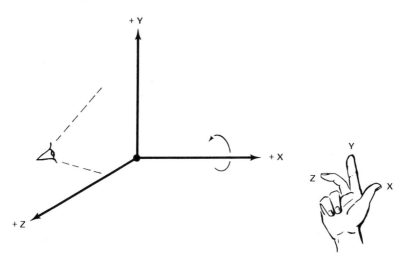

Figure 3-12a. Conventional "right-handed" coordinate system rotated around X-axis.

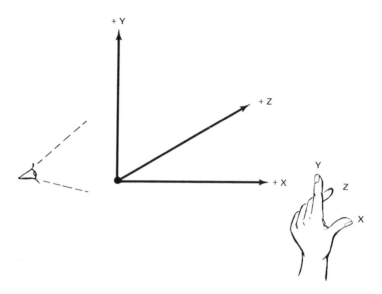

Figure 3–12b. "Left-handed" coordinate system with + Z values measured away from the viewer.

To avoid this limitation, graphics system designers and programmers often choose to transform "right-handed" world coordinates to "left-handed" values during the viewing operations. As shown in Figure 3–12b, the left-handed scheme allows positive Z-axis coordinates to increase infinitely—"into" the monitor screen—with distance away from the viewer.

There is another raster graphics Z dimension which has nothing to do with space coordinates. Raster resolution is frequently defined by the number of Y-axis raster lines and the number of addressable X-axis pixel locations along each line. In addition, the individual pixels have a "Z" value which indicates the number of bits used to define their intensity or color. Thus, any view-surface is, in theory, a plane with a Z-axis dimension of 0. But in raster graphics, the monitor screen has a minimum Z dimension of 1 (monochrome).

MULTIPLE TRANSFORMATIONS

Even the simplest raster graphics system will require one or more coordinate transformations.

Each information source, for example, may have its own "local" coordinate system. The data may represent flow rate versus time, shipments versus sales territories, or the X-Y-Z location of a bubble-chamber event. As a first step, all of this information must be manipulated into primitive elements—dots, lines, polygons, and text—using a uniform set of world-coordinate values.

In a relatively small two-dimensional system, the world coordinates may be identical to the display-memory coordinates. Primitives representing the source information can be simply "mapped" into the display memory. More likely, however, there will be one or more intermediate steps, each requiring a coordinate transformation. The displayed information may represent, for example, only a limited view of the world-coordinate data. Primitives viewed through a world-coordinate "window" must be converted to display-memory coordinates before they can be mapped into a display-memory "viewport."

Graphics software generally accomplishes this in two steps. To produce a "device-independent" package, adaptable to any type of display or hardcopy device, the system transforms the view through the world-coordinate window into a viewport expressed in Normalized Device Coordinates (NDC). Another transformation is then required to map the NDC-viewport data into the display memory (Figure 3-13).

The computational procedures and implementing hardware used to map the data into the display memory are critical to the performance of the graphics system. The algorithm that translates diagonal vectors into separate pixel locations on separate raster lines has, for example, a direct effect on the appearance of the display. The objectives are to

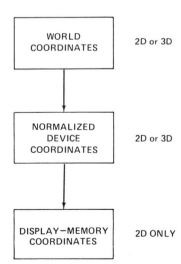

Figure 3-13. Coordinate transformation with device-independent intermediate step.

keep the stairstepping discontinuities to a minimum and, at the same time, avoid the varying line thicknesses caused by a "bunching" or skipping of pixels. A variety of digital-differential-analyzer (DDA) procedures have been developed for straight and curved lines, each with its strengths and weaknesses. Sophisticated procedures may even include the calculation of intermediate-intensity pixels at each stairstep to "soften" the irregularities.

If the display memory has a one-to-one correspondence with the monitor screen, no further transformations are required. By mapping the viewport data into an appropriate section of the display memory, the graphic content of the world-coordinate window will appear in the desired location on the screen.

The display memory may represent, however, considerably more pixel locations than the monitor can display. Portions of the display

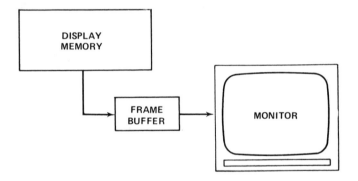

Figure 3-14a. Frame buffer as a physically separate "refresh memory."

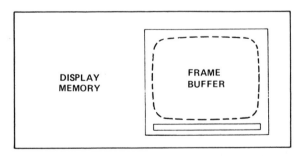

Figure 3-14b. Frame buffer simulated by addressing selected blocks within the display memory.

memory may, in fact, be stored on a disk. This means that the viewport, too, may also be larger than the monitor screen. A further transformation may then be required to convert the display-memory data to "frame buffer" coordinates which correspond to pixel locations on the monitor. The frame buffer may be a separate physical memory (Figure 3–14a), or its function can be simulated by addressing selected portions of a larger display memory (Figure 3–14b).

SCALE, TRANSLATE, ROTATE

During and between each conversion from one coordinate system to another, additional transformations may take place. The most important of these are scaling, translation, and rotation (Figure 3–15), and all are normally accomplished during the viewing operations—without affecting the objects defined in the world-coordinate space.

Rotation can be accomplished at separate stages in the viewing process. First, as shown in Figure 3–16, a rotation of *all* three-dimensional world objects can be simulated by tracing a circular "view point" path around the objects. Or individual objects can be rotated after they have been recreated in the three-dimensional NDC-viewport space. In the-

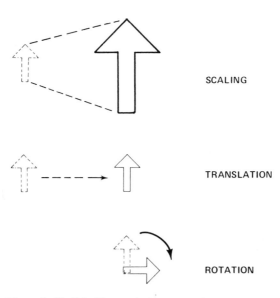

SCALING

TRANSLATION

ROTATION

Figure 3–15. Primitive and object transformations.

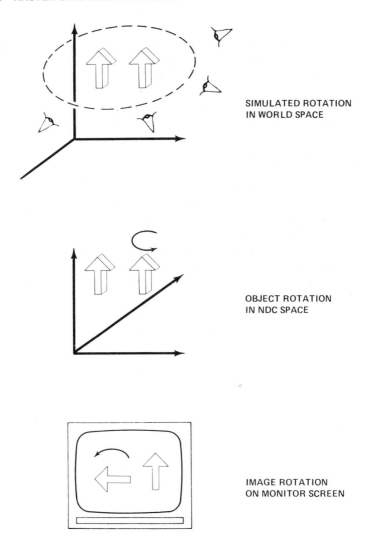

SIMULATED ROTATION
IN WORLD SPACE

OBJECT ROTATION
IN NDC SPACE

IMAGE ROTATION
ON MONITOR SCREEN

Figure 3-16. Rotation at different stages in the viewing operations.

ory, images of objects could also be rotated after they have been mapped into the display memory. This would require, however, an extensive recalculation of individual pixel values. It is normally simpler to rotate the objects at the NDC-viewport level and remap the results.

Similar options apply to the other two transformations. In every case, world objects are usually transformed as a group, while individual objects (or primitives) can be modified within the NDC-viewport space.

Translations, changes from one display location to another, can be accomplished (Figure 3–17) by shifting the world-coordinate window, by changing the location of separate objects within the NDC viewport, or by altering the position of the viewport when it is mapped into the

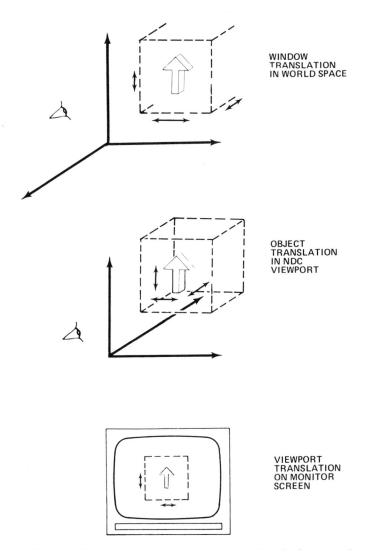

WINDOW
TRANSLATION
IN WORLD SPACE

OBJECT
TRANSLATION
IN NDC
VIEWPORT

VIEWPORT
TRANSLATION
ON MONITOR
SCREEN

Figure 3-17. Translation transformations during viewing operations.

display memory. The entire display can then be translated (scrolled or panned) by shifting the starting address of the refresh-cycle readout.

Scaling, or changing the displayed size of an object, is shown in Figure 3-18. Objects can be "scaled up" by decreasing the dimensions of the world-coordinate window, by expanding the size of the NDC viewport (or of specified objects within the viewport), or by increasing

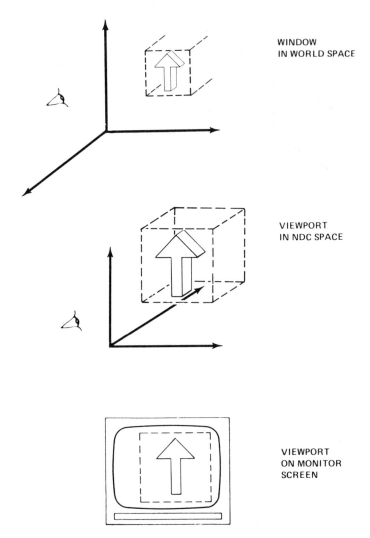

WINDOW
IN WORLD SPACE

VIEWPORT
IN NDC SPACE

VIEWPORT
ON MONITOR
SCREEN

Figure 3-18. Factors affecting the size of a displayed object.

the size of the viewport when it is mapped into the display memory. The display itself can also be scaled up by duplicating pixels and raster lines during the refresh-cycle readout—or scaled down by skipping pixels and lines.

DATA INPUT

Any information display system must start with *information*. Data input to a computer-based raster graphics system (Figure 3–1) can be in any form and from any type of device. With the exception of specialized interactive devices used by the operator, most of the data-input sources will be conventional computer peripherals, such as disks, tapes, data-communication modems, and instrumentation interfaces.

Information can also enter the raster graphics system at two other points (Figure 3–19a). One alternative is a direct input of digital pixel values into the display memory. This is the standard form of data input for systems designed primarily for image processing. Vector-graphic systems can also use the technique to advantage. Frequently used "forms, " legends, or overlays, for example, may be stored on disk or tape and loaded into display memory before variable information is added. The technique can significantly increase the effective throughput of the graphics system and reduce its world-coordinate and NDC-viewport memory requirements.

As a second alternative, non-digitized video signals can be mixed or combined with the display-memory output at the monitor interface. The only requirements are that all of the signals must be synchronized and meet the same display-signal standards. Figure 3–19b illustrates the mixing of a "live" video camera signal with the output of a graphics system. The operator could use such an arrangement to "trace," for example, the three-dimensional shapes of objects in the camera's field of view.

Stored Input Data

Raster graphics data can be read out, stored, and re-entered at any stage in the modeling, viewing, and display operations (Figure 3-20). Stored digital data can represent source information, world-coordinate primitives and attributes, NDC-viewport data, and the contents of the display memory. The storage medium can be any convenient type. The principal concerns, when making a choice, are the storage requirements, transfer rates, and cost.

Stored analog data could include the output of analog instruments,

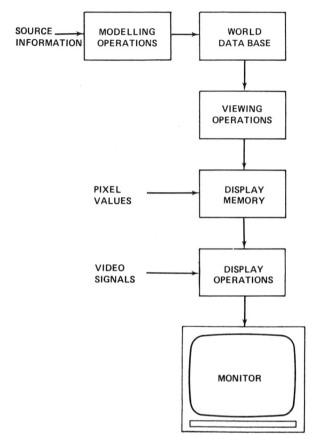

Figure 3–19a. Alternate entry ports for display-data input.

signals generated by video sources, and display signals previously generated by the raster graphics system itself.

Real-Time Input Data

Figure 3–21 indicates the wide variety of digital and analog devices that can serve as real-time information sources for a raster graphics system.

Digital data can come from process control and scientific instruments such as digital multimeters, counters, and frequency meters. Data-processing digital sources would include keyboard terminals, telephone-line modems, character-recognition subsystems, and data links with other computers.

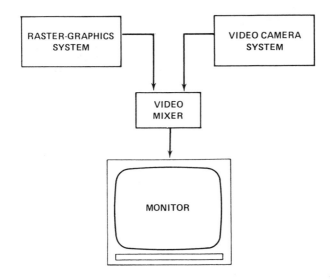

Figure 3-19b. Video image combined with graphics-system output.

Analog devices (including video cameras and spot scanners) can also serve as data sources. The input can be in the form of voltages, currents, resistances, capacitances, or frequencies. All of the signals (except for direct video inputs to the monitor) must be digitized before they can be processed by the raster graphics system.

Unless the information is to be used for other purposes, there is no reason to specify an analog-to-digital resolution beyond that required by the raster display. If the analog input is to be displayed as a diminsional value, conversion to 8-bit to 12-bit data words should be sufficient. If the analog value is to be displayed as a color or black-and-white intensity, the resolution can be reduced to 8 bits or less.

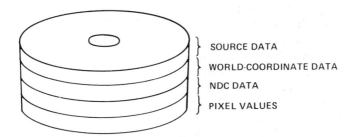

Figure 3-20. Types of stored data for entry or re-entry into graphics system.

DIGITAL SOURCES	DIGITAL VOLTMETERS COUNTERS FREQUENCY METERS KEYBOARD TERMINALS TELEPHONE MODEMS COMPUTER I/O CHANNELS ETC.
ANALOG SOURCES	VIDEO CAMERAS SPOT SCANNERS POTENTIOMETERS THERMOCOUPLES PRESSURE GAUGES PROCESS TRANSMITTERS ETC.
OPERATOR INPUT DEVICES	LIGHTPENS DATA TABLETS KEYBOARDS FUNCTION BUTTONS JOYSTICKS TRACKBALLS ETC.

Figure 3-21. Devices which can serve as sources of graphics data.

Interactive operator input devices can be either digital or analog. A keyboard, for example, produces a digital signal. Joysticks and track-balls are inherently analog.

MODELING OPERATIONS

"Modeling" includes all of the functions and tasks required to convert source information and computer-generated data into world-coordinate objects. The end product is a world data base, which serves as the starting point for subsequent viewing operations.

The information contained in the world data base is typically in the form of dots, lines, polygons, and other "primitive" elements. The modeling software defines the primitives and specifies their display characteristics—such as the width and color of lines, the type of symbol to be placed at each dot location, and the color or pattern of polygon areas. The modeling operations also position the primitives in either a three-dimensional world space or a two-dimensional world plane. Taken as a group, the assembled primitives establish the form of the objects in world-coordinate terms.

World objects can be changed, but only through additional modeling operations which may erase all trace of the previous forms. Meanwhile, multiple "views" of the world objects can be derived from the data base, and these can be modified through operator or application-program interactions without disturbing the world-object data.

Of course, not every application would require or benefit from this separation of modeling and viewing operations. Two-dimensional modeling, for example, could proceed directly to a mapped representation of the world objects in the display memory. There will also be instances when it would be more efficient to allow the operator to interact directly with the source or modeled data. As a general rule, however, the separation of functions and the "protection" of world-object data are worth the cost in processing time and memory resources.

Alternate Uses for Data

Modeling operations are very specific to the application, and could include every type of business, engineering, and scientific data-processing function now performed by digital computers. The generation of a graphics display will be, in most cases, only a peripheral aspect of the basic tasks performed by a computer system. The system designer has to consider, therefore, other uses for the information available to, or resulting from, the modeling operations.

For example, a voltage input may be the analog of a process-control pressure reading (Figure 3-22). But the graph, which may be scaled in pounds per square inch, is itself an analog of the pressure, and this raises a question. Is there any reason to convert the voltage to psi values as a part of the modeling operations?

The answer is yes, if the engineering-unit values are needed for other computations performed by the system. But if the only additional use is to provide a permanent record of the pressure, it may be more cost-effective to generate a hard copy of the displayed information on the monitor screen at periodic intervals.

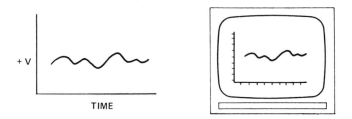

Figure 3-22. Analog voltage (left) reproduced as an analog display.

This is a trivial example, but when it is multiplied by hundreds or thousands of data points, plotted repeatedly over the course of months, the savings in processor time could become significant.

Hardware or Software

Similar choices apply to the hardware implementation of modeling functions, and whether the hardware (or equivalent software) functions should be performed at the modeling or viewing stages.

Computer graphics are usually composed of repeated elements— lines, curves, symbols, and alphanumeric characters. Not surprisingly, then, a number of software subroutines for generating such elements are commercially available, both as modules and as parts of a larger graphics package. Many are also available in the form of hardware function generators. Speed, system throughput, and cost will generally dictate the choice.

But this leaves open the question whether character generation, for example, should be treated as a modeling or viewing operation. Should a capital letter "E" be stored in the world data base as a construction of four strokes? Or should the data consist only of the ASCII code for "E" and an indication of its location in world-coordinate space? The actual form of the letter would not exist, in the latter case, until the character is mapped into a bit-map display memory or read out of a character-map memory (Chapter 7). It is also possible that some of the viewing operations, such as three-dimensional rotation and scaling, may be difficult to implement when a portion of the world-coordinate information is available only in an abstract, coded form. Again— speed, throughput, cost, and in this case, the visual appearance of the display, will dictate the choice.

WORLD DATA BASE

The world data base defines, in two-dimensional or three-dimensional world coordinates, all of the objects to be depicted by the raster graphics output.

Subsequent viewing operations may change portions of this description, but without altering the original definitions. Such changes are treated as "experimental," subject to the operator's value judgments. If there is a decision to retain a change, the new definition can be fed back through the viewing operations, altering the values stored in the world data base.

Primitives and Attributes

The form of the data in the world data base is established by the graphics software. The GKS and Core System specifications described in Chapter 4 both limit the descriptive data to six primitive graphic elements. The six Core primitives are illustrated in Figure 3-23.

A *marker* is a point defined by its world coordinates. When displayed on the monitor screen, it takes a form established by its "attributes," which can include a specified symbol, such as a cross, diamond, or dot (Figure 3-24). Several points, defined as a group, are called a *polymarker.*

A *line* is defined in world coordinates by its starting and end points. When displayed, it can have a number of different attributes, including a specified weight (thickness), color or intensity, and whether it is dashed or solid. A *polyline* consists of several connected lines, with a beginning and end.

A *polygon* is an area enclosed by three or more connected lines. It is defined by the vertices formed by adjoining lines, as expressed in world coordinates. Both the boundary lines and the enclosed area can be separately assigned a variety of display attributes, such as color and texture.

The sixth primitive is *text,* a string of alphanumeric characters and symbols positioned in world-coordinate space or on a world-coordinate plane. Text attributes include character size and font, color or

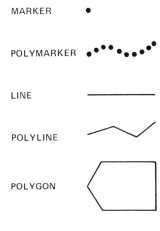

Figure 3-23. Primitives defined by Core System software.

Figure 3-24. Marker symbols defined by system-implementation software, application program, or controller hardware.

intensity, character spacing, direction (up, down, right, or left), and justification.

Individual primitives can also be assigned a "pick" identification number, simplifying the software processing of a single primitive selected by a pick-type device, such as a lightpen.

Commercially available graphics software systems have expanded broadly on the basic set of primitives defined by the Core and GKS specifications. Rectangles and circles, for example, are often specified as primitive forms. Three-dimensional systems may also include three-dimensional primitives, such as spheres, cylinders, cones, and rectangular parallelepipeds. Application-oriented systems can also treat standard graphic elements (e.g., transistor symbols) as primitives. The software system may, in fact, allow the programmer or operator to define any graphic sub-picture as an "instance" or "subroutine". The shape of a gear tooth, for example, may be described once in memory, then positioned repeatedly around the circumference of a circle to form a complete gear description.

VIEWING OPERATIONS

Viewing operations reproduce a part or all of the world-coordinate data and process the information for presentation on the monitor screen. The operations also allow the operator or application program to make selected changes in the displayed images. The result is an almost infinite variety of potential display outputs, all derived from the same world data base.

The viewing operations can be "two-dimensional" or "three-dimensional," depending on the system software capabilities and whether the information in the world data base is restricted to a single, two-dimensional plane, or is expressed in three-dimensional coordinates.

Image Segments

The primitive descriptions stored in the world data base are grouped into segments during the viewing operations. Each segment represents a separate "image." A segment can include all of the primitives that compose one or more objects, or a segment may consist of separate but similar primitives, originally located anywhere in the world-coordinate system.

Segments can be identified by name and are also given specified attributes, such as visibility or invisibility, and whether or not they can be transformed by the operator or the application program. Allowable segment transformations include rotation, translation, and scaling—applied simultaneously to all of the primitives included in the specified segment.

Two-Dimensional Viewing

Views of a two-dimensional world plane are relatively restricted. The principal decision to be made by the operator or application program is the location of a window (Figure 3–25) through which the contents of the world data base will be viewed.

The location and size of the window determine the primitives which will be displayed on the monitor screen. Portions of primitives lying outside the window are "clipped" by the software program.

The window can be large or small, and located anywhere within the bounds of the world-coordinate plane. The window can also be rotated. The effect is to rotate the displayed view through the window in the opposite direction (Figure 3–26).

The view through the window, as displayed on the monitor screen, is called a viewport. The Core System and GKS specifications process the viewport in two steps. First, the clipped contents of the world-coordinate window are reconstructed on a Normalized Device Coordinate (NDC) plane. Then, as a second step, the NDC viewport data is mapped into the display memory.

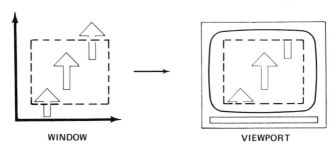

WINDOW   VIEWPORT

Figure 3-25. Effect of clipping at world-coordinate window boundaries.

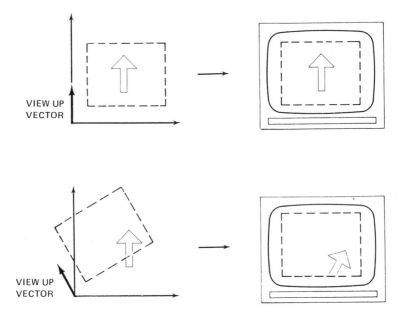

Figure 3-26. Effect of view up vector on position of window and the resulting counter-rotation of the displayed image.

The transformation from world to NDC coordinates can have a scaling effect. A small window and large viewport will produce an expanded image on the screen. A large window and small viewport will have an opposite effect.

The X and Y dimensions can also be independently scaled as shown in Figure 3-27a to produce a viewport aspect ratio (width vs. height) that will be exactly proportional to the desired display area on the monitor screen. The contents of the viewport will be affected, of course, by this type of non-uniform coordinate conversion. A circle, for example, may become an ellipse.

The display viewport can occupy all or part of the monitor screen. There is, actually, no theoretical limit on the number of viewports which can be simultaneously displayed. The viewports can be separate from each other, as shown in Figure 3-27b, adjoining each other, or even overlapped. It may be more convenient, for example, to separate a business chart and its descriptive text into separate viewports, scaling them independently before merging them on the monitor screen.

An advantage of the two-step procedure is that a variety of experimental segment-by-segment transformations can be accomplished

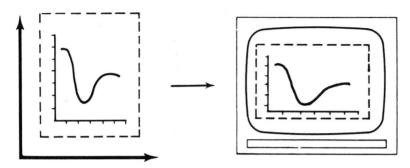

Figure 3-27a. Independent viewing transformation of X and Y coordinate values.

at the NDC-coordinate level without disturbing the world data base. Individual segments can be rotated, translated from one location to another, or scaled to a larger or smaller relative size. The results of the transformations are immediately mapped into the display memory, providing the operator with a nearly instant visual feedback.

The transfer of world-object and viewport images to the display memory raises a question of "priority." If overlapping occurs, should both images appear on the monitor screen? Or should one object or viewport block the view of the other? The choices are illustrated in Figure 3-28. Software may establish that the *latest* addition to the

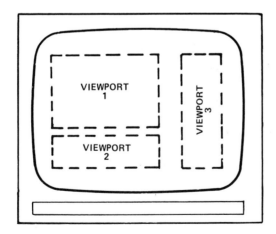

Figure 3-27b. Multiple viewports, independently scaled and positioned on display surface.

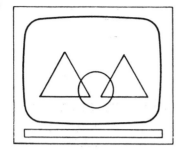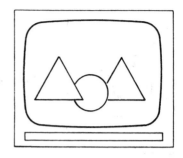

Figure 3–28. Two-dimensional priority or "2 1/2-D" logic. Overlayed objects (left) are given a relative display priority to give an impression of depth.

display memory has priority. Or provision may be made for setting the priority of each image—relative to others on the screen.

Three-Dimensional Viewing

The window in two-dimensional viewing lies on the same plane as the world-coordinate data. The only options are its size, location, and orientation. Three-dimensional viewing is not so simple. The window can be located on any plane in space. Objects in the world-coordinate space can be parallel-projected onto the view window at any arbitrary angle. Or, as an alternative, a center-of-perspective viewpoint can be located anywhere in front of the window, with expanding fields of view as the distance increases behind the window (Figure 3–29).

Core System viewing operations start with the establishment of a "view reference point," typically located on one of the objects in the world-coordinate space. (This is equivalent to focusing a camera on a particular detail in the scene to be photographed.)

The next step is to establish a world-coordinate vector, "view plane normal." The vector (Figure 3–30) originates at the view reference point and points in a direction that is perpendicular to the desired "view plane." The distance from the view reference point to the view plane is specified by a "view plane distance."

A "view up" vector is also established, with its origin at the view reference point. The projection of this vector on the view plane establishes a "vertical" axis on the view plane. A "horizontal" axis is established 90° from this vertical line. To avoid confusion, coordinates relating to the view plane are usually designated at U-V-W rather than X-Y-Z. A view window can now be specified, therefore, using U-V

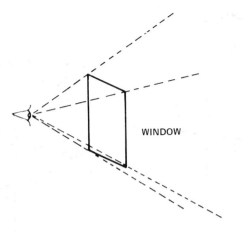

Figure 3-29. Perspective viewing through a world-coordinate window.

coordinate values (not to be confused with the U-V equal-chromaticity color chart coordinates described in the Appendix).

For parallel projections, a third vector, "direction of projection," is established in space with its origin at the view reference point. The combination of this vector and the window on the view plane produces an infinitely long parallelepiped (Figure 3-31).

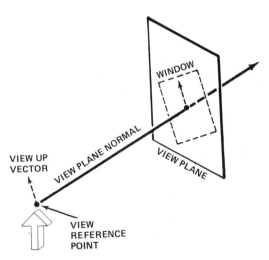

Figure 3-30. Steps in establishing a view plane and view-plane window.

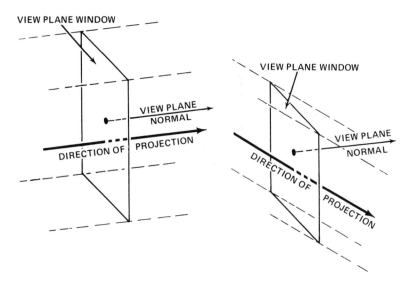

Figure 3-31. Parallel-projection viewing, perpendicular to the view plane (left) and at an arbitrary angle (right).

All portions of objects lying outside of this space are clipped by the software program. Additional clipping may be performed by front and back "clipping planes," parallel to the view plane and established by distances along the view plane normal measured from the view reference point (Figure 3-32).

Perspective-type views are established by a "center of perspective," which in combination with the view window establishes an infinitely extended four-sided view pyramid, as previously shown in Figure 3-29. The center of perspective can be anywhere in space to the front of the view-plane window. Front and back clipping planes are established to limit the view volume. The truncated pyramid is then transformed into a rectangular parallelepiped in NDC space (Figure 3-33). The contents are projected onto the front surface, which can now serve as a conventional two-dimensional viewport. The result of these transformations is an increase in the relative size of objects which are closer to the center of perspective—simulating the effect registered by the eye or camera when objects are viewed at different distances.

Questions of priority become much more complicated in the case of three-dimensional viewing. To what extent should objects in the foreground obscure those in the background? Should the software

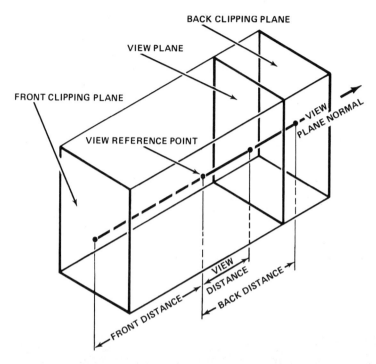

Figure 3-32. Front and back (hither and yon) clipping planes to create a three-dimensional world-coordinate "window."

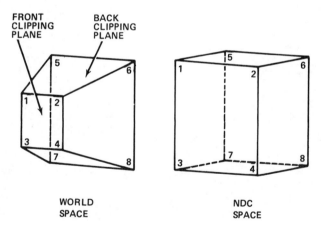

Figure 3-33. Transformation of perspective-view world-coordinate "window" to a three-dimensional NDC "viewport."

eliminate hidden surfaces—or hidden lines in the case of "wire-frame" outlined objects? Or should a level of "transparency" be established?

Software has been written to deal with all of these alternatives, plus such additional challenges as the shading of curved surfaces and the generation of shadows and reflections. Some of the effects which can be achieved are illustrated in Figure 3–34.

Display Memory

The display memory is the real-time source of information for generating the display signal which drives the CRT monitor.

The reduced cost of solid-state memories has influenced the design of raster-graphics systems in two ways. One has been an impetus to increase the horizontal and vertical resolutions of the display itself. With 1024 raster lines and 1024 addressable pixel locations along each line, a minimum of 1,048,576 bits must be stored in a "bit-mapped" display memory. This would have been prohibitively expensive a few years ago, but is now a practical reality.

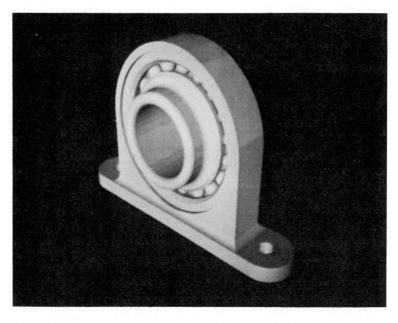

Figure 3–34. Shading and shadowing effects. Three-dimensional primitives were used to define world-coordinate object. (Source: Mathematical Applications Group, Inc.)

Coincident with this trend has been a move toward extremely large display memories—far beyond the requirements of the raster actually generated on the monitor screen. Oversize display memories allow the application program or operator to perform a variety of useful functions without rewriting pixel values. Information can be "scrolled" vertically or "panned" horizontally. Animation can be implemented by switching from one "frame-buffer" section of the memory to another. Alternate solutions to a design problem can be "toggled" for quick comparisons. A double-size memory can, as a very minimum, allow one complete frame of information to be assembled while another is being displayed—eliminating the distractions caused by partially mapped images.

The advantages of high resolution and increased memory must be balanced, however, against total system cost and, to a lesser extent, throughput. In many applications, cost is a critical factor, and alternative ways to reduce the memory size should be considered.

If the displayed information is relatively simple, "line mapping" can significantly reduce the memory requirements. Each scan line is divided into "runs" of a constant color or intensity. Instead of storing information on a pixel-by-pixel basis, each run is coded with just two parameters: the number of pixels in the run, and its color or intensity.

Another way to reduce the memory size is "character mapping." The monitor screen is divided into rectangular cells, each representing a number of individual pixels. The information stored in display memory is typically in the form of ASCII alphanumeric and "graphic" character codes, one for each rectangular unit. It may take some ingenuity to build a display using graphic characters, but the reduction in hardware costs can be significant.

Multiple Planes

The capabilities of a graphics system can be significantly enhanced by organizing the display memory into two or more duplicate "planes." The bits for each pixel in a bit-mapped memory are accessed in parallel to form a multi-bit "pixel word." Similar parallel accessing can be applied to line-mapped and character-mapped memories.

The multiple planes can be used to achieve a variety of effects. Each plane could hold, for example, a different image, generated by separate modeling and viewing operations. Figure 3–35 illustrates how one plane could be used to store a fixed background pattern or display outline that is not accessible to the operator—or superimposed images

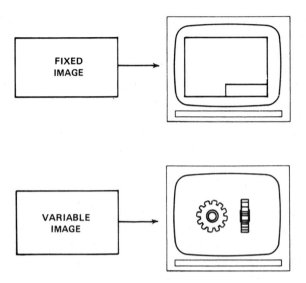

Figure 3–35. Separate display-memory planes for fixed and variable images.

could be combined through logic circuits to form another, completely different image.

The most general use for multiple planes is to create either intermediate gray shades on a black-and-white monitor or multiple hues on a color monitor. Eight display-memory planes, for example, will produce an 8-bit pixel word to define up to 256 shades of gray when processed by a digital-to-analog converter. Three planes, one assigned to each primary color, can be used to generate eight "colors" (including black and white). Two planes per color would allow the system to generate four different intensities of each color, or a total of 64 different hues and saturations on the monitor screen.

Display Cursor

The "cursor" is a universal communication link between the operator and an interactive graphics system. It is used to guide the operator to specific locations on the monitor screen. It can also be used by the operator to indicate where specified actions are to take place.

The cursor exists only in the display memory. There is no trace of it in the world-coordinate or NDC-coordinate environments. Its "current" location on the screen is used by the system, however, to implement a variety of interactive modeling and viewing functions.

Figure 3–36 illustrates the use of a cursor to "paint" graphic elements and designs on the display surface. At the top of the screen is a menu of painting "brushes." The system cursor can be used to control the movement of the brush, or the brush itself may serve as the cursor symbol. The circular arc at the left might have been traced by a conic function generator, while the freehand line was drawn by the operator, using any conventional type of cursor-control device.

The cursor can also be used to "drag" selected primitives, segments, or menu items, as shown in Figure 3–37. Another useful technique is to "rubberband" a line by using the cursor to reposition one endpoint while the other endpoint remains in a fixed position (Figure 3–38). In both of these cases, the operator's dexterity may be severely taxed by the resolution of the display. One way to resolve this problem is to apply "gravity" to the graphic element, shifting it automatically to the nearest coordinate intersection—as illustrated in Figure 3–39. The software may also dictate that all sketched lines are to be displayed exactly horizontal or vertical, or must always terminate at either the endpoint or along the length of an existing graphic element.

Almost any type of symbol can serve as a cursor. Figure 3–40 provides several examples. If high precision is required, a graphic arrow or

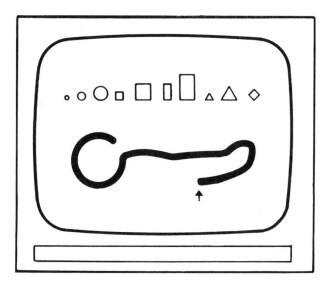

Figure 3-36. "Painting" with a cursor-controlled "brush" selected from menu at top of monitor screen.

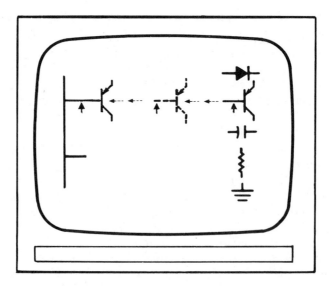

Figure 3–37. "Dragging" a software or hardware-defined electronics symbol selected from menu at right of screen.

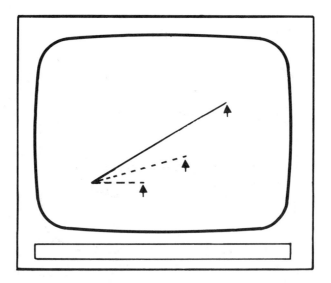

Figure 3–38. "Rubberbanding" a line with a fixed origin. Line is continuously redrawn as cursor is moved across the screen.

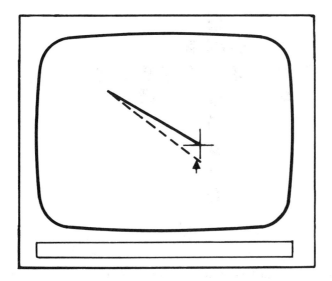

Figure 3-39. "Gravity" effect. Endpoint of line shifts to nearest coordinate intersection, independent of cursor positon.

cross is normally used. The true cursor is the tip of the arrow or the intersection point of the cross.

One problem with this type of cursor is that the balance of the symbol may interfere with other elements on the display screen. Figure 3-41 illustrates how "pixel-reversal" logic can minimize the loss of detail.

If lower resolution can be tolerated, the cursor can take the form of a square or rectangle, with a reversal of all pixel values in the area covered by the cursor. This technique is illustrated in Figure 3-42. There is little chance that a cursor of this magnitude will be "lost" on the monitor screen.

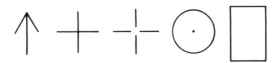

Figure 3-40. Examples of cursors for different levels of positioning precision.

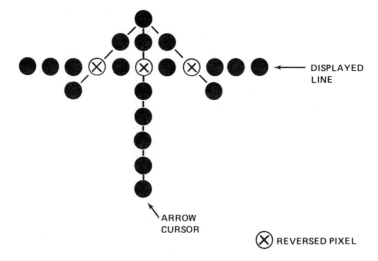

Figure 3–41. Pointer-type cursor with reversed pixels to avoid confusion with existing display elements.

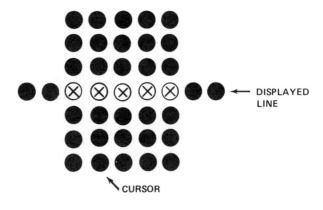

Figure 3–42. Character-space cursor with reversed pixels to prevent obscuring of previously written data.

DISPLAY OPERATIONS

Display operations start with the digital data stored in the display memory and end with an analog display-signal input to the display monitor. Between the two, several different types of processing may occur, both digital and analog.

Viewing operations provide dynamic control over the location of images on the monitor screen—as reflected by the state of the pixel values in the display memory. The pixel values also indicate such variables as the color or intensity of the primitives contained in the image. But changes in the color or intensity can be accomplished only by changing the primitive attributes—primitive by primitive.

Lookup tables, interposed between the display memory and the CRT monitor, permit dynamic "global" control over the color/intensity attributes for all primitives displayed on the screen. In the case of color displays, they can also increase significantly the "gamut" of potential colors which can be displayed. Lookup tables can also be used to increase or decrease contrast and perform other image-processing functions.

OPERATOR FEEDBACK

Actions by the operator complete the loop of an interactive raster graphics system. The operator responds to images on the monitor screen and takes appropriate actions, either on the operator's own initiative or in response to requests by the application program.

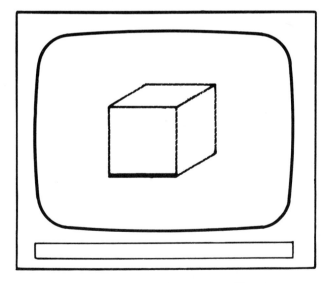

Figure 3-43. Intensity "echo." Visual feedback notifies the operator that a selected primitive has been identified by the system.

A number of different devices can be included in a graphics system to facilitate this interaction. These are described in Chapter 6, Accessories and Peripherals.

Echoing

Operator interactions require an immediate feedback to the operator that actions have taken place. Without an "echo," the operator is literally in the dark as to whether the system has responded. It is not enough for the software to store operator-supplied information away for later use.

Echos can take a variety of forms. If the information entered by the operator is not of immediate use, for example, it can be displayed for a few seconds, then erased from the screen. In similar fashion, the most recent entry or a "picked" primitive can be displayed with increased intensity—as illustrated in Figure 3–43. Error-message feedbacks can include a blinking display or an audible alarm.

4
Raster-Display Software

The software for a raster graphic system should provide for all the functions described in the previous chapter—to the level required by the application.

A total complement of graphics software would include the following elements:

- An operating system capable of supporting a graphics output.
- Applications specific to the type of graphics being generated.
- Display-memory mapping subroutines.
- Software or firmware (hardware) subroutines for generating alphanumeric characters, vectors, curves, and special graphic characters.
- Device drivers for CRT monitors, other raster-output devices, and any interactive-input devices included in the system.
- Facilities for storing and retrieving the graphic images that have been created.
- A "graphics package" that includes any or all of the above.

A full definition of a graphics package—even if it were possible—would be beyond the scope of this Handbook. Modeling operations, for example, can vary widely from application to application. Odds are high, then, that even if a graphics package includes modeling aids, at least a part of the specific modeling functions for an installation will have to be written by the application programmer.

Modeling can be generalized, however, if the "models" are defined in terms of a few "primitive" graphic elements such as points, lines, and enclosed areas. Moreover, viewing functions can be completely generalized, independent of the type of objects that have been modeled, and the same is true of a large set of attributes that describe the appearance of the primitive elements (such as the width of lines and their color) when displayed on a raster-monitor screen or reproduced by a hardcopy device.

Because these functions can be so easily generalized, independent of the application, it becomes not only feasible but mandatory that graphics software be written in a common language adaptable to the widest possible range of computer facilities, and reproducible on all present and future graphics-output devices. The benefits of such standardization are manifest: user familiarity, reducing the need for training and retraining; portability of applications from one type of computer installation to another; the assurance that as computer and graphics technologies continue to advance at a rapid pace, past investments in application software and generated graphics will not become obsolescent or lost.

SOFTWARE STANDARDS

Important progress has been made toward standardizing the principal graphics software functions. Reflecting both the range and rapid pace of developments in the graphics field, however, no single, all-encompassing standard now exists, nor, probably, will one ever be adopted. Instead, six major standards, proposed or officially adopted by national or international agencies, are shaping the future of graphics software.

Inevitably, varying degrees of overlap exist between the standards, and to the extent that each standard is based on a different set of primitives, for example, conflicts and incompatibilities result. Yet each has its place—and history. Moreover, the six standards can be readily divided into three subsets, each addressing a distinctly different set of software objectives.

Two of the standards, the Core System and GKS (Graphics Kernel System) are at the applications interface. They provide the applications writer with a comprehensive set of functions for interactively modeling, viewing, and describing objects. Both "deliver" to the system displayable views defined in NDC (normalized device coordinate) terms—an abstraction that can then be adapted by the balance of the system software to the requirements of specific display or recording devices.

Two other standards, VDM (Virtual Device Metafile) and IGES (Initial Graphics Exchange Standard) address the task of storing graphical data in a form that can be transferred from one computer installation to another—of the same or different type—or regenerated by the original system at a later date. VDM has been designed for maximum compatibility with both Core and GKS. IGES, with its roots in CAD/CAM, features a much wider variety of primitives in order to describe efficiently complex mechanical and electrical parts and assemblies.

The remaining two standards, VDI (Virtual Device Interface) and NAPLPS (North American Presentation-Level Protocol Syntax) apply to the graphical-output-device interface.

VDI, the least defined of the six standards, is intended as a companion specification to VDM and will share many of its features, including its compatibility with Core and GKS. The "virtual device" of both VDI and VDM is an abstraction of all present and likely future output devices. Most physical devices would therefore require a specific device driver as a further software interface between the host software and each attached device.

NAPLPS, by comparison, has a narrower, but potentially even more important mission. It establishes a standard for communicating with the millions of videotex and teletext terminals that may soon populate homes, schools, and offices around the world. It concentrates, therefore, on efficient utilization of relatively narrowband communication links (e.g., telephone lines) and economical, easy-to-implement graphic-generation facilities at each receiving station.

THE CORE SYSTEM

The Core System reflects its origin (1975–1977). Line drawing devices and applications dominated computer graphics. Memory modules were too expensive to make "jaggies"-free, high-resolution raster displays with over a million pixel-data locations a practical reality. Color monitors capable of such resolution were also a scarce commodity.

Core also reflects the number-crunching capabilities of the large computers that were the principal domain of line-drawing CAD/CAM systems. As a result, Core started as a three-dimensional graphics standard with sophisticated viewing functions and a full repertoire of interactive input functions. Two-dimensional capabilities were defined as a specified subset or lower "level."

Pixel-array and color functions were added later, but as the industry moves toward raster displays as a standard, Core's principal role would appear to be in the arena of high-performance stroke-writers for demanding applications, such as those involving a very high density of linear information, dynamic image manipulations, and three-dimensional rotation.

The Core System continues to serve, too, as a "template" for other standards, incorporating a variety of features that have become accepted throughout the industry. As GKS, for example, is expanded to a three-dimensional standard, it will likely include most of Core's three-dimensional viewing functions. Other features, such as the concept of "segments"—groups of primitives that can be manipulated as units—are already embedded in GKS.

Core supports six graphic primitives—marker, polymarker, line, polyline, text, and polygon—and one additional geometry-defining function: move, which repositions a hypothetical "pen" (or stroke-writing electron beam) to a new "drawing location" or "current position." Extending on this pen-position concept, moves and primitives can be defined in either absolute coordinates or relative distances based on a current-position starting point.

Primitives take on currently defined attributes when they are created. Only segments can be "dynamically" or interactively altered by changing the size, position, orientation, visibility, highlighting and pick-device detectability of the primitives within each segment.

Core supported input devices fall into the six classes—locator, stroke, valuator, button, keyboard, and pick—described in Chapter 3.

The following sections describe these and other functions provided by the Core System, arranged for easy comparison with the corresponding functions provided by GKS, VDM, and the remaining graphics standards.

Core Control and Descriptor Functions

INITIALIZE CORE. Must be the first function called during application-program initialization.

TERMINATE CORE. Closes any open segments, terminates all initialized displays and input devices, and releases all other resources being used by the Core System.

INITIALIZE VIEW SURFACE. Performs whatever run-time operating system functions are required (and have not already been performed) to obtain access and initialize the specified display.

TERMINATE VIEW SURFACE. Terminates access to the specified display. Segments whose images appear only on this display are deleted.

SELECT VIEW SURFACE. Adds the specified display to the set of selected view surfaces.

DESELECT VIEW SURFACE. Removes the specified display from the set of selected view surfaces.

CREATE RETAINED SEGMENT. Creates a new, empty retained segment with a specified name.

CLOSE RETAINED SEGMENT. Closes a currently open retained segment. Output primitives can no longer be added to the list of primitives for the retained segment.

DELETE RETAINED SEGMENT. Deletes the specified retained segment.

DELETE ALL RETAINED SEGMENTS. Deletes all retained segments. If there is an open retained segment, it is closed and deleted.

RENAME RETAINED SEGMENT. The specified retained segment is assigned a new name.

CREATE TEMPORARY SEGMENT. Creates a new, empty, temporary segment.

CLOSE TEMPORARY SEGMENT. Closes a currently open temporary segment. Primitives can no longer be mapped into the display memory.

SET DISPLAY MODE. Specifies the display mode:

Fast—Draw only the wire-frame contour of polygons.
Fill—Fill polygons, but do not perform hidden-surface removal.
Hidden-line—Remove hidden lines from the wire-frame version.
Hidden-surface—Remove hidden surfaces.

BEGIN BATCH OF UPDATES. Denotes the beginning of a batch of mapping updates.

END BATCH OF UPDATES. Denotes the end of a batch of mapping updates.

MAKE PICTURE CURRENT. Overrides the immediate-visibility off state.

NEW FRAME. Clears display memory of both retained and temporary segment images. All "visible" retained segments are immediately remapped and displayed.

REPORT MOST RECENT ERROR. Returns the error report for the most recently detected error and flushes the report from the Core System.

LOG ERROR. Used by the application program only as part of its error-handling function.

ESCAPE. Invokes a specified non-standard function and also specifies an array of parameters applicable to this function.

Core Coordinate and Viewing Functions

SET COORDINATE SYSTEM TYPE. Selects whether the world-coordinate system is right-handed or left-handed.

SET NDC SPACE (TWO-DIMENSIONAL). Defines the extent of the viewport within the NDC plane. The viewport's sides are vertical, and its top and bottom are horizontal.

MAP NDC TO WORLD (TWO-DIMENSIONAL). World coordinates corresponding to the specified NDC position are calculated, using the current viewing parameters and the inverse of the current world-coordinate transformation.

MAP WORLD TO NDC (TWO-DIMENSIONAL). The NDC values corresponding to the specified world-coordinate position are stored in the parameter file.

SET VIEW UP (TWO-DIMENSIONAL). Specifies an up vector in world coordinates. The up vector originates at the world-coordinate origin and is used to effect the rotational transformation of the view window.

SET WINDOW (TWO-DIMENSIONAL). Specifies a rectangle in world coordinates. Left and right sides are vertical; top and bottom are horizontal. The rectangle is then rotated around the world-coordinate origin until the left and right sides are parallel to the up vector.

SET NDC SPACE (THREE-DIMENSIONAL). Defines the size of the three-dimensional NDC space which will be mapped into the display memory.

MAP NDC TO WORLD (THREE-DIMENSIONAL). World coordinates corresponding to the specified NDC position are calculated, using the current viewing parameters and the inverse of the current world-coordinate transformation.

MAP WORLD TO NDC (THREE-DIMENSIONAL). The NDC values corresponding to the specified world-coordinate position are stored in the parameter file.

SET VIEWPORT (THREE-DIMENSIONAL). Gives the minimum and maximum bounds of the viewport in three-dimensional NDC space.

SET VIEW REFERENCE POINT. Gives the view reference point in world coordinates.

SET VIEW PLANE NORMAL. Determines a vector in world coordinates relative to the view reference point. The view plane is perpendicular to the view-plane normal vector.

SET VIEW PLANE DISTANCE. Specifies the distance between the view reference point and the view plane, measured along the view-plane normal.

SET VIEW DEPTH. Specifies the front and back planes for depth clipping. Planes are parallel to view plane. Front distance and back distance are measured from the view reference point along the view-plane normal.

SET VIEW UP (THREE-DIMENSIONAL). Determines a view up vector in world-coordinate space, relative to the view reference point. Projection of the view up vector on the view plane in the direction of the view-plane normal establishes the positive-V axis of the U-V view-plane coordinates (see Chapter 3).

SET WINDOW (THREE DIMENSIONAL). Defines the window in view-plane coordinates.

SET WINDOW CLIPPING. Used to enable or disable clipping against the window in the view plane.

FRONT/BACK CLIPPING. Used to enable or disable clipping against the front and back clipping planes.

SET PROJECTION. Sets the type of projection, parallel or perspective, and establishes a center-of-perspective point relative to the view reference point.

SET VIEWING PARAMETERS. Sets all viewing parameters with a single call.

SET WORLD-COORDINATE MATRIX. A world-coordinate transformation matrix specified by the parameter file is composed with the viewing-operation matrix to obtain a composite viewing-operation matrix.

Core Output-Primitive Functions

MOVE. The Current Position is set to the specified or relative X-Y-Z values in the world-coordinate system.

MARKER. The symbol defined by the current value of the Marker Symbol attribute is created at the updated Current Position.

POLYMARKER. The symbol defined by the current value of the Marker Symbol attribute is created at each of the specified positions.

LINE. Describes a line in world coordinates, extending from the Current Position to the position specified.

POLYLINE. Describes a connected sequence of lines in world coordinates, with a terminal line segment at each end of the sequence.

TEXT. A specified character string is drawn in the world-coordinate system.

POLYGON. Used to define a polygon with a vertex list in world coordinates. The vertex array defines a region enclosed by a connected sequence of lines. Because closure is implied, the Current Position is set to the coordinates of the first vertex at the completion of the primitive function.

Core Primitive-Attribute Functions

MARKER SYMBOL. Indicates the symbol used to denote the position of a displayed marker primitive.

LINE STYLE. Indicates the style of a displayed line (e.g., solid, dashed).

LINE WIDTH. Indicates the relative width or "weight" of a displayed line.

FONT. Indicates the style of a displayed character (e.g., Roman, Gothic, italic).

CHARACTER SIZE. Indicates the desired height and width of a character in world-coordinate units.

CHARACTER PLANE. Indicates, as a direction vector, the orientation in the world-coordinate system of the plane on which the character appears.

CHARACTER UP. Indicates the principal up direction in the plane on which the characters appear.

CHARACTER PATH. Indicates the string direction within the plane on which the characters appear (i.e., right, left, up, down).

CHARACTER SPACE. Indicates additional spacing between adjacent character boxes in a string.

CHARACTER JUSTIFICATION. Indicates the mode of string justification (i.e., right, left, up, down).

CHARACTER PRECISION. Indicates the "precision" of a displayed text primitive (i.e., character attributes apply to the appearance of the entire text string, individual characters, or individual character strokes).

SET COLOR MODEL. Specifies the color model. Two possible values are RGB (red, green, blue) and HIS (hue, intensity, saturation).

DEFINE COLOR (INTENSITY) INDEX. Defines an entry in the color (intensity) lookup table.

DEFINE COLOR (INTENSITY) INDICES. Defines all of the entries in the color (intensity) lookup table.

DEFINE STANDARD COLOR (INTENSITY) INDICES. Provides a standard assignment of the color (intensity) lookup-table values.

SET BACKGROUND INDEX. Specifies the background color/intensity index.

LINE INDEX. Used to select the displayed color or intensity of a line or marker. Line index also establishes the color or intensity of the edges of a polygon whenever the value of the polygon edge-style attribute is "solid."

TEXT INDEX. Used to select the color or intensity of a displayed text primitive.

POLYGON EDGE STYLE. Indicates the method for forming the image of the border of a displayed polygon (e.g., solid, dashed).

POLYGON INTERIOR STYLE. Indicates the method for filling the interior of a displayed polygon (e.g., plain, shaded, patterned).

FILL INDEX. Indicates the color or intensity used to fill the interior of a displayed polygon if the value of the polygon interior-style attribute is "plain."

VERTEX INDICES. Indicates a set of vertex color or intensity values used for shading displayed polygons whose polygon interior-style attribute is "shaded."

SET PIXEL ARRAY. Specifies the pixel "pattern" array to be used for filling polygon images.

SET PIXEL PATTERN ORIGIN. Establishes the origin for the mapping of the pixel array into the display memory.

PICK ID. Indicates the name of a primitive. The name is communicated to the application program whenever the primitive is selected by the operator using a Pick input device.

SET PRIMITIVE STATIC ATTRIBUTE VALUES. Specifies the system-maintained current attribute values for the specified primitive attributes.

SET PRIMITIVE ATTRIBUTES. Specifies the system-maintained current attribute values for all primitive attributes.

Core Segment-Attribute Functions

IMAGE TRANSFORMATION TYPE. Determines the image transformations that are valid for a specified retained segment. The four values of this attribute are:

a. No image transformation.
b. Two-dimensional translation.
c. Two-dimensional scale, rotation, translation.
d. Three-dimensional scale, rotation, translation.

IMAGE TRANSFORMATION. Indicates how the image of a specified retained segment is scaled, rotated, and translated.

VISIBILITY. Indicates whether or not a specified retained segment is to be displayed. It has two values: "visible" and "invisible."

HIGHLIGHTING. Indicates whether or not a specified retained-segment display is to be distinguished from those of other retained segments.

DETECTABILITY. Indicates whether or not a specified retained segment can be detected by a Pick input device.

SET IMAGE TRANSFORMATION TYPE. Specifies the current system-maintained attribute value for retained segments.

SET VISIBILITIES. Applies the visibility attribute to an array of specified segments.

SET IMMEDIATE VISIBILITY. Establishes the state of "immediate visibility" as on or off. In the off state, mapping into display memory can be arbitrarily delayed.

SET A RETAINED SEGMENT'S DYNAMIC ATTRIBUTE VALUES. Specifies attribute values for the dynamic attributes of the specified retained segment.

SET RETAINED SEGMENT DYNAMIC ATTRIBUTE VALUES. Specifies the current values for the specified dynamic attributes.

Core Input-Device Functions

INITIALIZE DEVICE. The specified device is initialized. A logical input device must be initialized before it can be enabled.

TERMINATE DEVICE. The specified device is terminated. The device must be initialized before it can be enabled again.

ENABLE DEVICE. The specified device is enabled. A logical input device must be enabled before it can be sampled or can cause an event.

ENABLE GROUP. All initialized but disabled devices in the specified group are enabled.

DISABLE DEVICE. The specified device is disabled.

DISABLE GROUP. All enabled devices in the specified group are disabled.

DISABLE ALL. Every enabled device is disabled.

TERMINATE GROUP. All initialized devices in the specified group are terminated.

ASSOCIATE. Logically associates the specified event device with the specified sampled device.

DISASSOCIATE. Deletes the specified association.

DISASSOCIATE DEVICE. Deletes all existing associations for the specified device.

DISASSOCIATE GROUP. Deletes all existing associations involving any device in the specified group.

DISASSOCIATE ALL. Deletes all existing associations.

SET LOCATOR. Sets the Locator (e.g., keyboard-controlled cursor) to a specified NDC position.

SET LOCATOR PORT. Sets NDC boundaries for a specified Locator device.

READ LOCATOR. The current NDC values of the specified Locator device are read and stored in the parameter file.

GET LOCATOR DATA. If there is sampled data for the specified Locator in the current event report, the data is returned in the form of NDC parameters.

SET STROKE. Sets the input buffer size (number of positions).

AWAIT STROKE. The system waits until an event occurs from a designated Stroke device or until a time interval elapses.

GET STROKE DATA. The sequence of coordinates entered with the Stroke device is returned in the form of NDC parameters.

SET VALUATOR. Sets an application-defined initial value and high-low range for the specified Valuator device.

READ VALUATOR. The current value of the specified Valuator device is read and stored in the parameter file.

GET VALUATOR DATA. If there is a sampled value for the specified Valuator in the current event report, the value is returned to the parameter file.

SET BUTTON. Invokes a prompting capability (e.g., a backlit function key).

SET ALL BUTTONS. Provides a convenient means for turning the prompt on (or off) for all Button devices.

AWAIT ANY BUTTON. The system waits until any initialized Button device is pressed by the operator or until a time interval elapses.

AWAIT ANY BUTTON, GET LOCATOR. The system waits for an event to occur for any initialized Button device or until a time interval elapses, then returns both the Button number and the position of a designated Locator device.

AWAIT ANY BUTTON, GET VALUATOR. The system waits for an event to occur for any initialized Button device or until a time interval elapses, then returns both the Button number and the value of a designated Valuator device.

SET KEYBOARD. Sets the input buffer size (number of characters).

AWAIT KEYBOARD. The system waits until a Keyboard event occurs for a designated Keyboard device or until a time interval elapses.

GET KEYBOARD DATA. The parameter file indicates both the space reserved for storing the entered string and an integer representing the number of characters that could fit in that space.

SET PICK. Allows the application program to define the "closeness" criterion for picking a specific display element (primitive or segment).

AWAIT PICK. The system waits until an event is caused by the designated Pick device or until a time interval elapses.

GET PICK DATA. Identifies a selected primitive by the name of the segment containing it and the primitive's Pick ID attribute value.

AWAIT EVENT. Removes the top element of the event queue at a specified wall-clock time or when there is at least one element on the queue.

FLUSH DEVICE EVENTS. Removes all events from the event queue that were generated by any device in a specified group.

FLUSH ALL EVENTS. Deletes all events in the event queue.

SET ECHO. Identifies the type of echo to be utilized for a specified device (e.g., for a Locator device, designate current position, a horizontal line, a vertical line, a rectangle, or drag a segment).

SET ECHO GROUP. The echo type for all the devices in the specified group is set to the designated echo type.

SET ECHO SURFACE. The echo for the specified device is performed on the designated display surface.

SET ECHO POSITION. Sets an echo NDC reference position.

Care Inquiry Functions

Output Capabilities
Selected Surfaces

Control Status
Retained Segment Surfaces
Retained Segment Names
Open Retained Segment
Open Temporary Segment
Escape (Level of Support)
Text Extent
Current Position
Primitive Static Attribute Values
Primitive Attributes
Image Transformation Type
Segment Image Transformation Type
A Retained Segment's Dynamic Attribute Values
Color Model
Background Index
Display Mode
Pixel Array
Color (Intensity) Index
Color (Intensity) Indices
Standard Color (Intensity) Indices
Individual Viewing Parameters (2D)
Individual Viewing Parameters (3D)
Viewing Parameters (3D)
Viewing Control Parameters
World Coordinate Matrix
Input Capabilities
Input Device Characteristics
Dimension
Device Status
Device Associations
Input Status Parameters
Echo Segments

Core Metafile

The original Core System proposal included a Metafile—a device-independent display-record format designed to facilitate the transfer of graphic images between sites—as a data source for making hardcopy images, as an archival medium, and as the basis for an interface standard for intelligent terminals and other peripherals.

These objectives are now being more closely met by the proposed

VDM (Virtual Device Metafile) standard described below. The Core Metafile is essentially an audit trail of a Core session and can be processed, therefore, only by the same or another Core-based system with equal or greater capabilities.

The Core Metafile is essentially a bit stream partitioned into fixed-size records. Each record contains 5760 bits, 720 8-bit bytes, 360 16-bit chunks or 180 32-bit words. The records are composed of commands, partitioned into positioning commands and non-positioning commands. Positioning commands are a compact notation for representing MOVE and DRAW operations. Non-positioning commands represent all other Metafile capabilities and consist of a command "chunk" and a variable number of parameter chunks.

The first command in a Metafile must be BEGIN METAFILE; the last must be END METAFILE. All commands following the END METAFILE command are ignored until a new BEGIN METAFILE command is encountered.

Each record must begin with a command chunk. A single command may not overlap two consecutive records, although a CONTINUE PREVIOUS COMMAND capability is provided. A NO OPERATION command is provided for padding records to the fixed length.

The graphics output commands are partitioned into one or more pictures. A picture consists of all the graphics output generated between two new-frame actions. Each picture must begin with a BEGIN PICTURE command and end with END PICTURE.

Pictures in the Metafile are mutually independent. The system must be able to output any picture in the Metafile without knowledge of either prior or subsequent pictures.

Metafile coordinates are represented in NDC fractions with a precision of either 15 bits or 31 bits, as defined in the BEGIN METAFILE command.

GKS

GKS (Graphics Kernel System) is, like Core, an applications-interface standard, developed at a later date and reflecting the new importance and higher resolution of raster-type devices and the availability of intelligent peripherals with extensive graphics capabilities of their own.

GKS also supports, like Core, a total of six graphics primitives: polyline; polymarker; text; fill area (similar to the Core polygon); cell array (a raster-like array for defining pictures on a cell-by-cell basis); and a generalized drawing primitive (GDP) that allows the programmer or user to invoke functions and pass along parameters to a device that has, for example, a built-in capability for generating circles or splines.

Unlike Core, GKS is presently limited to two-dimensional images. Counterbalancing this limitation, however, is a much more sophisticated technique for assigning attributes to individual primitives when they are created, and changing the appearance of the primitives either interactively or when the images are output on devices with different capabilities (e.g., a color monitor and a black-and-white printer).

Key to this ability is the concept of logical workstations, each with its own defined facilities such as color lookup tables and "bundles" of attributes to match, for example, the line-weight and color of the available pens on a plotter. Six types of logical workstations are supported: output only (with only one output device per workstation); input only (any number of input devices); output-input (with the same limitations); metafile output (for "writing" a metafile); metafile input (for "reading" a metafile); and a WISS (workstation-independent segment storage) workstation to facilitate the transfer of segments between workstations and to store previously generated segment images for future use on any workstation.

The workstation attribute bundles give the programmer or user the option of giving a primitive either a directly specified permanent attribute or its bundled equivalent. In the latter case, the appearance of the attribute can be changed by simply creating a new output-type logical workstation with the desired attribute combinations, or several workstations (e.g., one for color monitors, another for black-and-white printers) with different attribute bundles.

GKS input-device classes are identical to those of Core, although the "button" class has been changed to "choice," and the "keyboard" to "string." However, not every GKS system must have an interactive-input capability. Instead, the GKS standard provides for a matrix of nine input/output levels, as shown in Figure 4-1. The levels are additive; each of three output levels—0, 1, and 2—and the three input levels—a, b, and c—has the capabilities of any lower levels.

The following sections describe the presently defined GKS functions and the lowest levels at which they apply. All Level 0a functions, for example, would be included in any GKS system. A proposed American version of GKS would also allow a system to add higher-level capabilities selectively so long as all the requirements of a specified level have been met. The new version would also create an even lower, minimal "m" output level for graphics generated, for example, by personal or home computers.

OUTPUT LEVELS	a	INPUT LEVELS b	c
0	No input; only predefined bundles, multiple NDC transformation functions, all output functions; metafile functions optional	Request input, mode setting and initialize functions for logical input devices, no pick	Request, sample, and event inputs, no pick
1	Full output, including full bundle, multiple work stations; basic segmentation except WISS; metafile functions required	Request input, including pick	Request, sample, and event inputs, including pick
2	Workstation-independent segment storage (WISS)	Request input, including pick	Request, sample, and event inputs, including pick

Figure 4-1.   Matrix of GKS implementation levels.

GKS Control and Descriptor Functions

Level 0a. OPEN GKS. Changes the operating state from system-closed to system-open.

CLOSE GKS. Changes the operating state from system-open to system-closed.

OPENWORKSTATION. Requests the operating system to establish a specified connection with a specified workstation type characterized in the workstation description table.

CLOSE WORKSTATION. Updates the specified workstation (see below), then cancels the workstation file* and deletes the workstation name from the set of open workstations in the system file and from the set of associated workstations in each segment file.*

ACTIVATE WORKSTATION. Flags the specified workstation as active in the workstation file and adds its name to the set of active workstations in the system file.*

DEACTIVATE WORKSTATION. Flags the specified workstation as inactive in the workstation file and deletes its name from the set of active workstations in the system file.

UPDATE WORKSTATION. Executes all deferred actions for the specified open or active workstation (without intermediate clearing of the display surface).

CLEAR WORKSTATION. Executes the following actions in the given sequence:

a. All deferred actions for the specified workstation are executed.

b. If the control flag entered with the function calls for a conditional response, the display surface is cleared if the surface-empty switch in the workstation file is set to not-empty.

c. The workstation name is deleted from the set of associated workstations in each segment file containing the workstation name.

d. The set of stored segments in the workstation file is emptied.

e. The new-frame switch in the workstation file is set to no; the surface-empty switch is set to empty.

ESCAPE. Invokes a specified non-standard function. The form of the escape data record may vary for different functions.

EMERGENCY CLOSE GKS. Emergency-closes the system, even if the error state is on.

*File = state list.

ERROR HANDLING. Calls the error-handling procedure when a specified error situation results from a specified system action.

Level 1a. CREATE SEGMENT. Changes the operating state from workstation-open to segment-open. A segment file is allocated, initialized, and assigned a specified name.

CLOSE SEGMENT. Changes the operating state from segment-open to workstation-active. Primitives may no longer be modified, added to or deleted from the specified segment.

RENAME SEGMENT. Replaces each occurrence of a specified segment name with a specified new name in the set of segment names in the system file and in the set of stored segments in all workstation files.

DELETE SEGMENT. Cancels the specified segment file and deletes the segment from the set of segment names in the system file and from the set of stored segments in all workstation files containing the name.

DELETE SEGMENT FROM WORKSTATION. Deletes the specified segment from the specified workstation. The segment name is removed from the set of stored segments in the workstation file and the workstation name is removed from the set of associated workstations in the segment file.

SET DEFERRAL STATE. Sets the deferral-and regeneration-mode entries in the specified workstation file to a specified set of values.

REDRAW ALL SEGMENTS ON WORKSTATION. Executes the following actions in the given sequence:

a. All deferred actions for the specified workstation are executed.

b. The display surface is cleared, but only if the surface-empty switch is set to not-empty.

c. If the update-state switch is set to pending, current-window and current-viewport entries are changed to the requested values in the workstation file.

d. All visible segments contained in the workstation file are redisplayed or redrawn.

e. The new-frame switch in the workstation file is set to no; the surface-empty switch is set to empty.

MESSAGE. Displays a specified message at an implementation-dependent location on the viewport of the specified workstation or on a separate device associated with the workstation.

GKS Coordinate and Viewing Functions

Level 0a. SET NORMALIZATION TRANSFORMATION. Sets the normalization-transformation entry in the system file to a specified transformation number.

SET WINDOW. Sets the window-limits entry of the specified normalization transformation in the system file to a specified set of minimum and maximum X-Y world-coordinate values.

SET VIEWPORT. Sets the viewport-limits entry of the specified normalization transformation in the system file to a specified set of minimum and maximum X-Y world-coordinate values.

SET CLIPPING INDICATOR. Sets the clipping-indicator switch in the system file to a specified value: clip or no-clip.

SET WORKSTATION WINDOW. Sets the requested-window entry in the specified workstation file to a specified set of minimum and maximum X-Y NDC values.

Level 0b. SET VIEWPORT INPUT PRIORITY. Sets the viewport input priority of a specified normalization-transformation number in the system file to a specified next-higher or next-lower priority relative to a specified reference normalization-transformation number. Viewport input priority is relevant only to locator-device input.

GKS Output-Primitive Functions

Level 0a. POLYLINE. Generates a sequence of one or more connected straight lines, starting at a specified first point and ending at a specified last point.

POLYMARKER. Generates markers to identify one or more specified points.

TEXT. Generates a specified string of characters at a specified text-position point given in world coordinates.

FILL AREA. Generates a polygon-enclosed area defined by three or more specified points. A polygon boundary is drawn only when the interior style is hollow.

CELL ARRAY. Generates a rectangular colored-cell array with specified cell-number dimensions (DX, DY) and colors defined by a specified array of color-index pointers into the color table stored in each workstation file. Opposite corners of the array rectangle are specified by the coordinates of point P (PX, PY) and point Q (QX, QY).

GENERALIZED DRAWING PRIMITIVE (GDP). Generates a specified type of GDP function (e.g., circle, ellipse, or interpolating curve) on the basis of specified points and/or GDP data record.

GKS Primitive-Attribute Functions, Non-Bundleable

Level 0a. SET CHARACTER HEIGHT. Sets the text character height (the nominal height of a capital letter) to a specified world-coordinate value.

SET CHARACTER UP VECTOR. Sets the text character up vector (the up direction of individual characters) to a specified value.

SET CHARACTER PATH. Sets the text character path (sequential characters of a text string) to a specified value. The value can be right, left, up or down.

SET TEXT ALIGNMENT. Sets the text alignment to a specified set of values. The values define the horizontal and vertical alignments of a text string relative to the position point of a text primitive.

SET PATTERN SIZE. Sets pattern size to a specified set of world-coordinate dimensions for use when a fill-area primitive is filled with a colored-cell pattern.

SET PATTERN REFERENCE POINT. Sets the upper-left-corner reference point of the pattern rectangle to a specified world-coordinate value for use when a fill-area primitive has a patterned interior style.

SET ASPECT SOURCE FLAGS (ASF's). Sets the ASF value in the system file to individual or bundled for each nongeometric polyline, polymarker, text, and fill-area attribute.

SET POLYLINE INDEX. Sets the polyline bundle-table index in the system file to a specified value.

SET POLYMARKER INDEX. Sets the polymarker bundle-table index in the system file to a specified value.

SET TEXT INDEX. Sets the text bundle-table index in the system file to a specified value.

SET FILL AREA INDEX. Sets the fill-area bundle-table index in the system file to a specified value.

Level 1b. SET PICK IDENTIFIER. Sets the pick-identifier entry in the system file to a specified current value.

GKS Primitive-Attribute Functions, Bundleable

(Level 0a).   SET LINETYPE. Sets the linetype entry in the system file to a specified value.

SET LINEWIDTH SCALE FACTOR. Sets the linewidth scale-factor entry in the system file to a specified value. The scale factor is applied to a workstation's nominal linewidth.

SET POLYLINE COLOR INDEX. Sets the polyline color-index entry in the system file to a specified value. The polyline color index is a pointer into the color table stored in each workstation file.

SET MARKER TYPE. Sets the current marker-type entry in the system file to specified value.

SET MARKER SIZE SCALE FACTOR. Sets the marker-size scale-factor entry in the system file to a specified value. The scale factor is applied to the nominal marker size on a workstation.

SET POLYMARKER COLOR INDEX. Sets the polymarker color-index entry in the system file to a specified value. The polymarker color index is a pointer into the color table stored in each workstation file.

SET TEXT FONT AND PRECISION. Sets the text font-and-precision entry in the system file to a specified set of values. Font indicates the numbered text font to be used. Precision is string, character, or stroke.

SET CHARACTER EXPANSION FACTOR. Sets the character expansion-factor entry in the system file to a specified value. The expansion factor specifies a positive deviation from the established width-height ratio of individual characters.

SET CHARACTER SPACING. Sets the character spacing entry in the system file to a specified value. Added or subtracted character spacing is a positive or negative fraction of the nominal character height.

SET TEXT COLOR INDEX. Sets the text color-index entry in the system file to a specified value. The text color index is a pointer into the color table stored in each workstation file.

SET FILL AREA INTERIOR STYLE. Sets the fill-area interior-style entry in the system file to a specified value: hollow, solid, patterned or hatched.

SET FILL AREA STYLE INDEX. Sets the fill-area style-index entry in the system file to a specified value. When the interior style is patterned, the value is a pointer into the pattern table stored in each workstation list. When the interior style is hatched, the value determines the workstation-dependent hatch style to be used.

SET FILL AREA COLOR INDEX. Sets the fill-area color-index entry in the system file to a specified value. The index is a pointer into the color table stored in each workstation file.

GKS Segment-Attribute Functions

Level 1a. SET VISIBILITY. Sets the visibility entry in the specified segment file to a specified value: visible or invisible.

SET HIGHLIGHTING. Sets the highlighting entry in the specified segment file to a specified value: normal or highlighted.

SET SEGMENT PRIORITY. Sets the segment-priority entry in the specified segment file to a specified value. Segment priority affects the display of segments (and pick selection) if segments overlap on a workstation that can support two or more segment priorities.

EVALUATE TRANSFORMATION MATRIX. Generates a segment-transformation matrix based on a specified fixed point for scaling and rotation, a rotation angle (in radians), separate X and Y scale factors, and a shift (translation) vector.

ACCUMULATE TRANSFORMATION MATRIX. Composes a specified transformation matrix with a specified fixed point for scaling and rotation, rotation angle (in radians), separate X and Y scale factors, and a shift (translation) vector.

SET SEGMENT TRANSFORMATION. Sets the segment-transformation matrix in the specified segment file to a specified set of values.

Level 1b. SET DETECTABILITY. Sets detectability entry in the specified segment file to a specified value: detectable or undetectable. If the segment is detectable and visible, primitives in the segment are available for pick input. Detectable but invisible segments cannot be picked.

GKS Workstation-Attribute Functions

Level 0a. SET COLOR REPRESENTATION. Associates a specified color (red, green, and blue intensities) with a specified color index value in the color table of a specified workstation file. The color is mapped by the workstation to the nearest available color.

Level 1a. SET POLYLINE REPRESENTATION. Associates a specified polyline index value with a specified set of workstation-file values for linetype, line-width scale factor, and polyline color index.

SET POLYMARKER REPRESENTATION. Associates a specified polymarker index value with a specified set of workstation-file values for marker type, marker-size scale factor, and polymarker color index.

SET TEXT REPRESENTATION. Associates a specified text index value with a specified set of workstation-file values for text font and precision, character expansion factor, character spacing, and text color index.

SET FILL AREA REPRESENTATION. Associates a specified fill-area index value with a specified set of workstation-file values for fill-area interior style, fill-area style index, and fill-area color index.

SET PATTERN REPRESENTATION. Associates a specified style index value with a set of specified color index values and cell-number dimensions that define a colored-cell pattern (similar to the grid of a cell-array primitive) to be used when the interior-style attribute of a fill-area primitive is patterned. The values are listed as a single pattern-table entry in a specified workstation file.

GKS Input-Device Functions

Level 0b. INITIALIZE LOCATOR. Stores a specified initial locator position, initial normalization transformation number, prompt/echo type, echo area, and locator data record in a specified workstation file for a specified locator device.

SET LOCATOR MODE. Sets the operating mode entry for a specified locator device in a specified workstation file to a specified value:request, sample, or event; and sets the echo-state switch to echo or no-echo.

REQUEST LOCATOR. Requests the current position of a specified locator device connected to a specified workstation.

INITIALIZE STROKE. Stores a specified number of points in the initial stroke, initial normalization transformation number, prompt/echo type, echo area, and stroke data record in a specified workstation file for a specified stroke device.

SET STROKE MODE. Sets the operating mode entry for a specified stroke device in a specified workstation file to a specified value: request, sample, or event; and sets the echo-state switch to echo or no-echo.

REQUEST STROKE. Requests a series of points generated by a specified stroke device connected to a specified workstation.

INITIALIZE VALUATOR. Stores a specified initial value, prompt/echo type, echo area, and valuator data record in a specified workstation file for a specified valuator device.

SET VALUATOR MODE. Sets the operating mode entry for a specified valuator device in a specified workstation file to a specified value:request, sample, or event; and sets the echo-state switch to echo or no-echo.

REQUEST VALUATOR. Requests the current value of a specified valuator device connected to a specified workstation.

INITIALIZE CHOICE. Stores a specified initial choice number, prompt/echo type, echo area, and choice data record in a specified workstation file for a specified choice device.

SET CHOICE MODE. Sets the operating-mode entry for a specified choice device in a specified workstation file to a specified value: request, sample, or event; and sets the echo-state switch to echo or no-echo.

REQUEST CHOICE. Requests the current choice-number input from a specified choice device connected to a specified workstation.

INITIALIZE STRING. Stores a specified initial string, prompt/echo type, echo area, and string data record in a specified workstation file for a specified string device.

SET STRING MODE. Sets the operating-mode entry for a specified string device in a specified workstation file to a specified value: request, sample, or event; and sets the echo-state switch to echo or no-echo.

REQUEST STRING. Requests the current character-string input from a specified string device connected to a specified workstation.

Level 0c. SAMPLE LOCATOR. Returns the current position of a specified locator device connected to a specified workstation.

GET LOCATOR. Returns the locator-device input in the current-event report. The input includes the locator position in world coordinates and the normalization transformation number that was used to convert the position to world coordinates.

SAMPLE STROKE. Returns a series of points generated by a specified stroke device connected to a specified workstation.

GET STROKE. Returns the stroke-device input in the current-event report. The input includes a sequence of points in world coordinates, the number of points, and the normalization transformation number which was used in the conversion to world coordinates.

SAMPLE VALUATOR. Returns the current value of a specified valuator device connected to a specified workstation.

GET VALUATOR. Returns the valuator-device value in the current-event report. The value is in the range specified by the valuator-device data record stored in the workstation file.

SAMPLE CHOICE. Returns the current choice-number input from a specified choice device connected to a specified workstation.

GET CHOICE. Returns the choice-number input in the current-event report. Choice number 0 means no-choice.

SAMPLE STRING. Returns the current character-string input from a specified string device connected to a specified workstation.

GET STRING. Returns the character-string input in the current-event report. Length of the string is equal to or less than the current input-buffer size specified by the string-device data record stored in the workstation file.

AWAIT EVENT. Sets the system in a wait state if the input queue is empty. The wait state continues until an input event is written into the queue, or a specified timeout has elapsed.

FLUSH DEVICE EVENTS. Removes all entries in the input queue from a specified input device in a specified input class connected to a specified workstation.

Level 1b.   INITIALIZE PICK. Stores a specified initial status, initial segment, initial pick identifier, prompt/echo type, echo area, and pick data record in a specified workstation file for a specified pick device.

SET PICK MODE. Sets the operating-mode entry for a specified pick device in a specified workstation file to a specified mode: request, sample, or event; and sets the echo-state switch to echo or no echo.

REQUEST PICK. Requests the pick identifier and segment name of the primitive currently picked by a specified pick device connected to a specified workstation.

Level 1c.   SAMPLE PICK. Returns the current status and input of a specified pick device connected to a specific workstation.

GET PICK. Returns the pick-device input in the current-event report. Status is returned as no-pick (the device has not picked a primitive) or okay. An okay status is accompanied by the pick identifier of the picked primitive and the name of the segment containing the primitive.

GKS Segment-Storage Functions

Level 0a. WRITE ITEM TO GKSM. Writes a specified non-graphical data record to the metafile.

GET ITEM TYPE FROM GKSM. Inspects the type and data-record length of the current metafile item and returns type and length back to the application program.

READ ITEM FROM GKSM. Returns the current metafile item to the application program, then makes the next item current.

INTERPRET ITEM. Interprets the specified data-record item and makes appropriate changes in the system and workstation states to generate appropriate graphical output.

Level 2a. ASSOCIATE SEGMENT WITH WORKSTATION. Sends a specified segment previously stored in the WISS workstation to a specified workstation in the same form as if the workstation were active when the segment was created.

COPY SEGMENT TO WORKSTATION. Sends the primitives contained in a specified segment previously stored in the WISS workstation to a specified workstation after segment transformation and clipping.

INSERT SEGMENT. Sends primitives contained in a specified segment previously stored in the WISS workstation to all active workstations after segment transformation followed by a specified insert transformation.

GKS Inquiry Functions

Level 0a. Operating state value
Level of GKS
List of available workstation types
Maximum normalization transformation number
Set of open workstations
Current setting of primitive attributes
Current individual attribute values
Current normalization transformation number
List of normalization transformation numbers
Normalization transformation
Clipping indicator

Workstation state
Workstation connection and type
Workstation transformation
Text extent
List of color indices
Color representation
Maximum display surface size
Polyline facilities
Workstation classification
Polymarker facilities
Predefined polymarker representation
Predefined polyline representation
Predefined text representation
Fill area facilities
Text facilities
Predefined fill area representation
Pattern facilities
Predefined pattern representation
Color facilities
Predefined color representation
List of available generalized drawing primitives
Generalized drawing primitive
Pixel array dimensions
Pixel array
Pixel

Level 0b.   Locator device state
Stroke device state
Valuator device state
Choice device state
String device state
Number of available logical input devices
Default input device data

Level 0c.   Maximum size of input queue
More simultaneous events
Input queue overflow

Level 1a.   Workstation maximum numbers
Set of active workstations
Set of segment names in use
Name of open segment

List of polyline indices
Polyline representation
List of polymarker indices
Polymarker representation
List of text indices
Text representation
List of fill area indices
Fill area representation
List of pattern indices
Pattern representation
Set of segment names on workstation
Number of segment priorities supported
Maximum length of workstation state tables
Dynamic modification of workstation attributes
Dynamic modification of segment attributes
Default deferral state values
Set of associated workstations
Segment attributes

Level 1b. Pick device state

VDM

VDM (Virtual Device Metafile) is a proposed graphical-image storage
and transfer standard that is designed for maximum compatibility with
both Core and GKS.

Like Core, VDM accommodates both absolute and relative
geometric definitions and can therefore support the concept of "current position." Like GKS, attributes can be individually assigned to
primitives, or bundled to provide different combinations of attributes
for output on different devices.

VDM goes beyond both standards by adding three new primitives:
an arc line and two area-type primitives, circular and arc-close (closed
with either a straight-line chord or two pie-like segments). All three of
these, of course, could be simulated by Core and GKS primitives (including the GKS generalized drawing primitive).

Given these similarities, both Core and GKS systems can be adapted
to "write" VDM elements and "read" a VDM file through a metafile
interpreter—outputting the result, with or without modification,
through a device interface that meets the equally compatible features
of the proposed VDI (virtual device interface) standard described later
in this chapter.

Two "bindings" of the two-dimensional VDM standard have also been proposed: a character encoding scheme similar to that of the NAPLPS standard, and a binary encoding which generates a bit stream containing a descriptor component that provides information on how to interpret correctly the VDM and the body of the VDM itself. The following sections describe the standard VDM elements that are accommodated in both encoding techniques.

VDM Control and Descriptor Elements

BEGIN METAFILE. Indicates the start of a specified metafile. Nesting of one metafile within another is not allowed.

END METAFILE. Indicates the end of a metafile.

BEGIN PICTURE. Indicates the start of a specified picture. Every picture in a metafile is totally independent from every other picture. All elements are returned to their default values at the start of each picture. If the picture begins with a cleared view surface, the view surface is set to a specified background color.

END PICTURE. Indicates the end of a picture. Only external elements are allowed between END PICTURE and the next BEGIN PICTURE.

BACKGROUND COLOR. Specifies the background color index or direct-color value and sets the background-color switch on (colored) or off (transparent).

VDC PRECISION FOR INTEGER POINTS. Specifies the precision of subsequent integer X and Y coordinates of a point in VDC space. Enables metafiles to change the VDC precision in the middle of a picture for more efficient data storage when less precision is required.

VDC PRECISION FOR REAL POINTS. Specifies the precision of subsequent real-number X and Y coordinates of a point in VDC space for more efficient data storage when less precision is required.

VDC EXTENT. Specifies the lower-left and upper-right corners of a rectangular extent in VDC space that is the "region of interest" or visible portion of the picture defined by succeeding VDM elements. The coordinate values of the two corner points also establish the sense (positive direction of X and Y axes) and orientation (direction of positive or negative angles) of the VDC space.

CLIP RECTANGLE. Specifies minimum and maximum X and Y coordinates of a clipping rectangle in VDC space.

CLIP INDICATOR. Sets the clip-indicator flag to on or off. VDM interpreter may continue to clip to some limit such as the VDC extent or the display surface boundaries, even when the clip-indicator flag is off.

VDM VERSION. Specifies the version of the VDM standard to which the metafile conforms.

VDM DESCRIPTION. Describes the contents of the metafile in a nonstandardized way. Allows the VDM to be identified with descriptive text such as author, date, and place of origin.

VDC TYPE. Specifies the data type of the virtual-device coordinates.

INTEGER PRECISION. Specifies the precision of subsequent integer-type operands (numbers with no fractional parts).

REAL PRECISION. Specifies the precision of subsequent real-type operands (numbers with integer and fractional parts).

INDEX PRECISION. Specifies the precision of subsequent index-type operands (integers that point into a table of values or select from a set of enumerated values).

COLOR PRECISION. Specifies the precision of subsequent color-direct operands (three-tuple of red, green, and blue values).

COLOR INDEX PRECISION. Specifies the precision of subsequent color-index operands (integers pointing into a color table).

MAXIMUM COLOR INDEX. Specifies the upper bound of the color-index values that may be encountered in the metafile.

VDM ELEMENT LIST. Lists all of the elements that may be encountered in the metafile. Can be used by the interpreter to determine the minimum facilities necessary for interpreting the VDM, but may include elements not found in the VDM.

VDM DEFAULTS REPLACEMENT. Specifies substitute or replacement values for the default values established by the VDM standard.

FONT LIST. Lists the font names that can be accessed by a text-font index number. The first font in the list is assigned to index 1, the second to index 2, etc.

CHARACTER SET LIST. Lists the character sets that can be accessed by a character-set index number. The first set in the list is assigned to index 1, the second to index 2, etc.

SCALING MODE. Indicates whether the VDC space is "abstract" or "metric." If set to "abstract," VDC space is dimensionless and the picture is correctly displayed at any size. If set to "metric," each VDC unit represents a display dimension of one millimeter times a specified metric scale factor. Thus, a scale factor of 25.4 would imply display coordinates measured in inches.

COLOR SPECIFICATION MODE. Indicates whether colors are to be specified by color table entries ("indexed") or by red, green, and blue color values ("direct"). Only one color mode may be used within a picture.

LINE WIDTH SPECIFICATION MODE. Indicates whether line widths are to be specified in absolute VDC units ("absolute") or scaling factor is to be applied to the device-dependent nominal line width ("scaled"). Only one line-width mode may be used within a picture.

PERIMETER WIDTH SPECIFICATION MODE. Indicates whether perimeter widths are to be specified in absolute VDC units ("absolute") or a scaling factor is to be applied to the device-dependent nominal perimeter width. Only one perimeter-width mode may be used within a picture.

MARKER SIZE SPECIFICATION MODE. Indicates whether marker sizes are to be specified in absolute VDC units ("absolute") or a scaling factor is to be applied to the device-dependent nominal marker size. Only one marker-size mode may be used within a picture.

COLOR TABLE. Loads specified color-list elements in the specified order into consecutive locations in the color table beginning at the starting index. Only the specified color table entries are changed.

PATTERN TABLE. Defines a specified horizontal by vertical m by n array into which specified color values are mapped. The array is loaded sequentially by rows starting with the upper-left (maximum Y, minimum X) corner.

VDM ESCAPE. Allows use of device capabilities not specified by this standard.

VDM Output-Primitive Elements

POLYMARKER. Generates markers centered on one or more specified points. Implementation-dependent markers may have other non-centered alignments.

POLYLINE. Generates a sequence of one or more connected point-to-point straight lines, starting with the first point in an ordered list of specified points and ending with the last point in the list.

ARC. Generates a circular arc that begins at a specified starting point, passes through a specified intermediate point, and terminates at a specified ending point.

TEXT. Generates a specified string of characters at a specified text-alignment point. A text flag is set to "final" if the string constitutes the entire text to be displayed. If the flag is set to "not final," the character codes and current text attributes are accumulated (before being aligned as a block) to permit the text size, spacing, and appearance attributes to be changed before additional text is appended.

APPEND TEXT. Appends a specified final or not-final string of characters to a preceding not-final text or append-text element. If the text flag is set to "not-final," the character codes and attributes are again accumulated to permit the text size, spacing, and appearance to be changed before additional text is appended.

POLYGON. Generates a polygon-enclosed area defined by one or more connected straight lines, starting with the first point in an ordered list of specified points and ending with a line connecting the last point to the first. Edges of the polygon are allowed to cross, creating subareas. (A point is "inside" the polygon if an infinite straight line from the point intersects the polygon edges an odd number of times.) The appearance of the polygon boundary is controlled by the perimeter attributes and the perimeter-visibility component of the interior-style attribute.

CIRCLE. Generates a circular area of specified radius centered at a specified VDC position. Appearance of the circular boundary is controlled by the perimeter attributes and the perimeter-visibility component of the interior-style attributes.

ARC CLOSE. Generates an area enclosed by a circular arc and either a straight-line segment between the arc's specified starting and ending points (specified as "chord") or two straight lines between each of these two points and the computed arc center (specified as "pie"). Appearance of the closed-arc boundary is controlled by the perimeter attributes and the perimeter-visibility component of the interior-style attributes.

CELL ARRAY. Generates a rectangular colored-cell array with a separately specified number of cells dividing the distance between the specified maximum and minimum X and Y VDC values. The color of each cell in the array is specified by either a color index or a direct-color value in an ordered list running from left to right, top to bottom.

VDM Primitive-Attribute Elements, Non-Bundleable

CHARACTER HEIGHT. Sets the character height (in VDC units measured along the character-up vector) for subsequent text and append-text elements.

CHARACTER ORIENTATION. Specifies the X and Y components of two vectors: character up and character base. The two vectors define the orientation and skew of the character body (rectangle or parallelogram) in subsequent text and append-text elements.

CHARACTER PATH. Sets character path for subsequent text and append-text elements to "right," "left," "up," or "down."

TEXT ALIGNMENT. Sets text-alignment parameters for positioning the text-extent rectangle (or parallelogram) of subsequent text and append-text elements. Horizontal alignment with the text-element alignment point can be specified as "left," "center," "right," "normal horizontal," or "continuous horizontal." Vertical alignment can be specified as "top," "cap," "half," "base," "bottom," "normal vertical," or "continuous vertical." Normal alignments conform to conventional typesetting practices (e.g., flush "left" or "right" character paths). "Continuous" alignments allow a succession of text strings to be aligned to a single alignment point by specifying a different horizontal or vertical offset (based on the size of the text-extent rectangle) for each string.

CHARACTER SET INDEX. Specifies by index number a character set from the character-set list for subsequent mapping of character codes to character symbols.

PATTERN SIZE. Specifies the width and height of the colored-cell pattern rectangles positioned with one corner at the pattern reference point and replicated as necessary to fill the areas defined by subsequent polygon, circle, and arc-close elements with interior styles set to "pattern."

PATTERN REFERENCE POINT. Establishes a corner reference point for positioning the first colored-cell pattern rectangle that is then replicated as necessary to fill the areas defined by subsequent polygon, circle, and arc-close elements with interior styles set to "pattern." The reference point may also be used by the interpreter to position the start of a hatch pattern when the interior style is set to "hatch."

SET ASPECT SOURCE FLAGS. Sets each Aspect Source Flag (ASF) to "individual" or "bundled." If the attribute ASF for a particular attribute and type of graphic element is set to "individual," the individually specified attribute value is bound to all subsequent elements of that type and can not be changed. If the ASF is set to "bundled," the interpreter uses the currently specified bundle index value, also bound to all corresponding graphic elements, to point to a bundle-table entry containing the desired attribute value.

POLYMARKER BUNDLE INDEX. Sets the polymarker bundle index to a specified value. When subsequent polymarker elements occur, the values for marker type, marker size, and marker color are taken from the corresponding bundle if the ASF for the attribute is set to "bundled."

POLYLINE BUNDLE INDEX. Sets the polyline bundle index to a specified value. When subsequent polyline or arc elements occur, the values for line type, line width, and line color are taken from the corresponding bundle if the ASF for the attribute is set to "bundled."

TEXT BUNDLE INDEX. Sets the text bundle index to a specified value. When subsequent text or append-text elements occur, the values for text font, text precision, character expansion factor, character spacing, and text color are taken from the corresponding bundle if the ASF for the attribute is set to "bundled."

FILL AREA BUNDLE INDEX. Sets the fill-area bundle index to a specified value. When subsequent polygon, circle, or arc-close elements occur, values for interior style, fill color, hatch index, pattern index, perimeter type, perimeter width, and perimeter color are taken from the corresponding bundle if the ASF for the attribute is set to "bundled."

VDM Primitive-Attribute Elements, Bundleable

MARKER TYPE. Specifies by number the type of marker for subsequent polymarker elements. Assigned types include a dot, plus sign, asterisk, and x.

MARKER SIZE. Specifies the absolute marker size or marker-size scale factor (depending on the marker-size specification mode) for subsequent polymarker elements.

MARKER COLOR. Specifies a color-table index value or three direct-color values (depending on the color specification mode) for subsequent polymarker elements.

LINE TYPE. Specifies by number the type of line for subsequent polyline and arc elements. Assigned types include solid, dash, dot, dash dot, and dash dot dot.

LINE WIDTH. Specifies the absolute line width or line-width scale factor (depending on the line-width specification mode) for subsequent polyline and arc elements.

LINE COLOR. Specifies a color-table index value or three direct-color values (depending on the color specification mode).

TEXT FONT INDEX. Specifies by index number a font name from the font list for subsequent text and append-text elements.

TEXT PRECISION. Sets the text precision to "string," "character," or "stroke" for subsequent text or append-text elements. String precision guarantees only the starting position of subsequent strings. Character precision guarantees the starting position of each character and whole-character clipping at a clipping boundary. Stroke precision guarantees the placement, skew, orientation, and size of each character and partial-character clipping at a clipping boundary.

CHARACTER EXPANSION FACTOR. Specifies the character expansion factor for subsequent text and append-text elements. The resulting character width is the product of the current character height multiplied by the character width/height ratio multiplied by the character base-vector/up-vector ratio multiplied by the character expansion factor.

CHARACTER SPACING. Specifies added or reduced space between the characters of subsequent text and append-text elements. The added or subtracted space is specified as a fraction of the current character height.

TEXT COLOR. Specifies a color-table index value or three direct-color values (depending on the color specification mode) for subsequent text and append-text elements.

INTERIOR STYLE. Specifies by number the interior style for subsequent polygon, circle, and arc-close elements. Perimeter visibility is also set to "on" or "off." Assigned styles include hollow, solid, pattern, and hatch. Hollow-style elements are not filled. Solid-style elements are filled with the currently selected fill color. Pattern-style elements are filled with a colored-cell pattern currently selected from the pattern table.Hatch-style elements are filled with a fill-color hatch design selected from a device-level hatch table.

PATTERN INDEX. Specifies a pattern-table index value for filling subsequent polygon, circle, and arc-close elements when the interior style is specified as "pattern."

HATCH INDEX. Specifies a device-level hatch table index value for filling subsequent polygon, circle, and arc-close elements when the interior style is specified as "hatch."

FILL COLOR. Specifies a color-table index value or three direct-color values (depending on the color specification mode) for subsequent polygon, circle, and arc-close elements when the interior style is specified as "solid" or "hatch."

PERIMETER TYPE. Specifies by number the type of perimeter for subsequent polygon, circle, and arc-close elements when perimeter visibility is "on." Assigned perimeter-line types include solid, dash, dot, dash dot, and dash dot dot.

VDM External Elements

MESSAGE. Specifies a string of characters to communicate information to operators at metafile interpretation time through a path separate from normal graphical output.

An action-required flag signals the metafile interpreter to pause or not pause for an operator response.

APPLICATION DATA. Provides the metafile generator and interpreter with supplemental information in an application-dependent way. The element has no effect on the picture or its encoding.

IGES

IGES (Initial Graphics Exchange Specification) is a graphic-image storage and transfer standard of specific interest to users of CAD/ CAM systems. Its objective is to describe not only graphical objects but completely annotated drawings and engineering information on defined parts and assemblies.

The standard differs sharply in both contents and form, therefore, from the family of related software standards that would include Core, GKS, VDM, and VDI. There are, for example, 50 or more basic "primitives" such as conic arcs and surfaces of revolution, and 32 different types of "finite elements." If annotation devices such as labels and witness lines are viewed as primitives, the list is even greater.

Two data formats have been standardized. One consists of 80-column ASCII "card images"; the other is in a binary format and includes an initial binary section that defines how the data is to be interpreted. Five additional sections, common to both file types, include a start section that provides an English-language prolog to the file, a global section that identifies the file and describes how the data is to be interpreted, a directory section in which the entities that make up the file are listed, a parameter-data section that gives the specifics of each entity, and a brief file-terminator section.

There are, in effect, two entries for each entity: one in the directory section, and a second in the parameter-data section. The sequential order of entries in the directory section serves as an index for referencing the parameter-data entries.

Each type of entity is given an identification number. Each type of entity may also be specified in a variety of forms, as in the case of the

32 finite elements. The descriptive information in the directory entry for an entity is brief, however, and always in a fixed format common to all entities. The corresponding parameter-data entries, by comparison, may be very lengthy, and refer not only to its corresponding directory entry but to a number of other associated entities and "property" entities that further describe the original entity.

The entities themselves can be divided into three general categories: geometry-defining entities, annotation-type entities, and "structural" and definition entities that give form to the complete IGES file.

IGES Geometry Entities

CIRCULAR ARC (100). A portion of a parent circle with a specified center point. The arc is drawn counterclockwise from a specified start point to a specified terminate point.

COMPOSITE CURVE (102). A connected curve defined by an ordered list of pointers to entities of the following types: point, line, circular arc, conic arc, and parametric spline.

CONIC ARC (104). A portion of a parent conic curve (ellipse, parabola, or hyperbola) defined by six coefficients in a given polynomial equation. The conic arc is drawn from a specified start point to a specified terminate point (counterclockwise if the parent curve is an ellipse).

COPIOUS DATA (106). Specified data points in the form of pairs (points on a two-dimensional plane), triples (points in three-dimensional space) or sextuples (points in three-dimensional space with associated vectors). Parameter data includes an interpretation flag to indicate which of these forms is being used.

PLANE (108). An unbounded or bounded portion of a plane defined by four coefficients in a given parametric equation. Parameter data can include the location and size of a system-dependent display symbol to identify the plane visually. A bounded portion of the plane is defined by a pointer to any type of closed-curve entity.

LINE (110). A bounded portion of a parent straight line, drawn from a specified start point to a specified terminate point.

PARAMETRIC SPLINE CURVE (112). A sequence of parametric first-, second-, or third-degree polynomial segments. Parameter data includes the breakpoints between segments; four coefficients for each of three given polynomial equations for each segment; the type of spline (linear, quadratic, cubic, Wilson-Fowler, modified Wilson-Fowler, or B-spline); the degree of continuity at each breakpoint; and a dummy terminate segment.

PARAMETRIC SPLINE SURFACE (114). A grid of parametric bicubic polynomial patches. Parameter data includes the number and type of gridline splines (linear, quadratic, cubic, Wilson-Fowler, modified Wilson-Fowler, or B-spline); breakpoints between columns of patches; 16 coefficients for each of three polynomial equations for each patch; the type of surface (Coons, Bezier, B-spline, Ferguson, or Cartesian product); and dummy terminate patches at the end of each row and column.

POINT (116). A point defined by coordinates in definition space. Parameter data can include a pointer to a display-symbol (marker) subfigure entity.

RULED SURFACE (118). A surface formed by moving a line connecting points of equal relative arc length or equal relative parametric value from a specified start point to a specified terminate point on each of two parametric curves. The parametric curves may be points, lines, circles, conics, parametric splines, or any other defined parametric curves, planar or non-planar. Parameter data includes flags to indicate the relative directions of the two sequences of points and whether the surface is developable.

SURFACE OF REVOLUTION (120). A surface formed by rotating a generatrix (circular arc, conic arc, line, parametric spline curve, or composite curve) around a straight-line axis of rotation. The generatrix is rotated counterclockwise from a specified start angle to a specified terminate angle (relative to its originally defined position). Parameter data includes pointers to entities representing the generatrix and axis of rotation.

TABULATED CYLINDER (122). A surface formed by moving a straight-line generatrix parallel to itself along a directrix curve (circular arc, conic arc, line, parametric spline curve, or composite curve). Parameter data includes the terminate point of the generatrix line and a pointer to a curve entity representing the directrix. Start point of the generatrix line is identical to the start point of the directrix.

TRANSFORMATION MATRIX (124). A three-by-three rotation matrix and a translation vector move an associated entity from definition space to model space by first applying the rotation, then the translation. Alternatively, the transformation matrix defines a cylindrical, spherical, or cartesian coordinate system other than the standard definition space. Parameter data includes nine coefficients for the rotation matrix and three values for the translation vector.

LINEAR PATH (106). An ordered set of points in either two- or three-dimensional space. The points define a series of linear segments that may cross, be collinear, or form a closed path. (See Copious Data entity.)

SIMPLE CLOSED AREA (106). A bounded region of XY coordinate space represented by an ordered set of connected points. Line segments are not allowed to intersect or coincide except for the initial and final points. (See Copious Data entity.)

FLASH. A point in the XY plane that locates a closed flash area (circular, rectangular, donut, canoe or one defined by any type of closed-area or closed-curve entity). Parameter data includes values indicating the size and orientation of the standard flash areas.

RATIONAL B-SPLINE CURVE (126). An analytic curve of general interest (in order of preference; a line, circular arc, elliptical arc, parabolic arc, hyperbolic arc, or one defined by rational B-spline parameters). Parameter data includes upper index of sum, degree of basis functions, knot sequence, weights, control points, starting parameter value, ending parameter value, flags to indicate whether the curve is periodic with respect to its parameter, open or closed, rational or non-rational (equal weights), and planar or non-planar. If planar, a unit vector normal to the plane is specified.

RATIONAL B-SPLINE SURFACE (128). An analytical surface of general interest (in order of preference: a plane, right-circular cylinder, cone, sphere, torus, surface of revolution, tabulated cylinder, ruled surface, general quadric surface, or one defined by rational B-spline parameters). Parameter data includes upper indices of first and second sums, degrees of first and second sets of basis functions, first and second knot sequences, weights, control points, starting and ending parameters for the first and second bases, and flags to indicate whether the rational B-spline is periodic or non-periodic, open or closed in the first and/or second direction, and rational or non-rational.

NODE (134). A numbered geometric point used in the definition of a finite element. Parameter data includes a pointer to a nodal displacement coordinate system.

FINITE ELEMENT (136). A numbered element defined by its type of topology (node connectivity) along with physical and material properties. Parameter data includes a topology-type integer and name (one of 32 standardized, zero-, one-, two- and three-dimensional types, with defined nodes, edges, and faces), number of nodes, and a pointer to each node-defining entity.

IGES Annotation Entities

ANGULAR DIMENSION (202). Pointers to a general note, up to two witness lines, and two leader arcs, with arrowheads. Parameter data includes an angle vertex point and the radius of the leader arcs.

CENTERLINE (106). Lines that form either crosshairs (normally in conjunction with circles) or a construction of short and long segments between two endpoints. Each line segment is defined by a separate pair of specified points. (See Copious Data entity.)

DIAMETER DIMENSION (206). Pointers to a general note and one or two leaders. Parameter data includes the center point for the parent circle of the dimensioned arc.

FLAG NOTE (208). Pointer to a general note which determines, in turn, the dimensions of a flag-symbol outline. Parameter data includes the lower-left corner coordinates of the flag symbol, its rotation angle in radians, the number of leaders, and pointers to these leaders.

GENERAL LABEL (210). Pointers to a general note and one or more leaders. Parameter data includes the number of leaders.

GENERAL NOTE (212). A series of separately positioned text strings, each outlined by a hypothetical text box. Parameter data includes the number of text strings and, for each string, the number of characters, an integer-specified font (from an assigned list of fonts), a rotate-internal-text flag that indicates whether the text runs vertically or horizontally, the text-box height and width, a slant angle for the text within the box, a rotation angle for the box, and an X-axis or Y-axis mirror flag.

LEADER (ARROW) (214). One or more connected line segments (or circular arcs, when the leader is part of an angular dimension). The first segment begins with an integer-specified type of arrowhead (from an assigned list of 10 types of arrowheads). Parameter data includes the number of segments, the arrowhead, height, width, position, the terminate point of the first segment, and the terminate points of any additional segments.

LINEAR DIMENSION (216). Pointers to a general note, two leaders, and up to two witness lines.

ORDINATE DIMENSION (218). Pointers to a general note and a witness line or leader. The entity is used to indicate horizontal or vertical distances from a common base line.

POINT DIMENSION (220). Pointers to a general note, a three-segment leader, and an optional circle (circular arc) or hexagon (composite curve) enclosing the text. If the text is not enclosed, the final segment is a horizontal line underlining the text.

RADIUS DIMENSION (222). Pointers to a general note and a leader. Parameter data includes the center point of the dimensioned arc.

SECTION (106). Parallel or crosshatched lines, displayed or not displayed in a solid or centerline style, connecting pairs of specified points to form one of an assigned set of section patterns representing various materials of construction. (See Copious Data entity.)

WITNESS LINE (106). Two or more connected straight-line segments, alternately blank and visible, defined by an odd number of collinear points. The first point should be coincident with the geometry being dimensioned or with the second point if the geometry is unknown. (See Copious Data entity.)

IGES Structure and Definition Entities

ASSOCIATIVITY DEFINITION (302). Specifies a structure of associative data classes, each containing multiple entries with one or more items. (If an entry is a three-dimensional location, for example, each of the three coordinate values would be an item.) Parameter data includes the number of class definitions and, for each class, the number of items per entry (the number of entries per class is specified by the Associative Instance entity), flags to indicate whether back pointers are required and whether the class is ordered (sequence of entries is significant), and for each item in an entry, whether the item is a data value or a pointer to another entity. The other entity may or may not have a backpointer.

ASSOCIATIVITY INSTANCE (402). Establishes an associativity relationship based on either a pre-defined form or a pointer to a user-defined Associativity Definition entity. Parameter data includes the number of entries for each class and a data value or pointer for each item in each entry. Presently pre-defined forms include the following:

Group—A single-class associativity that collects a set of entities with back pointers into a single logical entity.

Group Without Back Pointers—A single-class associativity that collects a set of entities without back pointers into a single logical entity.

Views Visible—A dual-class associativity that identifies the views in which an entity is to be displayed (if displayed in more than one view) and the entities whose display is controlled by this associativity.

Views Visible, Pen Line Weight—A dual-class associativity that expands on the Views Visible relationship by specifying, if desired, a different pen value, line-font value (or pointer to a line-font entity), and line-weight value for each view in which an entity is displayed.

Entity Label Display—A single-class associativity that establishes, if desired, a different entity-label location and leader for each view in which the entity is displayed.

View List—A dual-class associativity that first identifies the view in which entities are to be displayed, then lists the entities included in the view.

Signal String—A four-class associativity that represents a single signal string. The first class is an ordered list of the names of the signal string. The second is a list of connection nodes. The third relates the string to geometric entities on a schematic drawing. The fourth translates this information to an implemented board or chip.

Single Parent—A single-class associativity that defines a logical structure of one independent "parent" entity and one or more subordinate "children" entities whose display parameters are governed by the parent entity.

Text Node—A dual-class associativity that relates the location and display parameters of a general note to multiple instances of itself when included in a subfigure definition. The first class consists of a pointer to a point representing the general note's original location followed by the locations of other existing instances. The second class consists of default general-note parameters such as box size, slant angle, and rotation angle.

Connect Node—A dual-class associativity that establishes a logical connection (e.g., electrical or piping) between one or more entity instances. The first class consists of a pointer to a point entity representing the original location of the connect node followed by pointers to point entities representing the connect-node locations in other existing instances. The second class describes properties of the connect node, but is presently undefined.

DRAWING (404). A collection of annotation entities and views of geometrical entities (including annotations) which together constitute a single representation of a part within a two-dimensional drawing space, which is different from the three-dimensional definition and model spaces. (A transformation matrix associated with each view entity transforms the entity from model space to drawing space.) Parameter data includes the number of views, pointers to individual view entities, the drawing-space location of the origin of each transformed view, the number of separate annotation entities, and pointers to each of these annotations.

LINE FONT DEFINITION (304). A user-defined line font consisting of either alternating visible and blank line segments or a repeating pattern of subfigure instances. Parameter data includes either the length and visibility of the segments that make up the minimum repeating line structure, or a pointer to the subfigure entity to be used in the repeating pattern, its orientation, a scaling factor, and the length of the pattern.

MACRO DEFINITION (306). Establishes a "new" type of entity in terms of other entities. Parameter data is limited to MACRO language statements written in the ASCII character set. The following basic statements can be used.

MACRO is used to signify the start of a MACRO definition. The statement includes a user-defined entity-type number in the range of 600 to 699.

LET is the basic assignment statement and is equivalent to the LET statement of BASIC.

SET establishes directory and parameter data entries for the entity.

REPEAT causes the following group of statements, terminated by a CONTINUE statement, to be repeated a specified number of times.

CONTINUE marks the end of a REPEAT group.

MREF is used to reference another MACRO from inside a MACRO definition.

ENDM signifies the end of a MACRO.

MACRO INSTANCE (600 to 699). Invokes the MACRO identified by a user-defined entity-type number. Parameter data includes values for all the arguments to the MACRO.

PROPERTY (406). Numerical or textual data with a predefined or user-defined meaning. Presently predefined forms include the following:

Definition Levels—Establishes a set of levels for entities that are defined by this set of multiple levels.

Region Restriction—Allows entities that can define regions to set an applications item restriction over the region (i.e., completely inside or completely outside the region).

Level Function—Provides a code which identifies the applications function of a level and a level-like source-system value to facilitate system-to-system transfers.

Region Fill Property—Helps to define the functional value of a closed region by indicating its "filled" status: unfilled, solid filled, or mesh filled. Includes a pointer to a section entity that defines a mesh pattern.

Line Widening—Defines the characteristics of "widened" entities when lines, for example, are used to locate such items as strips of metallization on printed wiring boards. Includes a cornering code (rounded or square) and "justification" (right, left, or center) relative to the defining line.

Drilled Hole—Defines the characteristics of a drilled hole located by, for example, a point entity. Includes drill and finish diameters and whether the hole is to be plated.

Reference Designator—Attaches a reference-designator text string to an entity being used to represent an electrical component.

Pin Number—Attaches a pin-number text string to an entity being used to represent an electrical component's pin.

Part Number—Attaches a set of part-number text strings to an entity being used to represent an electrical component.

Hierarchy—Indicates whether individual directory-entry attributes such as line weight or pen number are to be determined by global or subordinate-entity values.

SUBFIGURE DEFINITION (308). A collection of entities and other subfigures that, together, define a detail to be utilized in multiple instances in the creation of a whole picture. Parameter data includes the subfigure name, number of entities, pointers to these entities, and an indication of the subfigure "depth" (amount of nesting).

SINGULAR SUBFIGURE INSTANCE (408). Specifies the location and size of a single instance of a defined subfigure. Parameter data includes a pointer to the subfigure definition entity, a scaling factor, and a set of coordinates for locating the subfigure in model space. This may exist as a single instance or as a two-dimensional array of the same subfigure. Before placement by the subfigure instance, each entity is operated upon by any defining matrix that may be associated with the individual entity.

RECTANGULAR ARRAY SUBFIGURE INSTANCE (412). A rectangular array of copies of a base entity, arranged in equally spaced columns and rows. The base entity can be a group, subfigure instance, point, line, circular arc, conic arc, rectangular or circular array. Parameter data includes a pointer to the base entity, the coordinates of the lower left-hand corner of the array, the number of columns and rows, the separately defined distances between columns and rows, a rotation angle, and flags that permit individual copies within the array to be blanked or displayed.

CIRCULAR ARRAY SUBFIGURE INSTANCE (414). A circular array of copies of a base entity, arranged around the edge of an imaginary circle. The base entity can be a group, point, line, circular arc, conic arc, rectangular or circular array. The number of times that the base entity is replicated is given, together with the angle that the first replicated entity makes with the positive X-axis running through the center of the imaginary circle. Parameter data includes the center and radius of the array circle, a pointer to the base entity, the number of copies, a start angle for the first copy, the angular distance between copies, and flags that permit individual copies to be blanked or displayed.

TEXT FONT DEFINITION (310). Describes the appearance of characters in a new or modified text font. Each character is defined by straight line segments between grid points in an equally spaced square grid that includes the origin point for the next character in a text string. Parameter data includes the font number and name, the font this definition modifies or supersedes (if applicable), the number of text-height grid units, and for each defined character, its ASCII code, number of pen motions, and a pair of grid coordinates and pen updown flag for each pen motion.

VIEW (410). Defines a specific axonometric "look" at the model. The viewing direction is specified by a defining matrix of the form found in the transformation matrix entity. The default viewing direction is along the positive Z axis toward the X,Y plane in model space. Parameter data includes a view number, scale factor, and an optional clipping box consisting of pointers to planes that form the sides of the box, and as a further option, front and back planes normal to the viewing direction.

VDI

VDI (Virtual Device Interface) is a proposed graphical-device interface standard that is intended as a companion document for the VDM (Virtual Device Metafile) standard.

The VDI will provide a device-independent interface for the software device drivers needed to control displays, printers, and other peripherals with limited intelligence. It will also be able to drive any device that has sufficient intelligence to interpret the VDI commands and attribute instructions. As a third objective, the VDI could serve as an interface between a VDM interpreter and other such intelligent devices, allowing metafiles to be displayed or recorded without any intermediate steps.

It can be expected that the VDI standard, when published, will closely parallel the elements chosen for the VDM standard, including the same set of two-dimensional primitives and the option of individual or bundled primitive attributes. The major change will be the addition of facilities for interactive input. Core and GKS functions are very similar in this area, so that compatibility with both application-level standards should be readily achieved.

NAPLPS

NAPLPS (North American Presentation Level Protocol Syntax) is a graphical-device interface standard with a well-defined target: videotex and teletext terminals.

The NAPLPS standard takes two factors into account. First, communication lines with the graphical device are likely to be long and narrowband. Information should be transmitted with maximum economy, therefore, and as immune to error as possible. Second, a considerable amount of intelligence can be expected at the receiving station to reconstruct the graphic images that have been transmitted. Moreover, forces of the commercial marketplace provide assurance that the receiving station will have all the capabilities needed to implement the standard.

The NAPLPS transmits text and graphical information entirely in the form of 7-bit and 8-bit ASCII-like codes. The 7-bit format provides 128 code possibilities, of which 32 are reserved for a control-code set, and the remaining, for a 96-character graphic/text set. The 8-bit code doubles these capabilities, allowing two 32-code control sets to be resident in the system at the same time, along with two 96-character graphic/text sets.

Six graphic/text sets have been defined, including a PDI (Picture Description Instructions) set that describes six graphic "primitives" for creating graphic images.

Only one of these sets, described below, is "in use" at a time, but they can be rapidly shifted in and out of the graphic/text table in response to control codes transmitted by the data source. Moreover, additional user-defined graphic/text sets can be substituted for one or more of the six standard sets to expand greatly the capabilities offered by the system.

NAPLPS Control Codes

(C0 Set). ACTIVE POSITION SET. Sets the cursor to the character position specified by the following two bytes without resetting any parameters or attributes.

ACTIVE POSITION BACKWARD. Moves the cursor in a direction opposite to the character path a distance equal to the dimension of the current size character field parallel to the character path (backspace).

ACTIVE POSITION FORWARD. Moves the cursor in the direction of the character path a distance equal to the dimension of the current size character field parallel to the character path (horizontal tab).

ACTIVE POSITION DOWN. Moves the cursor in a direction perpendicular to the character path ($-90°$) a distance equal to the dimension of the current size character field perpendicular to the character path (line feed).

ACTIVE POSITION UP. Moves the cursor in a direction perpendicular to the character path ($+90°$) a distance equal to the dimension of the current size character field perpendicular to the character (vertical tab).

ACTIVE POSITION RETURN. Moves the cursor to the first character position on the current character path within the currently defined active drawing area (carriage return).

CLEAR SCREEN. Moves the cursor to the upper leftmost character position and clears the screen to black (color mode 0 or 1) or the current in-use background color (color mode 2).

SHIFT-IN, SHIFT-OUT, SINGLE-SHIFT 2, SINGLE-SHIFT 3, ESCAPE. Used to invoke active control and graphic/text sets into the in-use table.

CANCEL. Terminates the processing of all currently executing macros.

ACTIVE POSITION HOME. Moves the cursor to the upper leftmost character position on the screen.

NON-SELECTIVE RESET (NSR). Serves two functions: as a non-selective reset, or, if followed by two bytes representing character-position coordinates, as an alternative means to position the text cursor.

(C1 Set). DEFINE MACRO. Defines and downloads (but does not execute) a macro when followed by a macro-name byte and an arbitrary string of graphic/text codes. Up to 96 macros may be simultaneously defined.

DEFINE AND PROCESS MACRO. Simultaneously stores and executes the downloaded macro code.

DEFINE TRANSMIT-MACRO. Defines a transmit-macro which, when called, is not executed but is transmitted in its entirety to a host computer or local application process.

DEFINE DRCS. Defines and downloads a single DRCS (Dynamically Redefinable Character Set) character when followed by a DRCS character-name byte and an arbitrary string of graphic/text codes.

DEFINE TEXTURE. Defines and downloads texture-pattern mask A, B, C, or D when followed by a valid mask-identifying byte.

END. Terminates the current macro-, DRCS-, or texture-definition process.

PROTECT/UNPROTECT. Unprotects a rectangular area of the screen defined by a PDI FIELD command code, allowing the user to enter or edit data in that area. An unprotected field can be reprotected by a subsequent PROTECT/UNPROTECT control code.

REPEAT. Causes the last graphic/text character received to be repeated a specified number of times.

REPEAT TO EOL. Causes the last graphic/text character received to be repeated to end of line (the last character position along the current character path within the unit screen or active drawing area).

REVERSE VIDEO. Causes the terminal to enter reverse video mode.

NORMAL VIDEO. Terminates the reverse video mode.

SMALL TEXT. Sets the horizontal dimension of the character field to a value that will generate a nominal 80-character-per-row display.

MEDIUM TEXT. Sets the horizontal and vertical dimensions of the character field to values that will generate a nominal 32-by-16 screen format.

NORMAL TEXT. Sets the dimensions of the character field to their default values.

DOUBLE HEIGHT. Sets the vertical dimension of the character field to twice its default value, and the horizontal dimension to its default value.

DOUBLE SIZE. Sets both dimensions of the character field to twice their default values.

WORD WRAP ON. Causes the terminal to enter wordwrap mode. While wordwrap is on, graphic/text characters are not displayed one character at a time as received, but are buffered into complete "words."

WORD WRAP OFF. Causes the terminal to exit wordwrap mode.

SCROLL ON. Causes the terminal to enter scroll mode.

SCROLL OFF. Causes the terminal to exit scroll mode.

UNDERLINE START. Causes the terminal to enter underline mode. The mosaic graphics/text set is displayed in separated-graphics mode.

UNDERLINE STOP. Causes the terminal to exit underline mode. The mosaic graphics/text set is displayed in contiguous mode.

FLASH CURSOR. Turns on the cursor display and causes it to flash intermittently.

STEADY CURSOR. Turns on the cursor display and keeps it steadily visible.

CURSOR OFF. Causes the cursor display to be turned off (made invisible).

BLINK START. Turns on a blinking process, utilizing the current in-use drawing color as the blink-from color.

BLINK STOP. Turns off any currently active blinking processes.

NAPLPS Graphics/Text Sets

PRIMARY CHARACTER SET. Reproduces the standard 96-character ASCII alphanumeric set. Particular pixel patterns for the characters are not defined and are constrained only by the specified character field at each size for a given display resolution. Character legibility is not guaranteed for all sizes in all colors at all display resolutions. All display devices, however, must support at least the default character size.

MOSAIC SET. Contains 64 two-by-three block mosaic characters plus a second copy of the solid-mosaic character. Remaining character positions correspond to the space character and are not to be used for other purposes. Mosaic graphics characters can be displayed in two modes, contiguous or separated, depending on the underline mode. In contiguous mode, the mosaic should completely span the character field at any size. In seperated mode, each of the six mosaic elements in a character field is reduced in size by the width and height of the logical pel size.

SUPPLEMENTARY CHARACTER SET. Contains 96 assigned symbols, abbreviations, punctuation marks, accent marks, numerical fractions and graphic characters. Particular pixel patterns for the characters are not defined and are constrained only by the specified character field at each size for a given display resolution. Sixteen of the accent and symbol characters are different from other characters in that they are non-spacing (the cursor does not automatically advance when a non-spacing character is received).

MACRO SET. Allows up to 96 sequences of NAPLPS code to be simultaneously stored by the receiving device and individually executed upon command.

DYNAMICALLY REDEFINABLE CHARACTER SET (DRCS). A facility that allows a maximum of 96 user-defined pixel patterns to be downloaded and utilized in an identical manner as the other character sets. (All other pixel-pattern definitions are permanently stored in the terminal and can not be altered by the host computer.)

PICTURE DESCRIPTION INSTRUCTIONS (PDI) SET. Specifies six geometric graphic primitives: POINT, LINE, ARC, RECTANGLE, POLYGON, and IN-CREMENTAL, each of which has four forms. Also provides eight control codes: RESET, DOMAIN, TEXT, TEXTURE, SET COLOR, CONTROL STATUS (WAIT), SELECT COLOR, and BLINK. The remaining 64 character positions are reserved for numeric data in the form of six-bit data fields for each information byte. Unlike the calling syntax for the other character sets, which requires only one byte to produce a character-sized pixel pattern, PDI calls consist of multiple-byte commands and produce images not necessarily restricted to a single character field. A PDI command sequence starts with an op-code byte that represents either a graphic primitive or a control code. The balance of the command consists of one or more operands, each of which consists of one or more bytes of numeric data. The operands can take one of four forms:

Fixed format—One or more bytes whose length and meaning depends on the op code.

String—Any number of bytes whose interpretation again depends on the op code.

Single-value—One to four bytes interpreted as unsigned integers composed of concatenated bits taken from the consecutive bytes.

Multi-value—One to eight multiple-field bytes used to specify coordinate or color information. Each value is a signed or unsigned fraction composed of concatenated bits taken from corresponding fields in the consecutive bytes.

NAPLES PDI Primitives

POINT. Sets the current drawing point and optionally draws a dot. All four forms of the POINT command take one multi-value operand.

POINT SET (absolute) sets the drawing point at the absolute coordinates specified by the operand; it does not draw a dot.

POINT SET (relative) sets the drawing point at a specified displacement from the current drawing point; it does not draw a dot.

POINT (absolute) sets the drawing point at the specified absolute coordinates and draws a logical-pel dot.

POINT (relative) sets the drawing point at a specified displacement from the current drawing point and draws a logical-pel dot.

LINE. Draws a straight line between an initial drawing point and a final drawing point. LINE commands take a single multi-value operand; SET AND LINE commands require two multi-value operands.

LINE (absolute) draws a line from the current drawing point to a specified final absolute-coordinate drawing point.

LINE (relative) draws a line from the current drawing point to a specified final drawing point expressed as a relative displacement from the initial point.

SET AND LINE (absolute) draws a line from a specified initial drawing point to a specified final drawing point, both expressed in absolute coordinates.

SET AND LINE (relative) draws a line from a specified absolute-coordinate initial drawing point to a specified final drawing point expressed as a relative displacement from the initial point.

ARC. Draws circles or segments of circles from an initial drawing point to a final drawing point through a third point on the arc. The intermediate drawing point is specified as a relative displacement from the initial drawing point. The final drawing point is specified as a relative displacement from the intermediate point. If the three points defining the arc are collinear, a straight line is drawn between the initial and final points. If the final drawing point is either omitted or is coincident with the initial drawing point, a circle is drawn with the intermediate point halfway around the circle (i.e., on the diameter). If additional numeric data is transmitted beyond the final drawing point, a curvilinear spline is indicated with each succeeding point. With these exceptions, ARC commands take two multi-value operands; SET AND ARC commands require three multi-value operands.

ARC (outlined) uses the current drawing point as the initial drawing point for the arc.

ARC (filled) uses the current drawing point as the initial drawing point and fills the area bounded by the arc and a chord joining the endpoints of the arc with the currently specified color and texture.

SET AND ARC (outlined) starts the arc at a specified absolute-coordinate initial drawing point.

SET AND ARC (filled) starts the arc at a specified absolute-coordinate initial drawing point and fills the area bounded by the arc and a chord joining the end points of the arc with the currently specified color and texture.

RECTANGLE. Draws a rectangle of a specified height and width starting at an initial drawing point. The height and width are specified in relative coordinates as displacements measured from the initial drawing point. After the rectangle has been drawn, the new current drawing point is taken as the initial drawing point displaced horizontally by the width dimension. RECT commands take one multi-value operand; SET AND RECT commands require two multi-value operands.

RECT (outlined) uses the current drawing point as the initial drawing point for the rectangle.

RECT (filled) uses the current drawing point as the initial drawing point and fills the rectangle with the currently specified color and texture.

SET AND RECT (outlined) uses a specified absolute-coordinate point as the initial drawing point for the rectangle.

SET AND RECT (filled) uses a specified absolute-coordinate point as the initial drawing point and fills the rectangle with the currently specified color and texture.

POLYGON. Draws polygons from an initial drawing point through a series of up to 256 vertices back to the initial drawing point. The location of each vertex is specified as a relative displacement from the previous vertex. POLY commands take as many multi-value operands as there are vertices displaced from the initial drawing point; SET AND POLY commands require one additional multi-value operand.

POLY (outlined) uses the current drawing point as the initial drawing point for the polygon.

POLY (filled) uses the current drawing point as the initial drawing point and fills the polygon with the currently specified color and texture.

SET AND POLY (outlined) uses a specified absolute-coordinate point as the initial drawing point for the polygon.

SET AND POLY (filled) uses a specified absolute-coordinate point as the initial drawing point and fills the polygon with the currently specified color and texture.

INCREMENTAL. Describes images that consist of sequences of points, lines, or filled polygons. The commands take either multi-value or combinations of fixed-format, multi-value and string operands, depending on their form.

FIELD establishes a rectangular active drawing area within which the INCREMENTAL POINT command is executed. (FIELD also provides an active drawing area for columnated text and identifies regions that may be unprotected by the application to allow for user input and local editing.) The command takes two multi-value operands, one to specify the origin of the drawing area in absolute coordinates, the other to specify the width and height of the drawing-area rectangle as displacements from the specified origin.

INCREMENTAL POINT describes a string of color-specified points that are deposited in a raster-sequential manner within the active drawing area. The command takes two operands. The first is a fixed-format, single-byte packing counter that indicates the number of consecutive bits to be taken from the following operand to make up a single color specification. The second is a string operand of indeterminate length which contains the color specifications in sequential order without regard to byte boundaries.

INCREMENTAL LINE describes a string of lines drawn from point to point with a single set of color and texture. Not restricted to the active drawing area, the line drawing begins at the current drawing point and proceeds from one point to the next as specified by the relative positive or negative fixed-step displacements in X and/or Y from the previous point. The command takes two operands. The first is a multi-value operand that specifies the step-size parameters in X and Y. The second is a string operand of indeterminate length which consists of two-bit nibbles that indicate whether the next step should be X, Y, X/Y, or an escape to the next nibble which is a two-bit instruction indicating that the following lines should reverse visibility (on/off) or reverse the direction of the X, Y, or X/Y steps.

INCREMENTAL POLY (filled) uses the same multi-value and string operands as the INCREMENTAL LINE command to generate a closed polygon that is then filled with the currently specified color and texture.

NAPLPS PDI Control Commands

DOMAIN. Controls operand parameters and the logical-pel size. Once set, the parameters do not change until acted upon by either the RESET command, another DOMAIN command, or the NSR control code. The command takes two operands. The first is a single-byte, fixed-format operand that dictates the number of bytes in a single-value operand (up to 4), the number of bytes in a multi-value operand (up to 8), and whether the coordinates are two- or three-dimensional. The second is a multi-value operand that fixes the horizontal and vertical dimensions of the logical pel (which determines, for example, the width of lines generated by drawing commands).

TEXT. Controls parameters relating to text-character attributes and the cursor. The command takes two operands. The first is a two-byte, fixed-format operand that determines character rotation (0°, 90°,

180°, 270°), character path (right, left, up, down), inter-character spacing (1, 1.25, 1.5, proportional), inter-row spacing (1, 1.25, 1.5, 2), cursor display style (underscore, block, cross hair, custom), and the relationship between the cursor and the current drawing point (move together, move independently, drawing point follows the cursor or cursor follows the drawing point, but not vice versa). The second is a multi-value operand that specifies the width and height of the character field.

TEXTURE. Sets texture attributes for subsequent drawing commands. The command takes two operands. The first is a single-byte, fixed-format operand that determines line texture (solid, dotted, dashed, dot-dashed), highlighting (filled areas are outlined in black or background color), and the fill-area texture pattern (solid, vertical hatch, horizontal hatch, cross hatch, or one of four programmable texture masks). The second is a multi-value operand that specifies the displayed width and height of the texture mask when it is replicated to fill an area.

SET COLOR. Specifies actual color values either to load a color map or for direct display as the current color (until changed by another SET COLOR command, the RESET command, or the NSR control character). The command takes a single multi-value operand with up to two bits of color information for each primary color (red, green, and blue) in each byte. A color value of 0,0,0 is assigned the special meaning of "transparent" (allowing lower ordered planes or a video image, for example, to show through the display).

SELECT COLOR. Sets the color mode, and when applicable, specifies color-map addresses for the in-use drawing and background colors. The command takes zero, one, or two single-value operands. If the command is followed by zero operands, the system is in color mode 0 until a RESET command or a SELECT COLOR command with operands is received. Color selection in mode 0 can be accomplished only by SET COLOR commands. If the SELECT COLOR command is followed by one operand, the system is in color mode 1 until changed by a RESET command or a NSR command code, or a SELECT COLOR command with zero or two operands is received. The operand, in this case, is a color-map address that establishes the current drawing color. (Colors are loaded into the color map by specifying an address with a SELECT COLOR command and a corresponding color with a SET COLOR command.) If the SELECT COLOR command is followed by two operands, the system is in color mode 2 until changed by a RESET command or a NSR command code, or a SELECT COLOR command with one or two operands is received. The first operand is again a color-map address that establishes the current drawing color. The second operand is a color-map address for the current background color.

BLINK. Controls a blinking drawing-color process which periodically changes the current (blink-from) color-map address to a different (blink-to) address. After a specified "on" interval has expired, the process restores the color value that was overwritten. Multiple blink processes can be specified with defined phase delays measured from the start of the next "on" interval of the most recently received blink process. The command takes two operands. The first is a single-value operand that specifies the blink-to color-map address. The second is a three-byte fixed-format operand that specifies the on interval, off interval, and phase delay in tenths of a second.

CONTROL STATUS (WAIT). Indicates a programmed delay in the execution of the display code. The command takes two one-byte, fixed-format operands. The first operand contains a given bit pattern. The second operand specifies the delay in tenths of a second (additional bytes can be used to extend the delay).

RESET. Selectively reinitializes the control and atttribute parameters to their default values, clears the screen, sets the border color, homes the cursor, and clears the DRCS set, texture attributes, macro-PDIs, and unprotected fields. The command takes a two-byte, fixed-format operand that is decoded to determine which reset actions are to be taken. If the command is received with no operand, a complete reset is indicated.

5
Distributing the Intelligence

The two previous chapters have described the sequence of processing functions required to convert source data into a raster graphics display. Most of the initial steps can be equated with conventional data processing and could be executed efficiently by a host computer's operating system and application program. The final steps, mapping of the data into display memory and using this information to generate images on the monitor screen, are specifically oriented to the display task.

It would be wasteful of the host computer's resources to require its processor to perform all of the highly repetitive subroutines associated with display-memory mapping. It would be equally wasteful to use the computer's main-memory facilities to store the resulting display data and refresh the raster display. Such an arrangement would require, as a minimum, a dedicated direct memory access channel just to support the display function.

This is why we have selected the host-computer/graphics-controller configuration as our "model" graphics system (Chapter 1). In one form or another, virtually every system design off-loads the host computer by providing specialized graphics-generation hardware with its own firmware or software. Even a standalone graphics system will typically have a "communication" interface for receiving partially processed display information from another data source.

By implication, then, there is a distribution of the graphics intelligence between two or more processing centers. The objective of this chapter is to describe the variety of ways this division can be implemented. We will be concentrating, for the most part, on general-purpose hardware/software graphics systems, but the same principles apply to systems designed for specialized applications, such as computer-aided design, image processing, and process control.

160

SOFTWARE DIVISION

The most direct way to identify how a system's graphics-generation functions are distributed is to separate host-computer software from that of the controller. This is not always an easy task. Descriptive literature may list a wide range of programmable functions without any hint as to whether a particular function is executed by a host computer or by the graphics controller. It is even more difficult to determine, in a quick review, whether a particular function is performed by controller software and is theoretically accessible to the user, or is accomplished in hardware—with or without provision for user-defined firmware options. Moreover, the present trend in the design of graphics controllers is towards the use of multiple microprocessors, one or more of which may be incorporated into add-on options. Functions associated with these options must be further separated, therefore, from the capabilities offered by the basic system.

Most graphics-system suppliers provide full programming support for the graphics controller and, in addition, device drivers for the more "popular" host computers. Any additional host-computer software modules are generally written in a higher-level language, such as BASIC or FORTRAN. The result is illustrated in Figure 5–1, which shows the interrelationship between the user's application program, a "graphics package" (including a device driver resident in the host computer), and the graphics-controller microprogram.

A RANGE OF CAPABILITIES

A graphics controller may consist of one plug-in card, or racks of equipment—with capabilities to match. There are two reasons for this wide range of physical configurations and functional abilities. The first and most obvious is the variety of graphics requirements—from the simple presentation of data in the form of charts and graphs to the generation of complex three-dimensional drawings that require "real time" interaction with the operator. The second reason is the variety of companies engaged in the business of supplying graphics-system hardware and software.

Computer manufacturers, for example, are free to integrate the controller functions into their existing system architectures. Independent companies specializing in graphics hardware must, by contrast, maintain compatibility with the broadest possible range of computer systems. A market also exists for software that goes beyond the pro-

FORTRAN IV USER PROGRAM   Write a vector from (100,300) to (34,450).

```
            Integer X1, Y1, X2, Y2, Z
            X1 = 100
            Y1 = 300
            X2 = 34
            Y2 = 450
            Z = 1
            CALL DSVEC (X1, Y1, X2, Y2, Z)
```

NOVA/ECLIPSE Interface Software (FORTRAN IV Driver Program)

```
                        5
        DSVEC:   JSR@ .CPYL        ; Get arguments onto stack
        WAIT1:   SKPBZ 60          ; Wait for device to be ready
                 JMP WAIT1
                 LDA 0 C14         ; Get function code (14 octal)
                 DOAS 0 60         ; & send it to controller
                 LDA 0 C5
                 STA 0 COUNT       ; Initialize count to 5

        NXARG:   LDA 0@ - 167,3    ; Get next argument off stack
        WAIT2:   SKPBZ 60          ; Wait for device to be ready
                 JMP WAIT2
                 DOAS 0 60         ; Send argument to controller
                 INC 3 3           ; Advance argument pointer
                 DSZ COUNT         ; Any more arguments?
                 JMP NXARG         ; Yes, repeat this loop
                 JMP @ .FRET       ; No, return to main program
        COUNT:   0                 ; Loop counter
        C5:      5                 ; Initial value for counter
        C14:     14                ; Function code for VECTOR
```

CONTROLLER Microprogram

```
        VLP:     LDA SUM           ; Get running sum
                 ADD SMLINC        ; Add small increment to sum
                 JMPF CARRY, VL1   ; Is result positive?
                 ADD BIGINC        ; Yes, subtract big increment
                 STA SUM           ; & store new sum.
                 LDA BOTHDIR       ; Set to increment both X and Y
                 JUMP VL2

        VL1:     STA SUM           ; Negative result: store new sum
                 LDA BIGDIR        ; Set to increment larger direction
        VL2:     OTA MEMINC        ; Increment memory address
                 OTA SWRITE        ; Start memory write cycle
                 DSN COUNT         ; Any more points left?
                 JUMP VLP          ; Yes, repeat this loop
                 JMPI RETAD        ; No, return
```

Figure 5–1. Distribution of graphics-system software functions. (Source: Lexidata Corporation)

gramming aids provided by the host-computer or graphics-controller suppliers. And there are always niches for enterprising companies who offer products that meet a specialized requirement.

Computer users with a "dumb" Lear Siegler ADM-3A alphanumeric terminal can, for example, add a basic graphics capability to

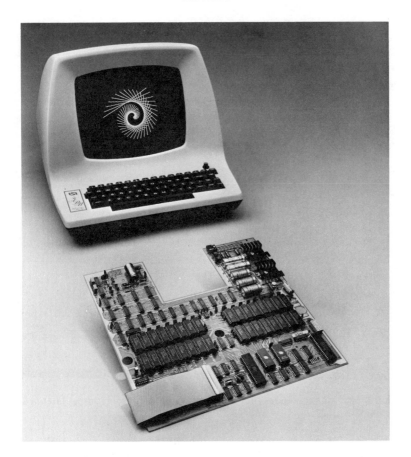

Figure 5-2. Graphics plug-in module for alphanumeric terminal. (Source: Digital Engineering, Inc.)

their systems by simply plugging in the card shown in Figure 5-2. The card is equipped with a microprocessor, 128,000 bits of RAM memory to support a 512-by-250 pixel array, and firmware for converting end-point coordinates into vectors displayed on the terminal CRT screen. The vector data can be received from the host computer or entered on the terminal keyboard, and the displayed vectors can be merged on the screen with alphanumeric annotations stored in the terminal's own character-mapped display memory. No software is supplied with the unit, but the microprocessor program has been written to provide software compatibility with a widely used graphics package (Tektronix Plot 10).

The circuit card shown in Figure 5-3 expands on this plug-in con-

Figure 5-3. Host-computer I/O-card graphics controller. (Source: Intermedia Systems)

cept. The card can be inserted into any available I/O slot in a Hewlett-Packard 2100/MX/E/F series computer using any version of the HP RTE operating system. The output drives any standard RGB color monitor, producing both an 8-color image and an independent monochrome overlay. Resolution is 768 by 512 pixels. Function calls from the host computer consist of a 16-bit control word followed by a data string representing points, vector coordinates, or text. The stored microcode implements standard display functions—with space reserved for user-defined special functions. The supplier also provides a device driver for the graphics-controller cards, but the balance of the graphics software must be provided by the user.

GRAPHICS TERMINALS

A similar dependence on the host computer applies to the "graphics terminal" shown in Figure 5-4. Any operator interaction with the

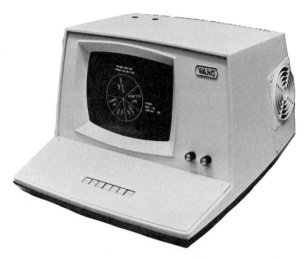

Figure 5-4. Non-interactive graphics terminal. System uses plotter software and line-printer interface. (Source: Wang Laboratories, Inc.)

display is through a separate keyboard terminal. The only operator controls provided by the graphics terminal are on/off, contrast, brightness, and clear screen—plus printer-select and copy controls for a dot-matrix printer attached to the terminal. The monochrome display has a resolution of 800 by 512 pixels, and illustrates the integration that can occur when the graphics system is supplied by the host-computer manufacturer. Interfacing with the host is through a line-printer controller; most of the graphics software consists of standard plotter utilities.

The color graphics terminal shown in Figure 5-5 adds a degree of interactive independence to the display station. The terminal includes not only a character-map display memory (Chapter 7), but also provides optional storage for over a thousand user-defined graphics-character masks. The terminal keyboard has special facilities for selecting programmed symbols and colors. Again, however, a standard printer-type controller provides the interface with the host computer, and all of the graphics software is resident in the host computer. A Graphical Data Display Manager (GDDM) package provides the basic functions required to construct an image from source data.

Added "intelligence" can free a graphics terminal from any dependence on the host computer—provided the graphics display is relatively simple. Figure 5-6 shows a terminal designed for both interaction with a host computer and independent BASIC programming of the terminal microprocessor. Features include English-like high-level graphics com-

Figure 5-5. Character-mapped, 8-color terminal, designed primarily for business graphics. (Source: International Business Machines)

Figure 5-6. Graphics terminal with standalone capabilities. (Source: Hewlett-Packard)

mands and menu-driven "automatic" plotting of pie charts, bar charts, and Cartesian-coordinate graphs.

GRAPHICS CONTROLLERS

As a class, graphics controllers have a far greater programming capability—compared to terminals—but still serve in a subsystem role. Ultimate control over the graphics-generation task remains with the host computer.

Graphics controllers vary widely in terms of both the functions they can perform and the degree to which the user can modify or expand on the controller's capabilities. The first clue is the instruction list which serves as the communication medium between host computer and controller. Figures 5–7 and 5–8 provide two typical examples. Both controllers support monochrome and color raster displays.

A cursory review of the two lists would indicate that despite a difference in terminology, very similar functions are being performed. But a closer examination of the instruction sets and the controller specifications will indicate fundamental differences that reflect tradeoff decisions by the designers of the two systems. The commands listed in Figure 5–7 are identified as "macro" instructions which invoke controller subroutines accessible to the user. This means that each subroutine can be rewritten, if necessary, to meet the requirements of a specific application. And in principle at least, new macros can be created and incorporated into the device driver to expand on the number of programmed controller functions.

The instruction set in Figure 5–8 does not provide the user with this flexibility. The controller software is relatively fixed. But embedded in the instructions are several capabilities not offered by the first controller. For example, the aspect ratio, resolution, and bits-per-pixel values can be altered by relatively simple wiring changes to the display memory; "major" and "minor" channel instructions are then used to map data into the altered memory without affecting, in any way, the balance of the controller functions. A single controller design can accommodate, therefore, a variety of display formats—from a single 512-by-512 monochrome raster to 16 independent 256-by-256 displays with three bits defining the color of each pixel.

"CONVERSATIONAL" SOFTWARE

Nearly all of the software functions described in this and previous chapters have related to interactive systems in which the operator uses

CHANNEL SELECT
Selects the display memory plane(s) associated with a channel on which an operation is to be performed.

PRIMARY MODE SELECT
Selects the mode of operation for the operating system.

SUB-MODE SELECT
Selects a sub-mode of operation (reverse write, long/short dash, fixed origin, etc.)

LOAD X OFFSET
Loads a 10-bit X offset value into the controller X offset register; when the indexing sub-mode is specified by the SMS instruction, the X offset value is added to initial X values and end X values.

LOAD Y OFFSET
Performs the same function as the LXO instruction for Y values.

LOAD INITIAL X
Loads a value defining the X coordinate of the operating point.

LOAD INITIAL Y
Loads a value defining the Y coordinate of the operating point.

LOAD END X
Loads a value defining the X coordinate for the endpoint in point-to-point vector and Cartesian modes.

LOAD END Y
Loads a value defining the Y coordinate for the endpoint in point-to-point vector and Cartesian modes. Initiates the operation upon completion of loading.

LOAD RELATIVE X
Loads a value which, when added to the X operating point, defines the X coordinate for the end point in point-to-point vector and Cartesian modes.

LOAD RELATIVE Y
Loads a value which, when added to the Y operating point, defines the Y coordinate for the endpoint in point-to-point vector and Cartesian modes. Initiates the operation upon completion of loading.

LOAD ZOOM FACTOR
Loads a zoom factor of X2, X4, X8, or X16 when in the zoom mode; resets the zoom mode when value of zero is entered.

LOAD BLOCK COUNT
Loads a block count of 1 to 4096 16-bit words for writing into or reading from the selected display memory plane(s).

TRANSFER CONTROL WORD
Multi-word construction; transfers control words to the controller to control display-signal gating, cursors, hardware scrolling and hardware zooming.

WRITE TRANSFER CONTROL
Two-word instruction, in which second word contains a buffer memory, lookup table, or I/O port address. Controller reads a word from host CPU and writes it into device address selected by second word. Continues until all specified data is written into selected device addresses.

TRANSFER CONTROL WORD, HALT, AND READ
Two-word instruction, in which second word contains a buffer memory, lookup table, or I/O port address. Controller reads a word from the device address selected by the second word, and writes the data into the host CPU memory. Continues until all specified data is read from addressed device and written into host CPU memory.

Figure 5-7. Controller macros, 1 or 2. (Source: Genisco Computers)

END OF GRAPHIC FILE
Terminates the graphic file. This instruction causes the controller to halt and interrupts the host CPU.

SPECIAL INSTRUCTION
When in the clear/set mode, specifies clear memory (all zeros) or set memory (all ones). For all other modes, this is a no operation (NOP) instruction.

PRIMARY MODES

X/Y Raster—Writes 16-bit data words in display memory. The raster write and advance directions are user-selectable.

Z Raster—Writes pixel data in the Z direction. The raster write and advance directions are user-selectable.

Alphanumeric & Symbol—Writes a 5x7 alphanumeric character in a 7x12 matrix for 7-bit ASCII codes.

Cartesian—Draws a rectangle between the operating point and the endpoint using the differences between the coordinates of the starting point and endpoint as the dimensions for the rectangle.

Memory Readback Primary Mode—Reads display memory data back to the host CPU in raster format.

X/Y Coordinates Primary Mode—Draws a vector between two points defined by the X and Y coordinates.

Incremental Vector Primary Mode—Determines one of eight possible directions on the basis of a three-bit code, and then moves the operating point in that direction.

Multi-Cursor Tracking Primary Mode—Enables user to control up to seven cursors by using joysticks, trackballs, or digitizer tablets.

Single-Cursor Tracking Primary Mode—Enables user to control up to four cursors, one at a time, using joysticks or trackballs.

Figure 5-7. Controller macros, 2 of 2. (Source: Genisco Computers)

LOAD RECTANGULAR LIMITS
The ten least significant bits of the limit instructions are the binary values of the rectangular limits. The origin of X,Y coordinates is in the upper left-hand corner of the CRT screen.

CURSOR POSITIONING
The start address of display memory read and write operations is specified by the cursor X and Y coordinates.

MODE CONTROL WORD
If bit 0 is set, graphic information may be written into the display memory. If bit 0 is reset, alphanumerics may be written. In the alphanumeric mode, bits 3 and 4 are decoded to select the outputs of one of four character fonts.

AUTOMATIC CURSOR ADVANCE
The instruction specifies the amount by which the cursor is to be moved each time a memory write operation is performed in the graphic mode.

CHANNEL SELECTION AND MASKING
A Select Major Channel instruction enables the inputs of up to twelve 512x512 display memory channels. A Select Minor Channel instruction is used only with the 512x256 or 256x256 scan formats.

Figure 5-8. Controller instruction set, 1 of 2. (Source: Aydin Controls)

LOAD INDEX REGISTERS
The least significant 10 bits specify the contents of the X and Y index registers.

SCROLLING, CLEARING - EDIT INSTRUCTION
The instruction provides for clearing any combination of selected channels simultaneously, either to all ones or all zeros. Zeros in bits 1 and 2 define the scroll instruction. Bit 1 specifies that a memory clear operation is to be performed.

LOAD ALPHANUMERIC CHARACTER
The seven least significant bits specify one of 128 possible character codes. Associated with each character font is a fixed character block area within which the character is written.

LOAD GRAPHIC ELEMENTS
The instruction writes 8 bits of picture element data into all selected memory channels.

BLOCK TRANSFER MODE
The instruction is used to transfer a block of data words from the host computer to the display memory.

CURSOR POSITION READBACK
The instruction causes the controller to transmit the current contents of the cursor X and Y registers to the computer.

MEMORY DATA READBACK
The instruction causes the controller to transmit the data within the truncated rectangular limits in each selected memory channel. Data returned is picture element information for each raster line of each memory channel.

KEYBOARD TRANSMIT STATUS
Each keystroke received by the controller may be handled in one of three ways: (1) transmitted to the computer, and not executed in the controller; (2) transmitted to the computer and executed in the controller, thus relieving the computer of the task of echoing the keystroke; (3) executed in the controller, but not sent to the computer.

LOAD KEYBOARD CURSOR
The command causes the current content of the cursor counters to be loaded into one of twelve keyboard cursor latches and thus enables the computer to move the operator's cursor.

LOAD PROGRAMMABLE FONT
This is a multiple word instruction used to specify any one of the 64 characters in the programmable font.

LOAD LOOKUP TABLE
The programmable lookup table is a random–access read/write memory which translates the combined serial outputs of up to 6 display memory channels into red, green, and blue color intensity information. Two-word instructions are used to initially define the color data words stored in the lookup table.

READ LOOKUP TABLE
The instruction causes the controller to transmit to the computer the contents of the lookup table.

EXECUTE CONIC INSTRUCTION
Discrete approximations to vectors, circles, ellipses and rotated ellipses are computed and written into all selected memory channels. Since conics are drawn only within rectangular limits, arcs can be generated by properly setting these limits before executing a conic instruction. Vector endpoint coordinates are loaded into the index X and Y registers; the start point is the cursor location. The radius of a circle is stored in the index X register, and the center point is the cursor location. Ellipses are specified by the semi-major and semi-minor axis lengths, the center point, and (if desired) the angle of rotation.

Figure 5–8. Controller instruction set, 2 of 2. (Source: Aydin Controls)

a keyboard, digitizer tablet, or other interactive-input device to generate and modify a graphics display. In fact, a principal rationale for having a physically separate controller is to provide a vehicle for such interactions, separate from the host computer.

There exists, however, a large and important class of systems in which the graphics are generated almost solely by "conversational" software in the host computer. The graphics controller is reduced to little more than a display generator, as was the case in several of the examples given earlier in this chapter. Operator interactions, if any, are through a conventional data-entry terminal. The graphics relate primarily to business, scientific, and geographic reports, and most of the creativity is exercised by the programmer who designed the software.

Software packages in this class tend to make up in sophistication and breadth what they lack in flexibility and depth. Figure 5-9, for example, illustrates how one system allows the user to generate a variety of charts through simple, higher-level statements. The parameters defining the form of the selected graphic can be entered in any "conversational" syntax; the system recognizes the key words it needs to create an acceptable image. If any instructions are missing, the system provides its own "default" alternatives.

The Figure 5-9 statements are implemented by subroutines drawn from a massive graphics-software resource with nearly four hundred FORTRAN-coded subroutines grouped into the following categories:

- Plot initialization and termination.
- Linear, logarithmic, semi-log, monthly, polar, degree-minute, and user-labeled axes.
- Line-drawing and data-curve routines, including curve fitting and smoothing, dot-dash lines, and arrows.
- Shaded areas and grids, parallel-lines and cross-hatched.
- Titles, headings, legends, character strings, and blocks of text.
- Translation, rotating and scaling transformations.
- Three-dimensional surfaces drawn on a mesh defined by a two-dimensional array, with hidden-line suppression.
- Special routines for drawing world maps and other cartographic images.

The subroutines are linked together by approximately 200 display variables. The system also supports over 50 character sets in eight dif-

GENERATE statements are used to give an overall description of the graph to be created. It sets up a standard plot that is normally acceptable but which might need additional specification to "customize" it, such as a TITLE describing what it depicts, or AXIS LABELS stating the units of the graph axes.

	X Axis Type	Y Axis Type	Line Type	Text Type	
GENERATE	X NUMBERED	Y NUMBERED	CONNECTED	FANCY	PLOT
	X LOG	Y LOG	SCATTERED	SIMPLE	
	X MONTHLY		REGRESSION		
	X LABELED				

X NUMBERED Divisions of the X axis are numbered with rounded values to fit the range of the data.

X LOG Divisions are numbered and logarithmically spaced.

X MONTHLY Divisions of the X axis are labeled with 3-letter abbreviations for months.

X LABELED Divisions are labeled in a fashion similar to the month axis. The division labels must be provided.

Y NUMBERED The divisions are numbered, similarly to X Numbered.

Y LOG Similar to X Log.

CONNECTED LINE TYPE The points defined by the X and Y coordinates are connected with a line.

SCATTERED LINE TYPE The points are not connected by lines. Instead each point is marked with a marker symbol, different for each curve, and identified in the legend.

REGRESSION LINE TYPE The points are not connected, but represented in the SCATTERED fashion. A best-fitting straight line (regression line or trend line) is drawn through the data.

FANCY TEXT TYPE Publication quality characters are used to give professional appearance to the plot.

SIMPLE TEXT TYPE Single stroke "stick" characters are used to minimize the display task.

	X Axis Type	Arrangement	Text Type	
GENERATE	LABELED	CLUSTERED	FANCY BAR	BAR
	MONTHLY	HIDDEN	SIMPLE	
	NUMBERED	STACKED		

X AXIS TYPE The meanings of the alternatives are identical to those for PLOT.

CLUSTERED BAR ARRANGEMENT The bars for a given X value (e.g., month or year) are clustered around that X value.

STACKED BAR ARRANGEMENT The second set of bars is stacked on top of the first, the third is stacked on top of the second, etc.

HIDDEN BAR ARRANGEMENT The bar with the largest value is the tallest, and the bars with smaller Y values are superimposed on it. Thus it appears as if all the bars are standing in front of one another.

SIMPLE AND FANCY TEXT TYPE Same as for PLOT.

	Text Type	
GENERATE	FANCY	PIE
	SIMPLE	

The FANCY/SIMPLE alternatives are the same as those for the PLOT statement.

Figure 5-9. Higher-level graphics statements. (Source: ISSCO)

ferent styles. Many, perhaps most, of these functions could be replaced or supplemented by hardware or firmware function generators under the control of a separate (i.e., controller) CPU. But in high-volume, non-interactive graphics applications, economies of scale tilt the scales toward a concentrated, non-distributed graphics "intelligence."

6
Accessories and Peripherals

A raster-graphics system can incorporate nearly every type of computer peripheral or mass-storage device used in data processing. Device interfacing may be with the graphics controller or the host computer, depending on the system configuration. Controller software, for example, may be stored on a flexible disk, while display data is stored on a large-capacity disk connected to the host computer.

A graphics system can also include a number of specialized accessories and peripherals designed to facilitate the graphics-generation task. In this category would be various interactive and data-input devices, such as keyboards, digitizer tablets, joysticks, light pens, television cameras, spot scanners, video tape recorders, and videodiscs. Graphics output devices could include—in addition to the monitor—large-screen projectors, photographic hardcopy systems, and a wide variety of printers.

KEYBOARDS

Nearly every graphics system has a keyboard. It is the universal operator input device. The graphics keyboard can serve as both a display-data source and as an interactive control device. It may also be used to control and support other input devices, or to simulate their functions.

The physical form and location of the graphics keyboard will depend on the system configuration. Its functions may be implemented, for example, by the host computer's console keyboard, or by one or more keyboard/CRT terminals. In most cases, however, the graphics system will have its own separate, specialized keyboard, closely associated with the graphics-display monitor.

The operative word is "specialized." Keyboard designs reflect both the special requirements of the application and the personal preferences of the system designer or user. Descriptive literature for one commercial graphics system offers a choice of 18 different "standard" keyboards. Most designs are centered, however, on the standard alphanumeric touch-typewriter arrangement illustrated in Figure 6-1. It is the assignment of the extra keys, shown as blank rectangles in this drawing of a standard, off-the-shelf keyboard module, which distinguishes one graphics-system keyboard from another.

The additional keys can be divided into functional groups:

Numeric keypads are designed for high-speed, single-handed entry of numerical information, such as vector-endpoint coordinates and statistical data. The keys are normally arranged in one of two standard patterns—business machine or touch telephone—depending on which is likely to be the most familiar to the operator. If the keyboard has a capitals-only output, an "uppercase" numeric keypad may be embedded in the alphanumeric array to reduce costs and conserve space.

Cursor control keys move the cursor symbol on the display screen to the right, left, up, down, or "home"—which may be the center of the screen or the upper left corner. Provision may also be made for fast or slow cursor movement. Normally the cursor continues to move in incremental steps as long as one or two keys are depressed. Cursor controls can also take the form of joysticks or trackballs, mounted directly on the keyboard or connected to the controller by a separate cable. Often both types of control mechanisms are provided—"digital" keys for processing text and "analog" devices for generating graphics.

Special function keys may carry specific legends or simply numbers. The significance of a numbered function key is defined by either the system software or the application program—and may differ from one program to the next.

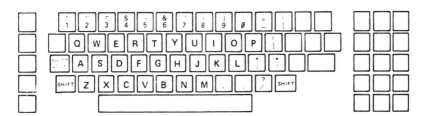

Figure 6-1. Standard off-the-shelf keyboard layout. (Source: Datanetics Corporation)

Coded Output

The output of a keyboard module is typically a combination of 8-bit character bytes and control-signal contact closures. Depending on the design of the keyboard circuits, the character-byte bits may be transmitted on eight parallel lines or serially on a single line. Parallel-line outputs are normally TTL/DTL compatible; a serial output is usually designed to meet the voltage-level, impedance, and polarity conventions established by the EIA RS-232C standard.

Character coding may be implemented by an on-board microprocessor or by a user-defined PROM, both of which allow the user to assign any code to any key. Alternatively, as in the case of the off-the-shelf keyboard shown in Figure 6–1, a standard IC encoder chip can be used to generate 90 different four-code combinations, each one of which can be assigned to one or more individual keys. The code generated by a specific key is determined by the keyboard "mode": non-shift, shift, control (by the simultaneous depression of a "control" key), or shift-control. Code combinations for alphanumeric keys are assigned at the factory. Codes for the remaining 28 keys can be assigned by inserting jumper wires in a circuit-board matrix. Keys without an assigned code combination can be optionally brought out as contact closures.

The codes represent a full ASCII (American Standard Code for Information Interchange) character set. ASCII is a 7-bit, 128-character code designed originally for teleprinter networks. The five least-significant bits define the codes within each of four 32-character blocks. The remaining bits form a 2-bit code to select one of the four blocks. The first 32-character block consists entirely of teleprinter control codes. The other three blocks represent codes for numerals and punctuation marks, uppercase letters, and lowercase letters. (If the ASCII code is contained in an 8-bit byte, the most-significant eighth bit is reserved for optional use as an odd-or-even parity check or as an indication of a function key).

Only a few of the teleprinter control codes have any significance in the operation of a graphics system. Several of the punctuation-mark and special-symbol codes may also be expendable. All of these codes are therefore available for other purposes, such as the generation of special control commands or graphic characters. In one graphics-system implementation, for example, the cursor up, down, left, and right commands are represented by the ASCII codes for shift out, line feed, backspace, and horizontal tabulation.

Keyboard outputs can also be coded in EBCDIC (Extended Binary Coded Decimal Interchange Code)—a 256-character set consisting of

8-bit coded characters—or a specially designed 8-bit code for graphics applications.

Keyboards may also be designed to communicate with programs written in APL (A Programming Language). APL is a character-oriented language which gains much of its utility through the use of special character symbols. The keyboard may be limited to capital letters and APL symbols or the operator may be able to switch at any time from a standard upper- and lowercase mode to a capital letters/APL mode.

In similar fashion, keyboards may be designed to provide a switch-selectable "all-caps" TTY mode which combines, without shifting, capital letters and "lowercase" numerals and punctuation marks.

Special Keyboard Features

A variety of other features can be incorporated into the keyboard design:

- Illuminated keys can be used to indicate the current code-generated mode.
- Signals from the graphics system can be used to illuminate "prompt" keys, to inhibit or "lock out" a portion of the keyboard (e.g., to prevent the entry of alphabetic characters during the entry of numeric data), or to generate an audible "echo" when a valid character has been received.
- Output codes may be stored in a single-character or multi-character buffer until they are transmitted in response to strobe signals from the system.
- Continued pressure on selected keys may result in a repeated character output, with repetition rates from 10 to 500 character codes per second.
- The balance of the keyboard may be designed with a "rollover" capability. An output code is generated with each key depression, even if another key (2-key rollover) is still depressed. An N-key rollover capability means that any number of keys can be depressed without inhibiting the generation of an output code with each new keystroke.
- The keyboard switching mechanism may be solid-state for theoretically infinite life, or mechanically designed for an operational life extending up to tens of millions of on/off cycles. Feedback to the operator may be audible or tactile.

- The key caps may be flat or sculptured, parallel to the keyboard surface (best for numeric entries) or tilted to form stepped rows of keys on a sloping keyboard (simulating the keys on a conventional typewriter).

Keyboard Logical Functions

A graphics keyboard can serve as a universal input device because it can perform every type of logical input function (Chapter 4). It is, by definition, a logical keyboard for entering alphanumeric information. The operator can also simulate the function of a valuator device by entering a single scalar value or the function of a stroke device by entering a series of coordinate values. Individual keys can serve as logical buttons; cursor-control keys can be used to simulate a pick device by superimposing the cursor on a selected display segment or primitive; the cursor-control keys can also act as a locator device by moving the cursor to a specified coordinate position.

SWITCHES AND POTENTIOMETERS

A variety of other switch-type devices can be added to the graphics system to supplement or supplant the keyboard. These may be assembled from individual key switches or off-the-shelf keypads with many of the features of a fully implemented keyboard, including a choice of binary-coded serial or parallel outputs, repeat functions, lockouts, and rollovers. Standard configurations range from 5 to 32 keys.

Another alternative is the use of thin-profile "touchboards." Unencoded touchboards can be designed with an array of contact points and a single common—a thin sheet of metal directly underneath a flexible touchboard surface—or a grid of metal strips can be used to form a coded matrix output.

Valuators can be simulated by rotary digital switches or by potentiometer dials. Two or more potentiometers can also be used in combination with analog-to-digital circuitry as high-precision cursor controls or to implement continuously variable zoom, rotation, or color controls.

DIGITIZER TABLETS

Digitizer tablets have become the second most important interactive graphics accessory, next to the keyboard itself. A digitizer tablet can, in fact, duplicate many of the keyboard's logical functions, including those of a pick, stroke, valuator, or locator device. If an area of the tablet is set aside for a permanent or overlay menu, the tablet can even serve as a logical button, or to a more limited extent, a logical keyboard.

The versatility of the digitizer tablet starts with the fact that it has a two-dimensional surface analogous to that of the graphics display screen—with the added advantage that it can be positioned horizontally, vertically, or at an angle for maximum hand-arm convenience and comfort. The one-for-one correspondence between the two surfaces creates a direct, unambiguous feedback loop between manual input and visual output. No "logic" on the part of the operator is required, minimizing the training interval and increasing the trained operator's efficiency and throughput.

The basic function of a digitizer tablet is to convert the position of a "probe" on the tablet surface into digital X-Y coordinate values which are then interpreted by the graphics system in a variety of ways, depending on the task being performed.

The probe can take several forms—with corresponding levels of precision. The simplest is the operator's finger, touching the tablet surface. A similar "pointing" function may be accomplished by a pencil-like stylus, optionally equipped with a marking pen which can both eliminate the need to glance at the monitor screen for visual feedback and also provide a hardcopy record of the input. Maximum precision, often exceeding that of the graphics system, is provided by a cross-hair probe—frequently called a "cursor"—with a flat or magnifying-glass lens at the center of a circular wire loop. The advantage of this construction is that the distance from the circular transducer to the cross-hair center is constant, no matter how the probe is positioned on the tablet surface.

Both probe and tablet may be provided with pushbuttons and switches to facilitate the various tablet functions. As a minimum, the operator should be able to select a continuous stream of data or a single coordinate reading with a momentary switch closure (or when the probe touches the tablet surface). To reduce the data-processing task, the tablet subsystem may be programmed so that new coordinates are generated only when the probe is moved an incremental distance established by the operator or the application program.

The origin of the tablet's coordinate system may be fixed relative to the display-screen coordinates or adjustable to any point selected by the operator. The same may be true of the relative coordinate scales. For precision work, the operator may want to "shrink" the tablet so that it corresponds to only a small area of the display surface, allowing graphic elements to be positioned with pixel-by-pixel accuracy.

Tablet dimensions can range from a few inches to several feet. A small tablet, for example, may be used to select menu items while the same probe extracts coordinate information from a tablet the size of a drafting table. Transparent or frosted panels are also available for digitizing data from photographic transparencies, vellum drawings, or images projected onto the back surface. The interface with the host system may be serial or parallel, with X-Y coordinates expressed as binary values, binary-coded-decimal (BCD) digits, or ASCII characters. Data transfer rates can range, as noted above, from single asynchronous readings to 400 or more coordinate pairs per second.

Digitizer-Tablet Functions

Digitizer tablets were originally developed as all-electronic substitutes for electromechanical devices designed to perform functions that even today may have little to do with computer-generated graphics. This helps to explain both the variety of tablet technologies and the fact that digitizer tablets can range from simple accessories to highly sophisticated, standalone systems with their own microprocessors, memory, and software.

One impetus for the development of a high-precision digitizer tablet was the advent of numerically controlled manufacturing machinery. Tablets that stem from this source offer accuracies on the order of 0.001 inch—an important asset when the principal function is to digitize dimensional information from existing drawings or modeled parts. Systems in this category may have such features as digital displays—with coordinates expressed in inches or centimeters—and a built-in microprocessor for calculating distances between points, radii of circles, and angles between vectors. The graphic display of the information may be quite incidental to the task. High-precision tablets are widely used, however, as source-data input devices for such varied graphics-system applications as computer-aided design and manufacturing, medical instrumentation, and topographical surveys.

Another early non-graphic application for digitizer tablets was the facsimile transmission of handwritten messages. Here the emphasis was on simplicity, low cost, and reliable service, with positional accuracy as a secondary consideration. Again, the evolvement of this technology has led to developments of major import to the design of graphics systems. Tablet subsystems are now available with sophisticated character-recognition capabilities, allowing the operator to "free-hand" both alphanumeric information and frequently used graphic elements such as electronic symbols, architectural components, and pipe fittings.

Graphics-system designers have combined and extended these applications to make the digitizer tablet a nearly universal interactive device. Programs have been written so that the operator can "sketch" engineering drawings which are then transformed by the system into rigorously defined display images, suitable for analysis and documentation. The same type of tablet can also be used to "paint" artistic designs, or to define intermediate steps in a cartoon sequence.

Nearly all of these digitizer-tablet functions have been facilitated by the fact that the display-screen cursor already serves as a versatile communication link between system and operator. The manual positioning of a tablet probe is a natural extension of this link. The only software required is the conversion of tablet coordinates to cursor coordinates. Every cursor function has become, therefore, a potential tablet function. By controlling the cursor, the tablet can be used to drag graphic elements, rubberband lines, define viewports, pick segments and primitives, and select menu items.

Tablet menu selection has been a particularly beneficial development. Menus provide the systems designer with a versatile and effective medium for operator interactions. But menus can occupy valuable display space, or even require an occasional blanking of the displayed information. Digitizer tablets allow the entire process to be moved off-screen, with frequently used menu items, such as colors and textures, permanently printed on the tablet surface. Less frequently required items can be printed on overlay sheets and keyed to specific locations on the tablet surface by the application program.

Digitizer-Tablet Technologies

A number of different technical approaches have been taken in the design of commercially available digitizer tablets. These can be divided, however, into two basic types: grid and border tablets.

As the name implies, a grid-type tablet has two sets of parallel conductors positioned at right angles to each other to form an X-Y grid. A "probe" placed on or near the tablet surface is detected by one of several techniques. The X-Y coordinate location of the probe is then calculated by interpolating the distance between grid lines. Grid-line spacing can range from a tenth to a half inch, depending on the type of tablet.

Electromagnetic grid-type tablets have either an "active" or "passive" probe. An active probe generates a low-level RF signal which is picked up by the closest grid lines (Figure 6-2). The coordinate position of the probe is calculated from the relative strengths of the received

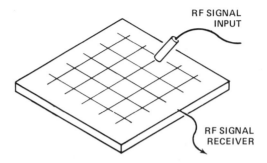

Figure 6-2. Grid-type digitizer tablet with active probe.

signals. A passive probe acts as an RF receiver (Figure 6-3). Continuous RF signals are transmitted along all of the grid lines with coded information to identify each line. Again, the probe position is precisely calculated from the relative strengths of the decoded signals—even when the probe is an inch or more above the tablet's surface.

Magnetostrictive tablets also have a grid-type construction, but the distance-measuring method corresponds more closely to that of border-type tablets. The grid consists of tensioned ferromagnetic wires (Figure 6-4) with separate transformer-coupled "send" wires on at least two adjoining sides. A current pulse is applied to one send wire, then the other, causing magnetostrictive perturbations that travel along the grid lines at an acoustic rate. A coil in the probe senses the traveling pulses and generates a series of reverse-magnetostriction output signals. The probe position is then calculated by measuring the time required for each pulse to travel from the edge of the tablet to the probe location.

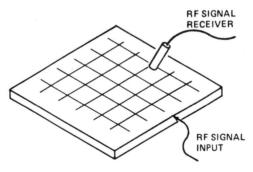

Figure 6-3. Grid-type digitizer tablet with passive probe.

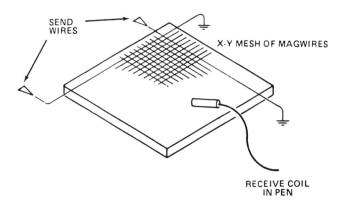

SEND WIRES

X-Y MESH OF MAGWIRES

RECEIVE COIL
IN PEN

Figure 6–4. Magnetostrictive digitizer tablet. (Source: Summagraphics Corporation)

A grid-type "touch panel"—without wires—has been designed for mounting directly in front of the display screen. Infrared LED's and photoelectric detectors are arrayed on the sides of the panel, forming an invisible light grid which can be interrupted by the operator's finger. The operator simply points at a displayed cursor, menu item, or graphic element to communicate with the controller or host computer.

Other types of touch panels are more closely associated with border tablets. One transparent, display-mounted tablet has piezo-electric transducers along the borders. A finger on the surface of the panel produces ultrasonic echoes which are timed and analyzed to provide positional information. Another border-type device is a dielectric-covered metal plate which acts as an electromagnetic antenna. A finger on the surface disturbs the radiated field, as sensed by receiver circuits at the corners of the tablet.

Perhaps the most versatile of the border-type designs is the acoustic tablet shown in Figure 6–5. A high-frequency spark at the tip of the probe generates acoustic waves which are sensed by strip microphones along two borders. The position of the probe is calculated from the timing relationships. A three-dimensional version of the tablet has microphones on all four borders. The spatial position of the probe is calculated on the basis of the three shortest timing intervals.

LIGHTPENS

Lightpens are hand-held devices that allow the operator to interact directly with the CRT display instead of indirectly through tablet probes or cursor controls.

STRIP MICROPHONES

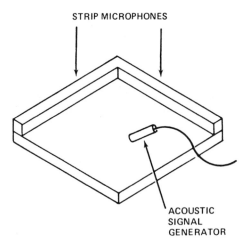

ACOUSTIC
SIGNAL
GENERATOR

Figure 6-5. Two-dimensional acoustic tablet. (Source: Science Accessories Corporation

The lightpen resembles a writing pen in appearance but operates in a reverse manner. Instead of "writing" on the screen, the lightpen "reads" displayed images, transmitting its position in the form of a "hit" pulse which the controller can correlate with the known raster-scan timing sequence.

The lightpen contains a photoelectric cell (Figure 6-6) which senses light entering through an aperture at the "writing" end. The aperture usually contains a lens to narrow the angle of light focused on the photocell surface.

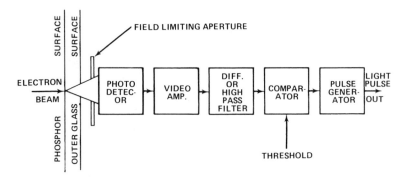

Figure 6-6. Lightpen signal-processing circuits. (Source: Information Control Corporation)

The graphics controller or host computer must be interrupted in order to accept information from the lightpen. A switch on the light-pen generates the interrupt and initiates a lightpen subroutine. Three types of switches may be encountered. The push-tip switch is the most widely used, but requires constant contact with the screen. The switch is activated by adding a slight amount of pressure to the pen tip against the screen. Pens that do not touch the screen use either a push-button or touch-tip switch. The touch-tip switch is actuated by using a finger to close a circuit between the main body of the pen and an isolated ring or the tip of the pen itself.

The output of the photoelectric cell is amplified and differentiated to isolate the signal transitions which occur when the electron beam passes in front of the lightpen aperture. The differentiated output is compared to a threshold voltage and when the threshold is exceeded a pulse is generated.

The threshold level must be set high enough to eliminate ambient brightness and noise. To test for inaccurate readings, several readings can be taken during successive raster scans. If the readings vary by more than a few pixels, an error message should be generated on the screen. A successful "hit" should be echoed in some form, such as an intensified or blinking display image.

The major disadvantage of the lightpen in raster-scan systems is that it can only identify pixels or graphic elements which are already dis-played; it can not "read" a dark area of the screen to position a new data point. One solution is to momentarily drive all of the pixels to the "on" state, bypassing the display memory. But this adds complexity to the system and the pen-search flash may be very distracting to the operator.

HARDCOPY OUTPUT DEVICES

Three types of accessories can be added to a raster graphics system to obtain hardcopy prints of the displayed images. Two are based on pho-tographic principles, the third encompasses a wide variety of printing techniques.

The simplest and, perhaps, least satisfactory method is to photo-graph the monitor screen itself. Camera attachments are available, but depending on the type of monitor and application, problems may be encountered with barrel distortions, ambient-light reflections, and de-saturation of colors due to the spatial separation of the red, green, and blue phosphor dots or stripes (Chapter 9).

The second photographic method starts with the separate red, green,

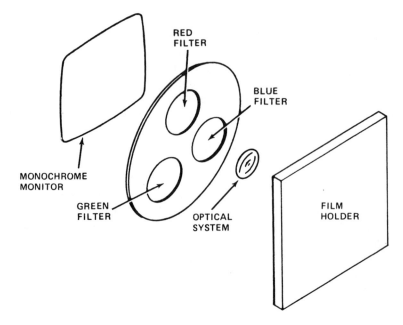

Figure 6-7. Photographic hardcopy system. Three exposures superimpose the red, green, and blue color information. (Source: Image Resource)

and blue display signals. Three "color" images are generated in sequence on an enclosed, flat-face monochrome monitor (Figure 6-7). A corresponding color filter is positioned as each image is displayed. The result, after three superimposed exposures, is a full-color reproduction without any loss of saturation due to spatial distribution of the color information.

Printing-type hardcopy accessories cover the full range of reproduction methods—with the display memory as the information source. Raster-line data is sequentially read out of memory at a rate determined by the hardcopy device. Available units include impact, ink-jet, laser scanning, xerographic, electrostatic, and thermal printing techniques, in both monochrome and color.

7
Designing the
Graphics Controller

The graphics controller is literally the central, controlling element in defining the performance of a raster graphics system. In Chapter 1 the controller was described as a programmable interface between the system's host computer and display monitor. Resident processors take the place of the host computer in standalone systems, but in both cases, computer and monitor are likely to have resolution, animation, and color-display potentials that significantly exceed the "system" specifications. It is the controller circuitry that sets the limits and determines the type of application for which the system is best suited.

These are not necessarily negative statements. Controller costs range from a few hundred dollars up to hundreds of thousands of dollars—with capabilities to match. Controller design or selection within this range is dicated by two independent variables. First, of course, is the nature of the graphics-generation task. Second, and equally important, is the relative importance of the graphics function compared to the other demands on the resources of the host computer. As noted in Chapter 5, most of the graphics-software "packages" supplied with commercially available controllers or from independent sources are designed to be executed by the host. If the computer's non-graphics load factor is negligible (as in the case of a standalone graphics system), a controller architecture with little or no programming flexibility may be adequate. But if the host is running at or near capacity, the extra cost of a more sophisticated controller design may be easily justified.

Similar options apply to the selection of the system monitor (Chapter 9). If the display data processed by the controller has other, more demanding applications, such as the generation of ultra-high-resolution hardcopy reproductions, it may be feasible to specify a monitor with limited resolution and color capabilities. In most cases, however, there are advantages to be gained by selecting a monitor with performance values beyond those of the controller. A monitor with enhanced resolution capabilities can provide improved legibility and appearance. Future upgrades would also be easier to implement. Form-fit problems created by a new monitor are generally much more severe than those imposed by new controller circuitry.

CONTROLLER CATEGORIES

In simplest terms, the function of a graphics controller is to receive display information and process it into a form which can be used to drive a raster-scan display monitor. The end product is the display on the monitor screen. One way to classify controller designs, therefore, is to identify the type of display which they generate: alphagraphic, vectorgraphic, or photographic. Too much overlapping occurs, however, to allow a distinct division at the display level. Alphagraphic displays can include simple vectorgraphic images. Sophisticated vectorgraphic software can be used to create images with photographic color and detail. Both vectorgraphic and photographic displays will usually include text and graphic symbols generated by exactly the same type of hardware used to create alphagraphic displays.

A more effective way to classify controllers would be to identify the type of data which the controller receives from the host computer. Controller inputs will generally fall into one of three distinctive categories: graphic characters, vector coordinates, or pixel values.

Graphic-character controllers receive display information in the form of binary-coded bytes or computer words, each of which represents a particular pattern of pixel values to be displayed within a specified character space (or "cell") on the monitor screen. The number of pixels represented by each character space can vary from 35 (5-by-7) to 100 or more—often under the dynamic control of the application program. The pixel patterns represented by each graphic character may be fixed by the controller hardware or "written" by the host computer or operator. In both cases, conversion to pixel values is performed "on the fly" as each raster line is traced on the display screen.

Vector-coordinate controllers may also contain hardware or software character generators for text and other graphic symbols, but most of the display data is in the form of bytes or computer words which represent the endpoints of straight-line vectors to be displayed at specified coordinate locations on the monitor screen. The coordinate values may also define such geometric forms as rectangles or conic sections (circles, ellipses, and arcs). The controller processes this information into a stream of pixel values which re-create the graphic elements each time the raster pattern is scanned.

Pixel-value controllers start with information which is already in a suitable form for raster-scan display. The source of the pixel data may be the digitized output of a television camera or spot scanner. The data may also be in the form of computer words generated, for example, by a CAT-scanner system. The principal function of the controller is to manipulate the pixel values in response to "image processing" instructions received from the host computer or interactively entered by the operator.

DISPLAY MEMORY

A basic characteristic of raster-scan systems (Chapter 2) is that information concerning every pixel on the monitor screen must be supplied to the monitor with every refresh cycle, typically 30 or 60 times a second, whether or not images are to be displayed at specific pixel locations.

To support this refresh requirement, every graphics controller must have, in one form or another, a quick-access display memory which can supply all of the information necessary to describe the state (intensity or color) of each pixel during the time the raster lines are being scanned. To simplify our discussion we will assume that the pixel state can be defined by a single bit—on or off. Even in the simplest case, however, the data storage and retrieval demands can be impressive. The display memory for a 512-by-512 pixel array must supply information for over a quarter million pixel locations. A 1024-by-1024 array increases this figure to over a million pixel values—as a minimum. Most systems have expanded display memories to support a variety of useful features, such as the scrolling and panning of images on the display screen. Expanded memories also allow new graphic images to be assembled in one part of memory while the display is driven by another set of memory addresses. Or several stored images may be displayed in sequence to provide a sense of animation.

Character Maps

Lower memory prices have made such expanded-memory systems feasible, but display storage still represents a major cost item in every controller design. A variety of ways have been devised, therefore, to reduce the display-memory requirements.

One of these is the character map—directly applicable to graphic-character systems but also used to store information in "split-screen" vector-coordinate systems which conserve memory by dedicating a part of the display surface to text and graphic symbols. A character map is simply an array of memory addresses corresponding to character spaces on the monitor screen. Graphic-character codes stored in the map identify the pixel patterns to be displayed in each character space. "Masks" for the coded patterns are stored elsewhere in the system, either in software or in a hardware character generator.

Figure 7–1 illustrates this concept and the type of "limited graphics" that can be created on the monitor screen. A controller assembles the mask patterns by addressing, for example, each of the top row of character-space codes in sequence. The codes reference the system to appropriate masks, and a complete raster line is generated by "shifting out" the top line of pixel values from each mask. The process is then repeated for the remaining mask lines and character rows.

The 3-by-3 patterns shown in Figure 7–1 would represent only a marginal memory saving since an 8-bit byte would be required for each 9-bit graphic pattern. But with a typical 8-by-10 character space (80 pixels), the savings escalate to 90 percent. The available preprogrammed graphic patterns also become much more limited, compared to the potential patterns that could be created. An 8-bit code can identify only 256 patterns, half of which must be devoted to alphanumerics and standard symbols. Even if several sets of patterns can be programmed, the total is still insignificant compared to the 2^{80} different

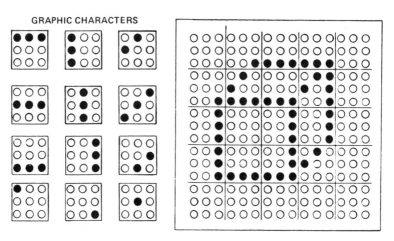

Figure 7-1. Typical graphic characters (left) for "assembling" vector-graphic images.

patterns which could be formed theoretically within an 8-by-10 pixel array.

Vector Maps

Character-mapped systems generate pixel values on the fly, one raster line at a time. Vector-coordinate data can also be transformed to pixel data on the fly, but the memory saving—compared to data for every pixel—imposes a heavy processing burden. Every vector must be re-processed and converted to a raster format with every refresh cycle.

One way to reduce this task is to "map" the graphic elements into an ordered vertical-coordinate listing. Only the vectors or conic sections which extend into the first ten raster lines, for example, would be processed while this part of the screen is scanned. Dozens or even hundreds of pixel values would still have to be calculated at high speeds for each graphic element, but the display memory requirements are reduced to the stroke-writing level. The future promise of the vector-map concept lies, in fact, in the development of 2048- and 4096-line raster-scan monitors which can challenge the ultra-high-resolution domain of storage-tube and refresh-vector systems. Controllers in this category could be readily used, in fact, to drive both raster-scan and stroke-writing displays, either alternately or simultaneously.

Bit Maps

Meanwhile, most vector-coordinate controllers convert incoming data to the raster format at once—and only once. The resulting bit values are mapped into display-memory addresses which can be correlated with pixel locations on the monitor screen (Figure 7–2). "Raster lines" are read directly out of memory by accessing a sequence of bytes or words, transferring them to one or more shift registers, then shifting out the bits to form a serial display signal.

Exactly the same type of bit-map display memory is used by pixel-value controllers. The digitized output of a television camera, for example, is stored in the same raster-scan format generated by the camera. The principal differences between image and vector controllers are in the preprocessing and postprocessing of the display data. A controller oriented to image processing concentrates, for example, on calculations performed on the pixel values *after* they are stored. Correlations, averaging, and other mathematical operations are performed on pixel-value "kernels" which may be several pixels wide and

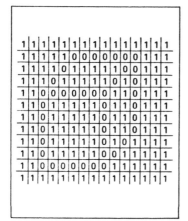 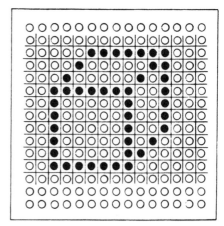

Figure 7–2. Section of bit map (left) with corresponding raster-scan image on display screen.

an equal number of raster lines deep. Speed is helpful in terms of operator response, but is not essential.

By contrast, most of the hardware and software computational capabilities of a vector-oriented controller are dedicated to the DDA (digital differential analysis) subroutines which convert graphic elements defined by endpoint coordinates into pixel values, and then perform such follow-up functions as filling a vector-defined polygon with a specified color or display intensity. Speed is essential, in this case, because image animation or change is limited to the rate at which new pixel values can be calculated and stored for display.

Various DDA algorithms have been developed. Most of them start with a test to determine whether a vector is generally horizontal or vertical. If horizontal, the DDA subroutine starts at one endpoint and progressively extends the vector along the initial raster line with repeated tests for plus or minus vertical displacements. More sophisticated routines may "trace" lines which are several pixels wide, or which include half-intensity pixels to soften the stair-stepping which occurs when a vector is drawn diagonally across raster lines.

Line Maps

Several techniques can be used to reduce the size of the display memory and still preserve the convenience of vectorgraphic data which has already been converted to pixel values.

One method is to divide the display screen into sections and limit the

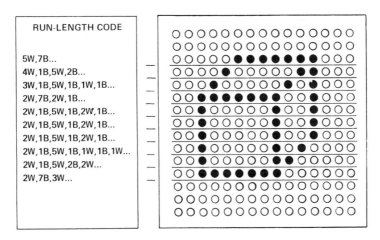

Figure 7-3. Line map stored in display memory (left) and resulting raster-line image.

bit map to only the sections that contain display images. The system automatically fills in empty sections with a specified background intensity or color.

Another technique is to convert a part or all of the bit-map data into a line map. Run-length codes, illustrated in Figure 7-3, are calculated for each raster line. In effect, only intensity or color transitions are stored in memory, eliminating the redundancy which occurs when a separate value must be stored for each pixel. Memory savings up to 97% have been claimed. Line maps are most effective when image transitions per line are at a minimum, as in the case of many computer-aided design applications.

MEMORY PLANES

All of the mapping methods described above can be extended to systems in which the pixels are displayed in a range of intensities or colors, requiring several bits to define the state of each pixel.

A graphics controller must generate pixel values at an instantaneous rate determined by the resolution and refresh frequency of the system. For a 512-by-512 pixel array refreshed at 60 Hz, data must be accessed from memory and processed into display-signal amplitudes at a rate approaching 20M pixel values per second. Conventional memory architectures combined with shift-registers can support such serial rates when each pixel value is represented by only a single bit. Multiple bits require multiple memory planes, accessed in parallel.

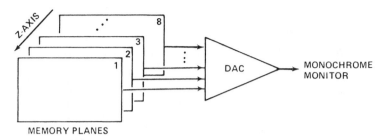

Figure 7–4. Eight memory planes and digital-to-analog converter for generating 256 different display intensities.

Figure 7–4 shows this arrangement. Each plane is, in effect, a separate character-mapped, bit-mapped, or line-mapped display memory. Coding for individual pixels is stored along the "Z" dimension. A single digital-to-analog converter (DAC) uses the parallel output from the eight planes shown in Figure 7–4 to generate up to 256 different display-signal amplitudes which translate into an equal number of different pixel intensities displayed on a monochrome monitor screen.

Other memory-plane configurations can be devised. Corresponding addresses on the multiple planes relate to a single pixel location but not necessarily to the same image. Each plane could be used to store, for example, the image of a separate multilayer printed-circuit pattern. By suitable gating and logic networks, the operator could "toggle" between two "overlay" layers for quick comparisons, or superimpose the layers with each layer set to a specified level of "transparency."

Figures 7–5 and 7–6 illustrate how three memory planes can be used to generate up to eight colors, including black and white. One variation on this basic configuration is to replace the blue signal and its corresponding phosphor dots (Chapter 9) with a "white" signal and phos-

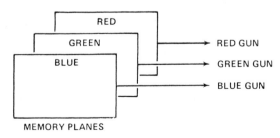

Figure 7–5. Three-plane display memory for 8-color raster graphics system.

RED GUN	GREEN GUN	BLUE GUN	PERCEIVED COLOR
OFF	OFF	OFF	BLACK
ON	OFF	OFF	RED
ON	ON	OFF	YELLOW
OFF	ON	OFF	GREEN
OFF	ON	ON	CYAN
OFF	OFF	ON	BLUE
ON	OFF	ON	MAGENTA
ON	ON	ON	WHITE

Figure 7-6. Colors generated by three-plane memory with one bit per primary color.

phor for alphanumeric notations, eliminating legibility problems created by misconvergence of the red, green, and blue electron beams.

Another technique is to use patterns of colors to form other colors. A blend of red and yellow pixels, for example, would produce an orange texture at normal viewing distances. The color range can also be expanded by multiple memory planes for each primary color. Up to 64 hues and saturations can be displayed by the six planes shown in Figure 7-7.

Lookup Tables

The inherent flexibility of multiple memory planes can be enhanced by the addition of a programmable lookup table such as the one illustrated in Figure 7-8. Instead of using the output of eight memory

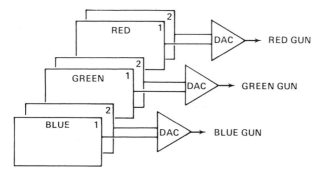

Figure 7-7. Display memory with two-bit code for each primary color. A total of 64 different colors can be programmed.

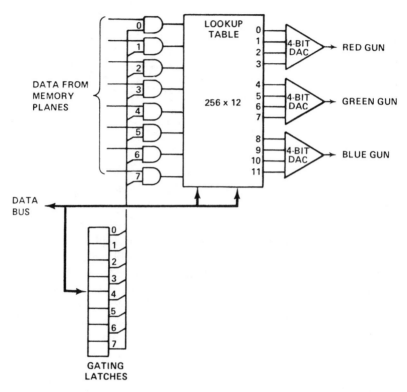

Figure 7-8. Programmable lookup table for generating up to 4096 colors and display intensities (Source: Genisco Computers)

planes to create 256 display intensities or colors, the bits for each pixel can address any one of 256 lookup-table locations. The 12-bit word currently stored at the specified location is then used to generate one of 4096 different display colors. In effect, the application programmer or operator has a palette of 256 different hues and saturations (or intensities) which can be "globally" changed at any time.

Lookup tables permit displayed images to be altered interactively without any rewriting of the pixel values. A selected band of tomography contrast levels can be expanded, for example, to reveal subtle variations in tissue density. Or colors can be changed experimentally during the course of a fabric design. Lookup tables can also be used to apply variable output-signal gamma corrections to accommodate a variety of display or recording devices.

Color monitors require separate red, green, and blue signals to generate a full range of colors. This does not mean, however, that the images created by the application-program or operator must always be transformed to values for these three "components," stored, for example, on red, green, and blue memory planes. Figure 7-9 indicates how the images could be just as readily transformed to hue, intensity, and saturation values. Lookup-table entries could then be selected by the more "natural" parameters of color shade, brightness, and vivid or pastel quality. The only additional system requirement would be a hardware or software transformation matrix to convert the HIS values to RGB signal levels. (Equations for this transformation are given in Appendix III.)

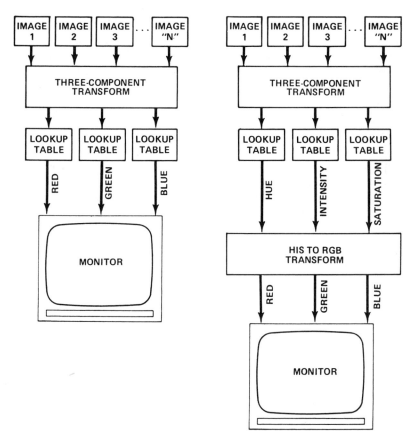

Figure 7-9. Comparison between RGB-programmed and HIS-programmed display systems.

CONTROLLER ARCHITECTURES

The earliest graphics controllers were hardwired and strictly limited in their ability to convert vector data into pixel values. Microprocessor technology increased the versatility of the controllers, but the straight-through architecture shown in Figure 7–10a was retained. As resolution, operator interaction, and other display demands grew, the microprocessor cycle time became a limiting factor. Repetitive operations, such as DDA conversions, were moved out of software and into special-purpose hardware function generators.

Controllers today incorporate a variety of such function generators, linked together and interacting with one or more microprocessors, memory modules, peripheral interfaces, and display-generator circuits. Multiple buses, such as those indicated in Figure 7–10b have become standard controller features. A separate memory bus, for example, can be extended to provide a feedback loop from the display output to the memory planes (Figure 7–10c). Iterative image-processing functions can be performed at "real time" rates—expanding the effective size of convolution kernels without any increase in the computational overhead.

To sustain the required refresh rates, a direct channel is usually provided between the memory planes and the display-generation interface with the monitor. Even at this stage, however, high-speed data processing can be implemented by hardware modules. Lookup tables are in this category, along with circuits to provide such special functions as "area fill."

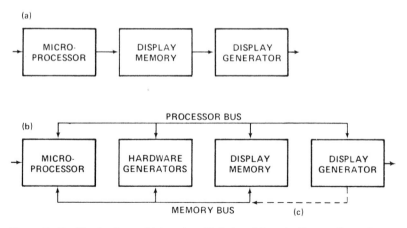

Figure 7–10. Single-channel (a) and multiple-bus (b) controller configurations, with display feedback loop (c).

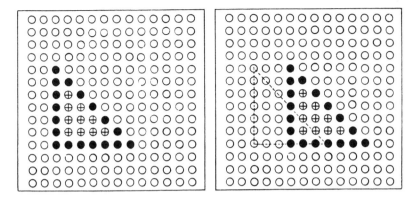

FILL GENERATOR
COLORS INTERIOR PIXELS
WITHIN OUTLINE

INTERIOR PIXELS RESTORED
TO BACKGROUND COLOR
AS OUTLINE IS REWRITTEN

Figure 7-11. "Filled" polygon, generated by hardware area-fill module. (Source: Genisco Computers).

Figure 7-11 shows how a hardware-fill module automatically changes the display color at boundary lines. Only the boundary-line pixels need to be rewritten in display memory in order to move blocks of color across the display screen—significantly increasing the rate at which animated sequences can be generated and displayed. The hardware-fill module also exemplifies the type of display-oriented sophistication which can be built into a controller to expand on the capabilities of the raster graphics system.

8
The Monitor Interface

The monitor interface consists of all the circuitry required to drive a raster-scan CRT monitor. Its principal functions are (1) to convert controller-generated digital data into an analog "display signal," and (2) to coordinate the display of this data by generating appropriate raster-scan synchronization signals. The interface may also include circuits to merge the controller-generated data with information from other sources, or to drive other output peripherals, such as raster-scan hardcopy devices.

Physically, a part or all of these functions may be incorporated into the design of the graphics controller. We have already discussed in the previous chapter, for example, the role of such display-signal sources as shift registers and digital-to-analog converters (DAC's). The same circuits could also be located within the monitor chassis to provide a digital display-device interface. For descriptive purposes, however, we will assume that the design of the interface is a separate task, with its own range of alternatives and options.

The interface design must take into account the output requirements of the controller and, to an even greater extent, the characteristics and signal-input requirements of the raster-scan monitor. The next chapter, Monitor Evaluation and Selection, indicates the wide range of capabilities represented by commercially available monitors. There may be a twenty-to-one difference in cost resulting from often-subtle performance, installation, or maintenance enhancements. Yet the highest performance monitor is, in almost every case, an essentially passive device—without intelligence, memory, handshaking, or status-feedback capabilities.

The monitor can limit, but not expand on the information content of the display. Interface sync signals determine, within limits, the size and aspect ratio of the visible raster pattern, the number of displayed raster lines, and whether the lines are interlaced or non-interlaced. Display-signal modulations establish the location and intensity of individual pixels along each raster line. The hues and saturations displayed by a color monitor are determined entirely by the display information received across the monitor interface.

In terms of interface design, however, the raster-scan monitor is anything but passive. Specific monitor models are generally restricted to a particular type of signal input—among dozens of possible display, sync, and color-encoding combinations. The monitor dictates, therefore, the form of the signal interface, which may or may not match the preferred output of the graphics controller. There may also be a need to switch or mix display signals from multiple sources with different signal outputs, or to distribute the display information to multiple monitors with different input specifications.

Signal conversion circuits can help to resolve all of these conflicting requirements—at a price in hardware costs and complexity. The result is an iterative design process, with interface decisions affecting the monitor selection and vice versa. The objective, of course, is to achieve a display-system design that delivers optimum performance at a minimum overall cost.

SYNCHRONIZING THE RASTER

Information is displayed on a raster-scan CRT monitor screen as a function of time. The CRT electron beam of a monochrome monitor is in constant motion, tracing a raster pattern on the phosphor surface. The same is true of the multiple beams in a color monitor. Display-signal modulations, controlling the intensity of the emitted light, must be precisely timed relative to the beam motion to produce a meaningful image on the screen.

Synchronization is achieved in two steps. Sync signals generated by the monitor interface establish control over the monitor's raster-scan circuits. Display information is then applied to the monitor's beam-modulation circuits within the timing framework created by the sync-signal input.

The sync signals take the form of voltage pulses and affect *only* the timing of the raster-scan process. Self-oscillating circuits within the monitor will, in fact, deflect the CRT electron beam to form a raster-like pattern on the phosphor screen—whether or not sync information is being received. A horizontal-deflection sawtooth signal (Figure 8–1) sweeps the beam from the left margin of the screen to the right, then returns the beam at an accelerated rate to the left. The scan to the right

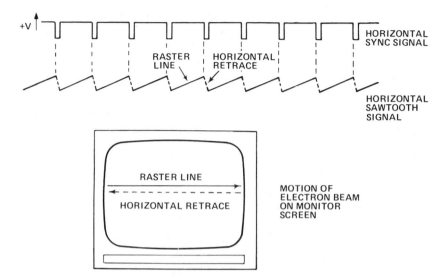

Figure 8-1. Horizontal-sync input and monitor beam-deflection waveforms.

is called a "raster line"; the return path is a "horizontal retrace." The time interval between the end of one raster line and the end of the next, including the initial retrace, is identified by the letter H. The frequency or H-intervals per second establishes the "line rate" of the display. Typical values lie in the range of 15 kHz to 31 kHz.

An independent vertical-deflection sawtooth signal sweeps the electron beam from the top of the screen to the bottom (Figure 8-2), then returns the beam at an accelerated rate to the top. The time interval between the end of one "vertical sweep" and the end of the next, including the "vertical retrace," is identified by the letter V. The frequency or V-intervals per second determines the "field rate" or "frame rate" of the display, depending on whether the lines are interlaced or non-interlaced (see below). International television standards have set this value at approximately 50 Hz or 60 Hz, but graphics system designers may elect to use a different figure, such as 80 Hz or 100 Hz, to meet a particular set of system requirements.

When the horizontal and vertical beam deflections are synchronized and occur simultaneously, a raster is generated on the monitor screen. Figure 8-3 shows the resulting pattern in simplified form. Raster lines are tilted downward to the right due to the downward vertical sweep of the electron beam. The raster retrace paths are nearly horizontal. During vertical retrace, both sets of lines are tilted steeply upward by the accelerated motion of the electron beam during its return to the top of the screen.

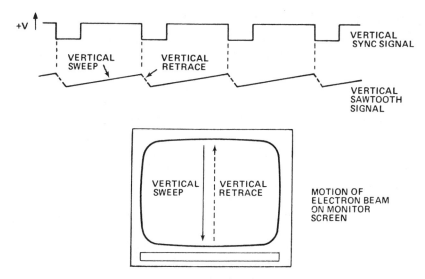

Figure 8-2. Vertical-sync signal input and monitor beam-deflection waveforms.

The Figure 8-3 drawings assume that two critical conditions exist. The first is that the V-interval is an exact multiple of the H-interval. The second is that the start of the downward vertical sweep coincides with the end of a raster line and ends with the completion of a raster line. Given these two conditions, the electron beam can start in the lower right corner of the display, zig-zag to the upper margin of the screen for the start of another raster scan, and end the raster pattern in the lower right corner.

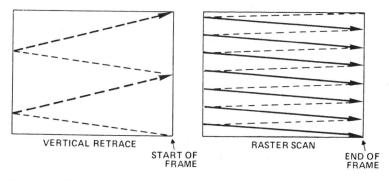

Figure 8-3. Path of electron beam in response to horizontal and vertical deflection signals.

Horizontal and Vertical Sync Pulses

The upward and downward slopes of the two beam-deflection saw-tooth signals establish the relative deflection rates. Peak-to-peak amplitudes of the sawtooth waveforms determine the width and height of the raster pattern created by the deflections. The relative frequencies of the two waveforms establish the H-to-V ratio, or number of raster lines which are scanned during each vertical retrace-and-sweep interval.

All of these relationships are established by the monitor design, subject to manual adjustment within a set of specified ranges. There is, however, *no* internal synchronization of the horizontal and vertical deflections with each other. Both are controlled by independent, free-running oscillator circuits. A stable and meaningful raster display requires precise coordination of the two deflections and, equally important, a precise time relationship between the deflections and the displayed information.

The negative-polarity pulses shown in Figure 8–1 and 8–2 provide the required synchronization. Generated by monitor-interface circuits, the sync pulses "trigger" the monitor's free-running horizontal and vertical oscillators, locking them into a fixed relationship to each other. Display-data synchronization is typically achieved by using a single graphics-system clock as the timing source for both sync signals and display-memory readout.

Horizontal-deflection sync pulses are very narrow, on the order of 3 to 5 microseconds. Vertical-deflection sync pulses are much wider, ranging up to 200 microseconds. Both pulse widths represent correspondingly small percentages of the H and V time intervals, but the most important characteristic of the pulse-width difference is that it allows the horizontal and vertical sync pulses to be combined into a single sync signal, as shown in Figure 8–4.

Two parallel filters can then be used by the monitor to separate the pulses. A high-pass filter "differentiates" the leading and trailing edges of the narrow horizontal-sync pulses. A separate low-pass filter extracts the vertical sync information, typically by "integrating" the signal in a capacitor. The long vertical sync pulses contain enough energy to charge the capacitor to a trigger level. The shorter horizontal sync pulses fall far short of this mark.

A major problem may be created, however, by this combining of the horizontal and vertical pulses into a single sync signal. The monitor's horizontal-deflection oscillator is "running free" during the time interval occupied by the extended vertical-sync pulse. The oscillator may be out-of-sync by the time horizontal-sync pulses reappear. The usual solution is to divide the vertical-sync pulse into "serrated" segments

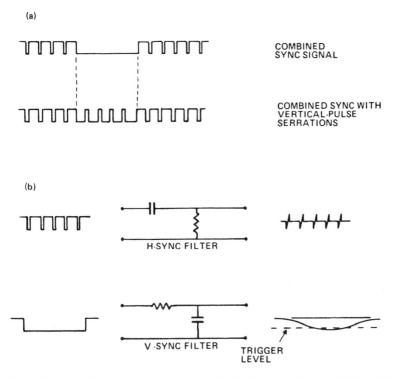

Figure 8-4. Combined sync signals (a) and typical horizontal and vertical sync-pulse filters (b).

(Figure 8-4). The serrations serve as horizontal-sync markers, maintaining synchronization throughout the vertical-sync-pulse interval.

A Flicker-Free Refresh Rate

The light emitted by the phosphors on the surface of the monitor screen decays rapidly, allowing a new image to be traced with the next raster "refresh." Light-initiated chemical reactions in the human eye decay at a slower rate, creating the *impression* of a continuous light emission—provided that the raster refresh rate is above the level where perceptible "flicker" occurs. The on/off rate at which flicker becomes perceptible can vary from 20 Hz to nearly 100 Hz, depending on the intensity of the light source (see Chapter 2, Display Principles). The higher the intensity, the higher the flicker-rate threshold.

A similar concern for flickering incandescent lights dictated the choice of ac line-voltage frequencies during the early years of the electrical power industry. U.S. power companies settled on 60 Hz; their European counterparts, expecting the public to use a lower level of illumination, chose 50 Hz. (The 10 Hz reduction translates into nearly a tenfold decrease in flicker-free luminance.)

Television system designers in Europe and the U.S. initially matched the refresh rate to the local power-line frequency to avoid power-line "beat" interference on the television screen. Present-day equipment is effectively isolated from power-line noise, but the 60 Hz and 50 Hz conventions have been carried forward in the form of international television standards. The same standards have also dictated the design of most of the monitors now available for raster graphics display.

Interlacing the Raster Lines

The longer image-to-image interval permitted by the European television standard—1/50 versus 1/60 of a second—permits more display information to be transmitted during each refresh cycle without increasing the bandwidth. European systems use the extra time to increase the vertical resolution of the display. Each raster "frame" contains 625 raster lines (including those "lost" during retrace). The U.S. frame is limited to 525 lines.

In both cases, however, only half of the lines are transmitted with each refresh cycle. By dividing the display into two interlaced "fields," each consisting of a separate set of odd or even lines, the horizontal resolution of the raster lines can be doubled without increasing the display-signal bandwidth. At a normal viewing distance, the interlaced lines tend to merge and the refresh rate appears to be a flicker-free 60 Hz or 50 Hz, even though the actual repetition rate of an individual raster line (and the complete raster frame) is only 30 Hz or 25 Hz.

The interlacing technique resembles the method used to produce a flicker-free motion picture at half the apparent frame rate (and with only half the required length of film). Frames move through the projector at a rate of 24 per second, but the image of each frame is flashed twice on the projection screen to produce a 48 Hz visual refresh rate—well above the flicker threshold for the reflected illumination. The comparison is important because an entire world population has been conditioned to animation based on 24 *new* images per second. An interlaced new-frame rate of 30 Hz or 25 Hz is therefore acceptable.

Interlacing represents a mixed blessing for the designer of a raster graphics system. It reduces by half the rate at which data must be read out of the display memory. Interlacing also reduces by half the bandwidth required to transfer the information to the monitor screen or, conversely, doubles the amount of information that can be displayed without increasing the bandwidth. The gains are partially offset by a doubling of the number of raster lines lost during the two vertical retraces, increasing the required data-transfer rate while the remaining "active" lines are scanned. A more important concern, however, is the fact that raster graphics displays are often characterized by abrupt color or intensity changes along raster-line boundaries. The result may be an objectionable 30 Hz or 25 Hz line-to-line flicker at close viewing distances.

Interlacing also complicates the form of the sync signals which must be generated by the interface circuitry. Monitor circuits are designed for uniform vertical retrace-and-sweep deflections which end at the top and bottom of the displayed rastern pattern. If an even number of lines are interlaced, the upper and lower boundaries will shift with each field and the length of the retrace path will change between successive fields. The preferred alternative is to specify an odd number of lines per frame (e.g., 525 or 625) with half of the time interval for the odd mid-frame line (line 263 or 313) allocated to each field. The resulting sweep-and-retrace patterns are illustrated in Figure 8-5 in simplified form.

Separate horizontal-sync and vertical-sync signals can accommodate

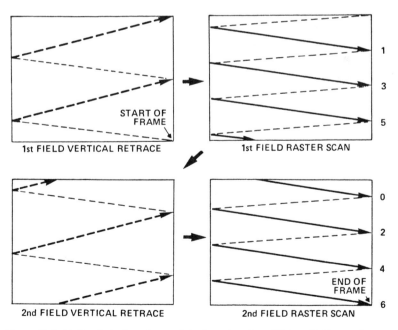

Figure 8-5. Path of electron beam, interlaced raster with two fields per frame.

the half-line shift in vertical-retrace timing without any problem. Complications are created, however, when the pulses are combined into a single sync signal. As shown in Figure 8–6, there is only a ½H interval between the final horizontal-sync pulse and the forward edge of the vertical-sync pulse at the end of the first field. Energy from the horizontal-sync pulse may be integrated with that of the vertical-sync pulse, producing a premature vertical-deflection trigger.

The conventional solution to this problem is to isolate the vertical-sync pulse with extended zero-signal intervals before and after the pulse. This expands even further, however, the amount of time during which the horizontal deflection may drift out of sync. Brief "equalizing pulses" at ½H intervals are usually added to the waveform, therefore, to maintain synchronization and provide a relatively uniform energy envelope, from field to field, on both sides of the vertical-sync pulse. Serrations within the vertical-sync pulse are also increased to ½H intervals to continue the synchronization pattern. Even-numbered ½H equalizing pulses and serrations maintain the horizontal sync at the end of the first field, odd-numbered at the end of the second field. The remaining intermediate signal transitions are too removed from the natural period of the horizontal-sync oscillator to have any effect.

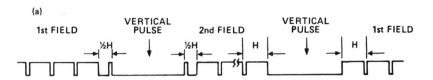

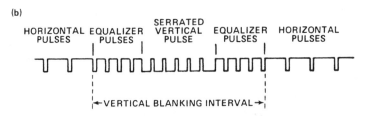

Figure 8–6. Interlaced sync signal (a) with added equalizer pulses and vertical-pulse serrations (b).

Superimposed Fields

A raster-scan CRT electron beam cycles between the top and bottom borders of the raster pattern at a constant rate—regardless of whether the raster lines are interlaced or non-interlaced. It is the ½ H shift in the vertical sync pulses generated by the interface circuits which interlaces the lines. This raises, then, the question whether a monitor designed for interlaced operation can be used to generate a non-interlaced display by simply changing the sync-signal input. The answer is a qualified "yes."

Two design features distinguish an interlace-type monitor. The first is the H-to-V frequency ratio of the beam-deflection oscillators. The ratio for an interlaced monitor is half the value of a non-interlaced monitor with the same number of lines per frame. For example, the H-to-V ratio for an interlaced 525-lines-per-frame monitor operating at a *field* rate of 60 Hz is 262½:1. The ratio is 525:1 for a non-interlaced monitor with the same number of lines per frame but operating at a *frame* rate of 60 Hz. Twice as many lines must be scanned during each vertical sweep interval—doubling the line rate of the display.

A second and more important difference lies in the physical design —and expense—of the horizontal-deflection circuits. Twice as much deflection power is expended when the line rate is doubled to produce a non-interlaced display. The power ratings for all circuit components must be higher, and significantly more heat must be dissipated.

Any interlaced-display monitor can be adapted to lower-resolution, non-interlaced operation, however, by reducing the lines per frame to an even number. Both fields would return, in this case, to the upper right corner of the display and trace identical raster patterns. The superimposed fields become, in effect, separate "frames" with half the vertical resolution of the original display. The change can be accomplished by simply decreasing the V interval for each frame by ½ H. The monitor's vertical-deflection oscillator normally has sufficient adjustment range to accommodate the slight shift in vertical-deflection timing. Black stripes between the superimposed lines can be minimized by reducing the vertical-deflection or expanding the electron-beam spot size.

Any application which can tolerate the reduction in vertical resolution would be a candidate for this type of monitor operation. The major advantage is that all line-to-line flicker is eliminated without the extra monitor costs and data-transfer rates imposed by a standard non-interlaced display. Typical would be a large-screen vector-graphic or alphagraphic application in which line-to-line flicker at the horizontal borders of graphic elements would be highly objectionable.

THE DISPLAY SIGNAL

Raster-scan display signals perform two functions. One is to provide "display" information in the form of a positive-polarity, amplitude-modulated voltage. The second function is to "blank" the electron beam during the horizontal and vertical retrace intervals so that no visible retrace paths appear on the monitor screen. Both functions require precise synchronization with the sync signals which control the generation of the raster pattern.

Typical display signals encountered in a raster graphics system are illustrated in Figure 8-7. The output of a shift register, for example, consists of discrete pulses with a constant amplitude that corresponds, we can assume, to the full-scale luminous output of the CRT monitor. The output of a DAC is a stairstepped signal, with each step generated by a binary-coded value at the DAC input. A 4-bit DAC can generate a 16-step signal, corresponding to 16 monochrome luminosities or gray-scale values. An 8-bit DAC increases the gray-scale range to 256. "Gray-scale," as used here applies to any graduated variation in the luminous output produced by a single electron beam. This would include both the grays displayed by a single-beam monochrome monitor and the intermediate red, green, or blue intensities produced by modulating one of the electron beams in a three-beam color monitor. (By contrast, a "video" signal is neither pulsed nor stair-stepped. It is, instead, a true analog signal representing, for example, the light intensities reflected into the optical system of a television camera.)

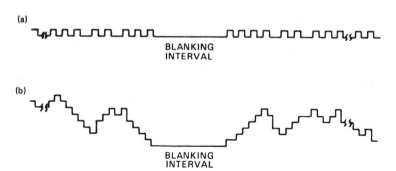

Figure 8-7. Display signals generated by shift register (a) and digital-to-analog converter (b).

Each digitally generated pulse or stair-step is related to a specific pixel location on the display screen. To maintain this relationship, the controller must read information out of display memory at exactly the same rate as the electron beam scans an active raster line. Display information for the first pixel location along a raster line must be delivered to the monitor at the precise moment when the electron-beam retrace has been completed and the blanking interval ends. Display information for the last pixel on the line must be received just before the start of the next retrace blanking interval.

The duration of the display time for each pixel, the display-memory readout rate, and the required display-signal bandwidth can all be calculated from three known values: (1) the horizontal resolution as defined by the number of pixel codes stored in the display memory for each raster line, (2) the H-interval determined by the horizontal-sync pulses, and (3) the duration of the horizontal-retrace blanking interval.

Figures 8-8a and 8-8b list the H-intervals and horizontal-retrace

	Monochrome Standards			
	U.S. Broadcast	European Broadcast	U.S. Closed-Circuit	U.S. High-Resolution
Lines/Frame	525	625	525	See Figure 8-8b
Field Rate (Hz)	60	50	60	60
V-Interval (us)	16,667	20,000	16,667	16,667
V Blanking (us)	833	1,200	1,250	1,250
V-Sync Pulse (us)	190.5	192	150	150
H-Interval (us)	63.5	64	63.5	See Figure 8-8b
H Blanking (us)	11.4	12.8	10	See Figure 8-8b
H-Sync Pulse (us)	5.1	5.8	4.8	2.8

Figure 8-8a. Display-signal parameters established by international standards.

U.S. High-Resolution Standards			
Lines/Frame	Active Lines	H-Interval	H-Blanking
675	650	49.5 us	7 us
729	702	45.7	7
875	842	38.1	7
945	909	35.3	7
1023	985	32.5	7

Figure 8-8b. Parameters established by U.S. high-resolution standard (EIA RS-343, Appendix II).

blanking intervals specified by several widely applied interlaced-monochrome standards. The time values allow us to make a sample calculation of the signal parameters. For example, the H-interval for an 875-line interlaced display is 38.1 microseconds. From this we must subtract a 7-microsecond retrace blanking interval, resulting in an active-raster-line duration of 31.1 microseconds. If the line is to contain 1024 addressable pixel locations, the per-pixel display time can be calculated as 31.1 microseconds divided by 1024, or 30.4 nanoseconds. Dividing this value into one second, we can conclude that during the time the electron beam is tracing an active raster line, pixel data must be read out of each display-memory plane at a rate of 32M bits per second. Allowing a half-cycle per bit, the bandwidth of the interface and monitor circuits would have to be at least 16 MHz, with 20 to 30 MHz as a more conservative estimate of the bandwidth requirement for "sharper" pixel-to-pixel transitions. Any increase in the number of visible lines would reduce the horizontal-line interval proportionately, requiring a corresponding increase in bandwidth to maintain the same image quality. Non-interlaced scanning would double the required bandwidth.

The horizontal and vertical blanking intervals listed in Figures 8–8a and 8–8b are minimum values and assume that the visible raster pattern is to occupy most or all of the CRT screen. One way to adjust the size and aspect ratio of the raster is to change the amplitudes of the beam-deflection sawtooth waveforms. Another and more flexible method is to alter, potentially under software control, the duration of the blanking intervals. Lengthening the vertical blanking interval, for example, has the effect of reducing the number of visible raster lines. A lengthened horizontal blanking interval will shorten the visible raster lines. The blanking intervals can also be shifted relative to the sync signals to place the visible raster anywhere on the surface of the monitor screen. The only constraint is that the blanking intervals must also coincide with and mask the retrace paths of the electron beam.

Composite Display Signal

Just as the horizontal and vertical sync pulses can be combined into a single sync signal, display and sync information can be merged into a single "composite signal" (not to be confused with the composite-sync term often used for a combined horizontal-and-vertical sync signal).

Figure 8–9 illustrates a typical composite waveform and the terminology used to identify the signal voltage levels. The blanking level serves as the benchmark for the other voltage values. By definition, a

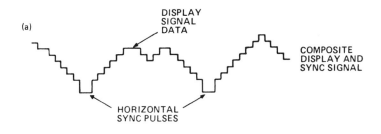

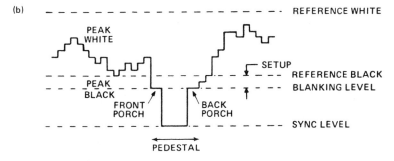

Figure 8–9. Composite display signal (a) and waveform nomenclature (b).

blanking-level voltage at the monitor input will reduce the CRT electron-beam current below the "cutoff" point, assuring that no visible trace of the electron beam will appear during the blanking intervals.

All of the display voltage levels have a positive polarity with respect to the blanking level. The lowest display level is reference black, defined and specified as a lower limit for "peak black" excursions. The highest positive level is reference white, defined and specified as an upper limit for "peak white" excursions. The display-signal "setup" is the ratio between the reference-black and reference-white voltage levels when both are measured from the blanking level. It is typically expressed as a percentage (e.g., 7.5 percent).

The vertical-retrace and horizontal-retrace blanking intervals are referred to as "pedestals" (for reasons that will become clear when we examine a modulated-RF composite signal). The horizontal-retrace pedestal has a "front porch" ahead of the sync pulse and a "back porch" following the pulse.

Sync voltage levels are negative with respect to the blanking level. The furthest negative excursion of the horizontal and vertical sync pulses is the sync level, also called the sync tip. The negative sync level is typically 40 percent of the reference white level when both are measured from the blanking level.

Display and Sync Signal Amplitudes

Because the display and syncs signal may vary in amplitude as they are processed through the interface and monitor circuits, an "IRE" scale has been established for defining the relative voltage levels of the signals, independent of their absolute voltage values. Reference white is given a value of +100 IRE units. The blanking level is set at 0 IRE units. Sync tips would typically have a value of −40 IRE units. A composite signal would therefore have a peak-to-peak (p-p) value of 140 IRE units.

Voltage levels at the monitor input can vary within wide limits and are specified in different ways. A typical practice is to define a nominal value and a range. The specification for a composite display/sync signal might be 1.0 V p-p nominal, 0.3 to 3.0 V p-p acceptable. A non-composite display signal could be specified as 0.7 p-p nominal, 0.3 to 2.0 V p-p nominal, 1 to 8 V p-p acceptable.

The input circuits of conventional monitors are designed to "terminate" a 75-ohm or 100-ohm coaxial cable. If the signal is "looped through" to one or more monitors, provision must be made for terminating the last monitor on the line. Monitors are also available with input-impedance and signal-level characteristics which are directly compatible with transistor-transistor-logic (TTL) circuits. A full-scale TTL-compatible signal input voltage level would typically be +5V.

Modulated-RF signal voltages (see below) are held to a much lower value to avoid radiation which could interfere with television receivers in the neighborhood. FCC regulations generally limit the peak-to-peak signal value to less than 500 microvolts. The RF signal levels are often specified in dBmV—the ratio between the signal level and 1 millivolt, expressed as dB. Figure 8–10 is a conversion table for dBmV signal values.

A number of monitors (and all television-receiver antenna terminals) are designed for a "floating" or "differential" input. Unless specified otherwise, however, it is assumed that the signal inputs are single-ended, with the coaxial-cable shields tied to the monitor ground. With a non-composite input, the display-signal blanking level and the sync-signal tips would therefore be at ground. With a composite input, only the sync tips would be at ground. In both cases, care must be taken to avoid ground-loop or common mode noise which could interfere with the sync and display signals.

dBmV	mV	dBmV	mV
-40	.010	2	1.259
-30	.032	3	1.413
-20	.100	4	1.585
-19	.112	5	1.778
-18	.126	6	1.995
-17	.141	7	2.239
-16	.159	8	2.512
-15	.178	9	2.818
-14	.200	10	3.162
-13	.224	11	3.548
-12	.251	12	3.981
-11	.282	13	4.467
-10	.316	14	5.012
-9	.355	15	5.623
-8	.398	16	6.310
-7	.447	17	7.079
-6	.501	18	7.943
-5	.562	19	8.913
-4	.631	20	10.00
-3	.708	30	31.62
-2	.794	40	100.0
-1	.891	50	316.2
0	1.000	60	1000
1	1.122		

Figure 8-10. Conversion table, dBmV to millivolts.

Gamma Correction

There is a direct relationship between the display signal and the voltage applied to the monitor CRT. The luminous output of the phosphors on the CRT monitor screen is not, however, directly proportional to either of these values.

Figure 8-11 plots the luminous output of the monitor as a function of the display-signal voltage. Both are shown as fractions of their full-scale values. The monitor output is less than linear at low display-signal values, more than linear at high display-signal levels. Monitors differ, but the international convention is to assume that the fractional value of the luminous output can be approximated by raising the fractional display-signal input to the 2.2 power. Thus, a 60%-of-full-scale input voltage will result in 33%-of-full-scale luminous output ($0.6^{2.2}$ equals 0.33).

The practice in the television industry is to correct for this "gamma" non-linearity at the signal source: the television camera. The signal out-

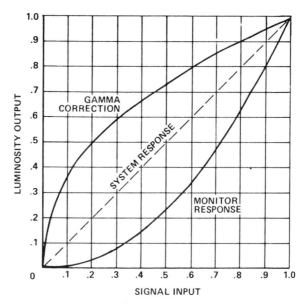

Figure 8–11. "Gamma" monitor response and correction, based on a gamma value of 2.2.

put of the camera tube (or each of the three tubes in the case of a color camera) is modified by taking the 2.2 root of its full-scale fractional value. The correction results in a linear *system* relationship, from camera to monitor screen.

There is considerable disagreement on the most appropriate "general-purpose" value for gamma. Values up to 2.8 have been cited, with 2.5 suggested as an average figure.

The designer of a graphics system with a DAC-generated display signal has three choices with respect to gamma. The gamma correction can be performed in software by recalculating the display-data values before they are stored in display memory or entered into a lookup table. As a second alternative, an analog gamma correction can be applied to the display signal generated by the graphics controller. The third option is to ignore the whole subject and accept the luminous output of the monitor screen as an inherent characteristic of the system.

COLOR SIGNALS

The discussion on visual perception in Chapter 10, The Human Interface, summarizes the experimental evidence for the theory that the

human eye perceives color as a three-dimensional quality. One characteristic of three-dimensional systems is that any three independent
parameters can be used to define the complete system specifications. A
rectangular box, for example, can be fully described by its length,
width, and height, or by the length of a single side and its area and
volume. In similar fashion, color information can be specified, coded,
and communicated in a variety of three-parameter combinations,
several of which have application in the processing of color information for a raster graphics display (see Appendices II and III).

Virtually all raster-scan color monitors incorporate three electron
guns, each directed at a separate array of red, green, or blue phosphor
dots or stripes. The simplest way to control the output of a color
monitor is to supply a separated display signal for each of these three
"primary" colors. An "RGB" monitor is designed for this type of signal interface. Each of the three color inputs is, in effect, a separate
monochrome signal, with all the characteristics described in the preceding paragraphs and pages. The only significant difference is that in
the case of a "composite" RGB input, sync pulses are frequently
added to only one of the display signals. As shown in Figure 8–12, one
convention is to combine the sync and green signals, with corresponding "blanking" intervals in the other two color signals.

Levels of *radiant* energy emitted by the color phosphors on a white-
aligned monitor screen (see Appendix III) will be generally proportional to the corresponding gamma-corrected color signal levels. The
luminous energies perceived by the human eye will not be proportional.
As described in Chapter 2, the eye is highly sensitive to the yellow-green

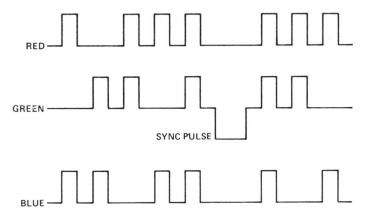

Figure 8–12. Composite RGB display signals with sync on green.

portion of the color spectrum, less sensitive to red, and much less sensitive to blue. Lower full-scale red and blue luminances must be generated, therefore, to obtain a balanced white.

The differences in color response also require a "weighting" of the RGB signals when they are combined into a single signal to drive a monochrome monitor. Figure 8-13 indicates how a selected percentage of each signal can be "summed" to produce a single gray-scale display signal which the eye can interpret as being correct in terms of the relative luminances of the original colors.

Color Encoding

There are, as noted, a variety of three-dimensional ways to "code" a color—other than specifying its red, blue, and green components. All of the present color-encoding techniques used in television and raster graphics include, as one of the coding parameters, the gray-scale or "luminance" signal produced by a summing circuit such as that shown in Figure 8-13. The other two "dimensions" are derived from red-minus-luminance and blue-minus-luminance values which can be added to (and the results subtracted from) the luminance to reconstruct the original red, green, and blue signal strengths.

The importance of the weighted luminance or gray-scale parameter stems from experimental evidence that the human eye can see only grays in the small details of a scene. The colors that can be perceived in larger details start with orange and its complement, blue-green, followed by a full range of all the colors in very large visual elements. Television color-encoding systems take advantage of this human char-

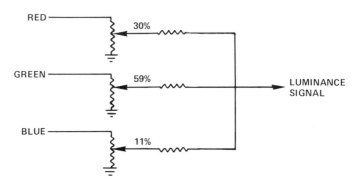

Figure 8-13. Summing circuit for monochrome-monitor input and luminance component of encoded-color signal.

acteristic. Only the gray-scale or luminous details are transmitted at the full carrier bandwidth allowed for television broadcasting (Figure 8-14). "Chrominance" information is superimposed on the luminance waveform in the form of a modulated subcarrier signal which, in the case of the NTSC (National Television System Committee) color-encoding technique, reduces the bandwidth of orange-cyan information to approximately ± 1.3 MHz and only ± 0.5 MHz for the remaining colors.

A description of the NTSC color-encoding method is given in Appendix II. Brief summaries are also presented for the other two major color-encoding techniques, PAL and SECAM. Countries which have standarized on the three methods are listed in Figure 8-15. The PAL and SECAM techniques are generally associated with the 625-line, 50-Hz European transmission standard. The NTSC system is associated with the 525-line, 60-Hz standard which originated in the U.S. The PAL and SECAM systems can, it is claimed, improve the fidelity of the color display. The two methods also expand on the effective bandwidth of the color-encoded information. In all three cases, however, the bandwidth is severely limited, compared to the bandwidth potential of an RGB system. This should be of major concern, therefore, to any system designer who is considering the use of color encoding in a raster graphics application. Encoding can preserve all of the *colors* represented by the digital data in a display memory, but much of the pixel-to-pixel color resolution may be lost in the transfer to a color monitor.

Conversion equipment is available for converting from one type of color-encoded signal to another. Conversions between PAL and SECAM are relatively simple; the original signal is decoded into its RGB components, then re-encoded to the new format. Conversions be-

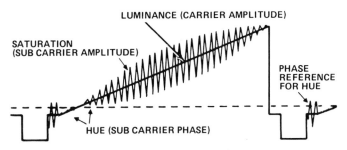

Figure 8-14. Three components of NTSC color-encoded display signal, including modulated chrominance sub-carrier.

INTERNATIONAL TELEVISION STANDARDS

Lines per Frame: 525 Field Rate: 60 Hz Color Coding: NTSC	Lines per Frame: 625 Field Rate: 50 Hz Color Coding: PAL	Lines per Frame: 625 Field Rate: 50 Hz Color Coding: SECAM
Antigua, West Indies	Algeria	Afars & Issas
Bahamas	Australia	Arab Republic of Egypt
Barbados	Austria	Bulgaria
British Virgin Islands	Bahrain	Czechoslovakia
Canada	Bangladesh	East Germany
Chile	Belgium	France
Costa Rica	Brazil (525/60)	Greece
Cuba	Brunei	Haiti
Dominican Republic	Denmark	Hungary
Ecuador	Federal Republic	Iran
El Salvador	of Germany	Ivory Coast
Guatemala	Finland	Iraq
Japan	Hong Kong	Lebanon
Mexico	Iceland	Luxembourg
Netherlands Antilles,	Ireland	Mauritius
West Indies	Italy	Monaco
Nicaragua	Jordan	Morocco
Panama	Kuwait	Poland
Peru	Malaysia	Reunion
Philippines	Netherlands	Saudi Arabia
St. Kitts, West Indies	New Zealand	Tunisia
Samoa (U.S.)	Nigeria	USSR
Surinam	Norway	Zaire
Province of Taiwan	Oman	
Trinidad, West Indies	Pakistan	
Trust Territory of	Oatar	
Pacific	Singapore	
United States of	South Africa	
America	Spain	
	Sweden	
	Switzerland	
	Tanzania	
	Thailand	
	Turkey	
	United Arab Emirates	
	United Kingdom	
	Yugoslavia	
	Zambia	

Figure 8–15. Nations which have adopted the NTSC, PAL, and SECAM color-encoding standards.

tween NTSC and the other two techniques are much more difficult. The number of lines per frame must also be increased or decreased. Systems have been built, but they are very expensive and complex. By contrast, a variety of encoders are available to convert RGB signals to one of the international standards. The same is true of decoders for converting the encoded signals to RGB.

Mixing and switching systems require that all of the signals have the same format. The relatively inexpensive RGB encoders and decoders can be of great value, therefore, in assemblying a raster graphics display from several sources of distributing the display signals to multiple monitors with different input requirements.

TELEVISION RECEIVERS

When the resolution and color-fidelity requirements are low, a mass-produced television receiver can often be considered as a cost-effective substitute for a raster graphics monitor.

A television receiver is, in effect, a monitor with tuning and RF-demodulation circuits at the input. There are two ways, therefore, that a receiver can be incorporated into the graphics system. The simplest but not necessarily the most inexpensive way is to use an RF modulator to convert a composite display signal into a "television signal." Low-cost RF modulators are available, designed principally for use with video tape recorders. The modulators generally invert the composite display signal before applying it to the RF carrier frequency for the selected TV channel. The result is shown in Figure 8-16 (which also visually explains why the horizontal retrace blanking interval is referred to as a "pedestal" with front and back porches). Inverted modulation helps to preserve picture fidelity in low-signal or noisy environments. Transient noise will produce black patterns on the receiver screen, which are less objectionable than white "snow." There is also less danger that synchronization will be lost. The sync tips are the strongest part of the signal.

Most commercial RF modulators can be switched to one of two adjoining TV channels (Figure 8-17). Very few communities in the U.S. have stations broadcasting, for example, on both channels 3 and 4. Switching to a vacant channel reduces the chance that neighboring receivers will be bothered by an interference signal. As noted earlier, the FCC requires that the output signal of the RF modulator be kept very low, below 500 microvolts or -6 dBm V, to avoid radiation problems.

The second way to incorporate a receiver into a graphics system is to bypass the unit's RF-demodulation stage. Advice should be obtained from the receiver manufacturer or at the very least, considerable caution should be exercised—especially in the case of ac-dc receivers or "hot-chassis" units with one side of the power line tied to ground. If such recievers must be used, they should either be isolated from line voltage with a transformer or the signal input should be protected with an optical isolator.

For monochrome and NTSC-encoded input signals, the bypass con-

DISPLAY
SIGNAL

INVERTED
DISPLAY SIGNAL

MODULATED-RF
DISPLAY SIGNAL

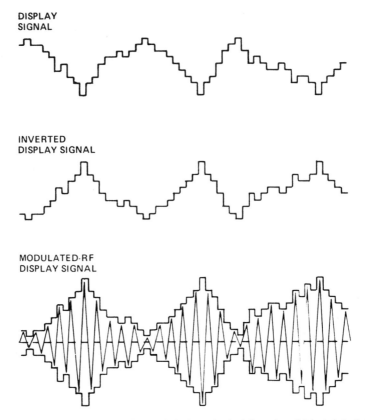

Figure 8–16. Inversion and RF-modulation of television signal. Modulated display signal is required for operation of receiver-type display unit.

nection should be at the input of the first video amplifier. RGB color signals can be applied directly to the three color amplifiers or the CRT grid inputs, depending on the receiver design. In both cases, the chrominance decoding matrix must be disconnected.

SPECIAL FEATURES MONITORS

A number of commercially available monitors offer special features which simplify the interfacing task:

Monitor/Receivers—These are combination units which can serve as either monitors or receivers. A front-panel switch selects the mode of operation. In the receiver mode, the channel-selection and RF-

Channel No.	Frequency Range (MHz)	Picture Carrier (MHz)
2	54-60	55.25
3	60-66	61.25
4	66-72	67.25
5	76-82	77.25
6	82-88	83.25
7	174-180	175.25
8	180-186	181.25
9	186-192	187.25
10	192-198	193.25
11	198-204	199.25
12	204-210	205.25
13	210-216	211.25

Figure 8-17. Range and carrier frequencies, VHF broadcast band defined by U.S. standards.

demodulator circuits are activated. In the monitor mode, the display signal is fed directly to the input of the first video amplifier.

Multiple Color Standards—Other combination units allow the user to change from one international color-encoding standard to another by simply turning a front-panel switch. The monitors are designed with three completely separate circuits for decoding NTSC, PAL, and SECAM input signals.

"Internal/External" Sync—Monitors with this input feature can accommodate both composite and non-composite display signals. The terminology is misleading; the "external" graphics system must *always* serve as the synchronization source. When a switch is set to "internal," the monitor strips the sync pulses from a composite display signal received through a single input connector. When the switch is set to "external," the monitor's horizontal and vertical beam-deflection oscillators are triggered by a sync signal received through a separate input connector.

Non-Combined Sync—Horizontal and vertical sync pulses are normally combined into a single sync signal. Monitors can also be designed to accept a "non-combined" sync input. There are several advantages to the use of separate horizontal and vertical sync signals. The horizontal and vertical pulses are normally formed by separate sync-generation circuits; the non-combined form eliminates the need to merge them into a composite signal. More importantly, the vertical-sync waveform can be simplified. Equalizing pulses and serrations are not required to maintain horizontal sync during the vertical-retrace interval. Monitor circuits to separate the horizontal and vertical pulses can also be eliminated, reducing the hardware costs.

Gray-Scale to Color Conversion—Color monitors with this feature produce color-coded displays from a gray-scale monochrome signal. Monitor circuits alter the displayed color as the signal amplitude increases from the black to white reference levels. Figure 8–18 shows how the primary colors could be used to "code" three gray-scale ranges. In theory, hundreds of different gray-scale graduations could be color coded to indicate, for example, tissue-density or temperature variations. The conversion parameters may be manually set by a pegboard matrix inside the monitor or remotely programmed by the raster graphics system.

INPUT-SIGNAL CONVERSIONS

There are a number of occasions when a conversion must be made from one type of display signal to another. It may be necessary, for example, to match a graphics system to existing display equipment. Or the installation may require a variety of display and recording devices, all to be driven by the same signal source. Or a single display may be driven by several signal sources, both digital and video.

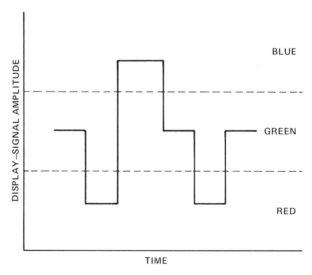

Figure 8–18. Monochrome-to-color conversion for coding displayed information. Display color is determined by signal-amplitude range.

DISPLAY DEVICE

INPUT SIGNAL(S)	Monitor						Receiver	
	Non-Composite			Composite			Modulated-RF	
	Mono-chrome	RGB Color	NTSC Color	Mono-chrome	RGB Color	NTSC Color	Mono-chrome	NTSC Color
Non-Composite:								
Monochrome	A1	A2	A3	A4	A5	A6	A7	A8
RGB Color	B1	B2	B3	B4	B5	B6	B7	B8
NTSC Color	C1	C2	C3	C4	C5	C6	C7	C8
Composite:								
Monochrome	D1	D2	D3	D4	D5	D6	D7	D8
RGB Color	E1	E2	E3	E4	E5	E6	E7	E8
NTSC Color	F1	F2	F3	F4	F5	F6	F7	F8
Modulated-RF:								
Monochrome	G1	G2	G3	G4	G5	G6	G7	G8
NTSC Color	H1	H2	H3	H4	H5	H6	H7	H8

Figure 8–19. Input-signal conversion matrix. Letter-number notations refer to descriptive paragraphs for each signal-device combination.

Such conversions are relatively simple to implement—especially if advantage is taken of off-the-shelf encoders, decoders, modulators, and demodulators. In many cases, there will also be a requirement for combining or distributing signals. Again, commericially available devices can be used. Hybrid couplers and splitters are the least expensive, but they have the effect of increasing the display-signal amplitude when two signals are combined or attenuating a signal when it is "split." Video mixers and bridging amplifiers avoid this problem.

Figure 8–19 is a matrix composed of eight of the most typical input signals and corresponding display devices. The following paragraphs describe how each type of input signal can be converted to an appropriate input for the indicated monitor or receiver.

Non-Composite Monochrome Signals (A)

Non-composite monochrome signals are carried on two cables: display and sync. The following procedures can be used to interface the signals with a selected monitor or receiver:

→ *Non-Composite Monochrome Monitor (A1)*—Connect display and sync cables to corresponding monitor display-input and sync-input connectors.

→ *Non-Composite RGB Color Monitor (A2)*—For black-and-white display, use hybrid splitter or bridging amplifier to distribute display signal to all three color-input connectors. Distribution to two color-input connectors produces one of three complementary colors. Connection to single color-input connector produces one of three primary colors. Connect sync cable to sync-input connector.

→ *Non-Composite NTSC Color Monitor (A3)*—Connect display and sync cables to corresponding monitor display-input and sync-input connectors.

→ *Composite Monochrome Monitor (A4)*—Use hybrid coupler or mixer to connect sync cable and display cable to monitor signal-input connector.

→ *Composite RGB Color Monitor (A5)*—For black-and-white display, use hybrid splitter or bridging amplifier to distribute display signal to all three color-input connectors. Use hybrid coupler or mixer to connect sync cable and "green-display" cable to green-input connector. See A2 above for other color options.

→ *Composite NTSC Color Monitor (A6)*—Use hybrid coupler or mixer to connect display and sync cables to monitor input connector.

→ *Monochrome Receiver (A7)*—Use hybrid coupler or mixer to connect display and sync cables to input connector of RF modulator for selected TV channel. Connect RF-modulator output to receiver input. As an option, bypass receiver RF detector stage. Use hybrid coupler or mixer to connect display and sync cables to input of first video amplifier.

→ *NTSC Color Receiver (A8)*—Same as A7 above for black-and-white display. For optional primary-color display, connect sync cable to input of first video amplifier and display cable to one of the color drive amplifiers (or color-gun grids). For complementary-color display, use hybrid splitter or bridging amplifier to distribute display signal to two color drive amplifiers (or color-gun grids).

Non-Composite RGB Color Signals (B)

Non-composite RGB color signals are carried on four cables: red display, green display, blue display, and sync. The following procedures can be used to interface the signals with a selected monitor or receiver:

→ *Non-Composite Monochrome Monitor (B1)*—Combine the three color-display signals in a summing circuit as shown in Figure 8–13.

Connect summing-circuit output cable to monitor display-input connector. Connect sync cable to sync-input connector.

→ *Non-Composite RGB Monitor (B2)*—Connect the four input-signal cables to corresponding monitor color-input and sync-input connectors.

→ *Non-Composite NTSC Color Monitor (B3)*—Connect the four input-signal cables to the corresponding color-input and sync-input connectors of an NTSC color encoder. Connect color-encoder display and sync output cables to corresponding monitor display-input and sync input connectors. If encoder output is a composite signal, use hybrid splitter or bridging amplifier to distribute signal to display-input and sync-input connectors.

→ *Composite Monochrome Monitor (B4)*—Combine the three color-display signals in a summing circuit as shown in Figure 8–13. Use hybrid coupler or mixer to connect sync cable and summing-circuit output cable to monitor signal-input connector.

→ *Composite RGB Color Monitor (B5)*—Use hybrid coupler or mixer to connect green-display cable and sync cable to green-input connector. Connect red-display and blue-display cables to corresponding monitor input connectors.

→ *Composite NTSC Color Monitor (B6)*—Connect the four input-signal cables to the corresponding color-input and sync-input connectors of an NTSC color encoder. Use hybrid coupler or mixer to connect color-encoder display and sync output cables to monitor signal-input connector. If encoder output is a composite signal, connect output cable directly to monitor signal-input connector.

→ *Monochrome Receiver (B7)*—Combine the three color-display signals in a summing circuit as shown in Figure 8–13. Use hybrid coupler or mixer to connect sync cable and summing-circuit output cable to input connector of RF modulator for selected TV channel. Connect RF-modulator output cable to receiver signal-input connector. As an option, bypass receiver RF-detector stage. Use hybrid coupler or mixer to connect sync cable and summing-circuit output cable to input of first video amplifier.

→ *NTSC Color Receiver (B8)*—Connect the four input-signal cables to the corresponding color-input and sync-input connectors of an NTSC color encoder. Use a hybrid coupler or mixer to connect color-encoder display and sync output cables to input connector of RF modulator for selected TV channel. If encoder output is a composite signal, connect directly to RF-modulator input connector. Connect RF-modulator output cable to receiver signal-input connector. As an option, bypass receiver RF-detector and color-decoding stages. Connect sync cable to input of first video amplifier and color-display cables to inputs of corresponding color drive amplifiers (or color-gun grids).

Non-Composite NTSC Color Signals (C)

Non-composite NTSC color signals are carried on two cables: display and sync. The following procedures can be used to interface the signals with a selected monitor or receiver:

→ *Non-Composite Monochrome Monitor (C1)*—Connect display and sync cables to corresponding monitor display-input and sync-input connectors.

→ *Non-Composite RGB Color Monitor (C2)*—Connect display and sync cables to corresponding input connectors of an NTSC color decoder. Connect color-decoder sync and three color-display output cables to corresponding monitor input connectors. If the decoder has a composite output, use a hybrid splitter or bridging amplifier to distribute green display/sync signal to monitor's green-input and sync-input connectors.

→ *Non-Composite NTSC Color Monitor (C3)*—Connect display and sync cables to corresponding monitor display-input and sync-input connectors.

→ *Composite Monochrome Monitor (C4)*—Use hybrid coupler or mixer to connect display and sync cables to monitor signal-input connector.

→ *Composite RGB Color Monitor (C5)*—Connect display and sync cables to corresponding input connectors of an NTSC color decoder. Connect color-decoder red-display and blue-display cables to monitor red-input and blue-input connectors. Use hybrid coupler or mixer to connect color-decoder green-display and sync cables to monitor green/sync-input connector. If color decoder has a composite output, connect green-display/sync cable to monitor green/sync-input connector.

→ *Composite NTSC Color Monitor (C6)*—Use hybrid coupler or mixer to connect display and sync cables to monitor signal-input connector.

→ *Monochrome Receiver (C7)*—Use hybrid coupler or mixer to connect display and sync cables to input connector of RF modulator for selected TV channel. Connect RF-modulator output to receiver input. As an option, bypass receiver RF detector stage. Use hybrid coupler or mixer to connect display and sync cables to input of first video amplifier.

→ *NTSC Color Receiver (C8)*—Use hybrid coupler or mixer to connect display and sync cables to input connector of an RF modulator for selected TV channel. Connect RF-modulator output to receiver signal-input connector. As an option, bypass receiver RF-detector stage. Use a hybrid coupler or mixer to connect display and sync cables to the input of first video amplifier.

Composite Monochrome Signal (D)

A composite monochrome signal is carried on single display/sync cable. The following procedures can be used to interface the signal with a selected monitor or receiver:

→ *Non-Composite Monochrome Monitor (D1)*—Use a hybrid splitter or bridging amplifier to distribute the display/sync signal to the monitor display-input and sync-input connectors.

→ *Non-Composite RGB Color Monitor (D2)*—For black-and-white display, use hybrid splitter or bridging amplifier to distribute display/sync signal to the red-input, green-input, blue-input and sync-input connectors. Connection to two color-input connectors and sync-input connector produces one of three complementary colors. Connection to a single color-input connector and sync-input connector produces one of three primary colors.

→ *Non-Composite NTSC Color Monitor (D3)*—Use hybrid splitter or bridging amplifier to distribute display/sync signal to monitor display-input and sync-input connectors.

→ *Composite Monochrome Monitor (D4)*—Connect display/sync cable to monitor signal-input connector.

→ *Composite RGB Color Monitor (D5)*—For black-and-white display, use hybrid splitter or bridging amplifier to distribute display/sync signal to red-input, blue-input, green/sync-input connectors. Connection to green/sync-input connector and one other color input connector produces one of two complementary colors (cyan or yellow). Connection to the green/sync-input connector alone produces green monochrome display.

→ *Composite NTSC Color Monitor (D6)*—Connect display/sync cable to monitor input-signal connector.

→ *Monochrome Receiver (D7)*—Connect display/sync cable to input connector of RF-modulator for selected TV channel. Connect RF-modulator output to receiver input. As an option, bypass receiver RF detector stage. Connect display/sync cable directly to input of first video amplifier.

→*NTSC Color Receiver (D8)*—Same as D7 above for black-and-white display. For monochrome primary-color display, use hybrid splitter or bridging amplifier to distribute display/snyc signal to first video amplifier and one of the color drive amplifiers (or color-gun grids). For complementary-color display, distribute signal to two color drive amplifiers (or color-gun grids).

Composite RGB Color Signals (E)

Composite RGB color signals are carried on three cables: red display, blue display, and green display/sync. The following procedures can be used to interface the signals with a selected monitor or receiver:

→*Non-Composite Monochrome Monitor (E1)*—Connect red-display and blue-display cables to red-color and blue-color input connectors of a summing circuit (Figure 8–13). Use a hybrid splitter or bridging amplifier to distribute green-display/sync signal to monitor sync-input connector and summing-circuit green-color input connector. Connect summing-circuit output cable to monitor display-input connector.

→*Non-Composite RGB Color Monitor (E2)*—Connect red-display and blue-display cables to corresponding monitor color-input connectors. Use hybrid splitter or bridging amplifier to distribute green-display/sync signal to monitor green-input and sync-input connectors.

→*Non-Composite NTSC Color Monitor (E3)*—Use hybrid splitter or bridging amplifier to distribute green-display/sync signal to the green-input and sync-input connectors of an NTSC color encoder. Connect red-display and blue-display cables to color-encoder red-input and blue-input connectors. Connect color-encoder display and sync output cables to monitor display-input and sync-input connectors. If color-encoder output is a composite signal, use hybrid splitter or bridging amplifier to distribute signal to monitor display-input and sync-input connectors.

→*Composite Monochrome Monitor (E4)*—Combine red-display, blue-display, and green-display/sync signals in a summing circuit as shown in Figure 8–13. Connect summing-circuit output cable to monitor signal-input connector.

→*Composite RGB Color Monoitor (E5)*—Connect all three signal-input cables to corresponding monitor signal-input connectors.

→*Composite NTSC Color Monitor (E6)*—Connect red-display, blue-display, and green-display/sync cables to the corresponding input connectors of an NTSC color encoder. Use hybrid coupler or mixer to connect color-encoder display and sync cables to monitor signal-input connector. If color-encoder output is a composite signal, connect output cable to monitor signal-input connector.

→ *Monochrome Receiver (E7)*—Combine all three signals in a summing circuit as shown in Figure 8–13. Connect summing-circuit output cable to input connector of an RF modulator for selected TV channel. Connect RF-modulator output to receiver input. As an option, bypass the receiver RF-detector stage. Connect summing-circuit output to the input of first video amplifier.

→ *NTSC Color Receiver (E8)*—Connect red-display, blue-display, and green-display/sync cables to corresponding input connectors of an NTSC color encoder. Use a hybrid coupler or mixer to connect color-encoder display and sync output cables to input connector of RF modulator for selected TV channel. Connect RF-modulator output to receiver input. As an option, bypass the receiver RF detector stage. Use a hybrid coupler or mixer to connect color-encoder display and sync output cables to input of first video amplifier.

Composite NTSC Color Signal (F)

A composite NTSC signal is carried on single display/sync cable. The following procedures can be used to interface the signal with a selected monitor or receiver:

→ *Non-Composite Monochrome Monitor (F1)*—Use hybrid splitter or bridging amplifier to distribute display/sync signal to monitor display-input and sync-input connectors.

→ *Non-Composite RGB Color Monitor (F2)*—Connect display/sync cable to input connector of an NTSC color-decoder. Connect color-decoder's sync output and three color-display output cables to corresponding monitor sync-input and color-input connectors. If color decoder has a composite output, use hybrid splitter or bridging amplifier to distribute green-display/sync signal to monitor green-input and sync-input connectors.

→ *Non-Composite NTSC Color Monitor (F3)*—Use a hybrid splitter or bridging amplifier to distribute display/sync signal to monitor display-input and sync-input connectors.

→ *Composite Monochrome Monitor (F4)*—Connect display/sync signal to monitor signal-input connector.

→ *Composite RGB Color Monitor (F5)*—Connect display/sync cable to input connector of an NTSC color-decoder. Connect color-decoder red-display and blue-display cables to corresponding monitor color-input connectors. Use hybrid coupler or mixer to connect color-decoder green-display and sync cables to monitor green/sync-input connector. If decoder has a composite output, connect green-display/sync cable to monitor green/sync-input connector.

→ *Composite NTSC Color Monitor (F6)*—Connect display/sync cable to monitor signal-input connector.

→ *Monochrome Receiver (F7)*—Connect display/sync signal to input connector of an RF modulator for selected TV channel. Connect RF-modulator output to receiver input. As an option, bypass receiver RF-detector stage. Connect display/sync cable to the input of first video amplifier.

→ *NTSC Color Receiver (F8)*—Connect display/sync cable to input connector of an RF modulator for selected TV channel. Connect RF-modulator output to receiver signal-input connector. As an option, bypass the receiver RF detector stage. Connect display/sync cable to the input of first video amplifier.

Modulated-RF Monochrome Signal (G)

A modulated-RF monochrome signal is carried on single display/sync cable. The following procedures can be used to interface the signal with a selected monitor or receiver:

→ *Non-composite Monochrome Monitor (GI)*—Connect display/sync cable to input of an RF demodulator, tuned to the appropriate TV channel. Connect RF-demodulator display and sync output cables to corresponding monitor display-input and sync-input connectors. If de-modulator output is a composite signal, use a hybrid splitter or bridging amplifier to distribute output to both monitor input connectors.

→ *Non-Composite RGB Color Monitor (G2)*—Connect display/sync cable to input of an RF demodulator, tuned to the appropriate TV channel. For black-and-white-display use hybrid splitter or bridging amplifier to distribute RF-demodulator display/sync signal to red, green, blue and sync-input connectors.

→ *Non-Composite NTSC Color Monitor (G3)*—Connect display/sync cable to input connector of an RF demodulator tuned to the appropriate TV channel. Connect RF-demodulator display and sync output cables to corresponding monitor display-input and sync-input connectors. If RF-demodulator output is a composite signal, use hybrid splitter or bridging amplifier to distribute signal to monitor display-input and sync-input connectors.

→ *Composite Monochrome Monitor (G4)*—Connect display/sync cable to input of an RF demodulator, tuned to the appropriate TV channel. Use hybrid coupler or mixer to connect RF-demodulator display and sync output cables to monitor signal-input connector. If RF-demodulator output is a composite signal, connect demodulator output cable to monitor signal-input connector.

→ *Composite RGB Color Monitor (G5)*—Connect display/sync cable to input of an RF demodulator, tuned to the appropriate TV channel. For black-and-white display use hybrid splitter or bridging amplifier to distribute RF-demodulator display/sync signal to red-input, blue-input, and green/sync-input connectors.

→ *Composite NTSC Color Monitor (G6)*—Connect display/sync cable to input connector of an RF demodulator tuned to the appropriate TV channel. Use hybrid coupler or mixer to connect RF-demodulator display and sync output cables to monitor input-signal connector. If RF-demodulator output is a composite signal, connect output cable to monitor input-signal connector.

→ *Monochrome Receiver (G7)*—Connect display/sync signal to receiver signal-input connector.

→ *NTSC Color Receiver (G8)*—Connect/display sync cable to receiver signal-input connector.

Modulated-RF NTSC Color Signal (H)

A modulated-RF NTSC color signal is carried on single display/sync cable. The following procedures can be used to interface the signal with a selected monitor or receiver:

→ *Non-Composite Monochrome Monitor (H1)*—Connect display/sync cable to the input of an RF demodulator, tuned to the appropriate TV channel. Connect RF-demodulator display and sync output cables to the corresponding monitor display-input and sync-input connectors. If demodulator output is a composite signal, use hybrid splitter or bridging amplifier to distribute output to both monitor input connectors.

→ *Non-Composite RGB Color Monitor (H2)*—Connect display-sync cable to input of an RF-demodulator, tuned to the appropriate TV channel. Connect RF-demodulator display/sync cable to input connector of an NTSC color decoder. Connect color-decoder sync and three color-display output cables to corresponding monitor input connectors. If color-decoder has a composite output, use hybrid splitter or bridging amplifier to distribute green-display/sync signal to monitor green-input and sync-input connectors.

→ *Non-Composite NTSC Color Monitor (H3)*—Connect display/sync cable to input connector of an RF demodulator tuned to the appropriate TV channel. Connect RF-demodulator display and sync output cables to corresponding monitor display-input and sync-input connectors. If RF-demodulator output is a composite signal, use hybrid splitter or bridging amplifier to distribute signal to monitor display-input and sync-input connectors.

→ *Composite Monochrome Monitor (H4)*—Connect display/sync cable to the input of an RF demodulator, tuned to the appropriate TV channel. Use hybrid coupler or mixer to connect RF-demodulator display and sync output cables to monitor signal-input connector.

→ *Composite RGB Color Monitors (H5)*—Connect display-sync cable to input of an RF-demodulator tuned to the appropriate TV channel. Connect RF-demodulator display/sync cable to input connector of an NTSC color decoder. Connect color-decoder red-display and blue-display output cables to corresponding monitor color-input connectors. Use hybrid coupler or mixer to connect color-decoder green-display and sync cables to monitor green/sync-input connector.

→ *Composite NTSC Color Monitor (H6)*—Connect display/sync cable to input connector of an RF-demodulator tuned to the appropriate TV channel. Use hybrid coupler or mixer to connect RF-demodulator display and sync output cables to monitor signal-input.

→ *Monochrome Receiver (H7)*—Connect display/sync cable to receiver signal-input connector.

→ *NTSC Color Receiver (H8)*—Connect display/sync cable to receiver signal-input connector.

9
Monitor Evaluation
and Selection

Throughout the preceding chapters there has been an implicit assumption that the design of a raster graphics system is a straightforward, linear process—from source data to visual display. Source information is modeled and viewed to obtain display data which is mapped into a memory capable of supporting the required display refresh rate. Interface circuits are designed with sufficient bandwidth to deliver the pixel data to a monitor without loss of resolution or color/intensity information. All that remains, it would appear, is to select a particular monitor model which will meet the predetermined display requirements and also offer maximum benefits in terms of economy, reliability, and performance.

Unfortunately, it is not that simple. Except for brief comments in Chapter 2, Display Principles, little attention has been paid to the most important single element in a graphics system—the observer or operator. A fuller description of this "human interface" will be given in the next chapter, but any discussion on monitor evaluation and selection must take into account both the environment within which the system will operate and the requirements—and limitations—of the people who will be interacting with the system on an hourly, daily basis.

Futher complications and constraints are created by the nature of the monitor "industry." A review of the technical literature would indicate an almost infinite range of monitor sizes, types, and display capabilities. On closer examination, however, repetitive patterns become apparent, limiting the choice and forcing compromises which may require a reexamination of earlier design decisions. There may be a few specialized applications which can justify the costs of a "custom-built" CRT, but competitive pressures will force most system designers to take advantage of the economies offered by CRT's which have been optimized for the mass entertainment marketplace. Monitor manufacturers may be able to add valuable graphics-display enhancements (e.g., long-persistence phosphors, extended-life cathodes), but the fact remains that the cake under the frosting was originally designed for a non-graphics application. The monitor-selection process becomes, therefore, a matter of finding the closest fit to a design objective, with the certain knowledge that price/performance tradeoffs will be required.

ASPECT RATIO AND ORIENTATION

Until recently, raster graphics system designers have had exactly two choices in the selection of aspect ratios (display-screen width divided by height) and orientation (horizontal or vertical). They could choose either a 4:3 horizontal or a 3:4 vertical configuration. Rasters with any other aspect ratio, including 1:1, would have to fit within the limits set by the available monitors.

CRT monitors with 5:4, 4:5, and other full-screen aspect ratios are now offered in a limited number of sizes and models, allowing us to generalize the raster selection to one of three choices: a horizontal rectangle, a vertical rectangle, or a square. Each has its place, depending on the application, and the selection of the most suitable configuration represents one of the most fundamental decisions a systems designer has to make at the start of a design project. Display-memory architecture, interface circuitry, and almost all of the other monitor-evaluation parameters are, in fact, directly impacted by this choice.

The dominant orientation has been, and will probably continue to be, the horizontal display rectangle. It matches the panoramic view provided by the human binocular visual system and can therefore serve as a natural "window" on reality—as evidenced by the theatrical stage, motion-picture screen, painted landscape, engineering drawing, and television picture.

Vertically oriented displays also have their antecedents in the form of printed pages of text and the illustrations designed to accompany text. Western typography is most legible and compact when it is organized into vertical columns composed of short horizontal lines. (Long lines require extra spacing for legibility, and this reduces the number of words which can be contained on a page.)

Square displays have their roots in the charting of scientific and financial information. Given a choice, similar or identical scales (coordinate lines or circular arcs) should always be used to represent two or more variables. Any departure from this convention incurs the risk of a visual distortion of the data. From clocks to compasses to oscilloscopes, the square or circle within a square has remained a basic display configuration.

Aspect-ratio and orientation decisions depend, then, on the type of information being displayed. If the graphics consist of representational views, such as those created by a computer-aided-design system, a conventional horizontal orientation would normally be specified. If the displayed information consists primarily of text, or if the graphics are being designed to accompany text when reproduced in another form, a vertical orientation can make more effective use of the monitor screen. If charted data is being displayed, the decision will often be to create a square raster in the center of a conventional, horizontally oriented monitor screen.

RASTER-LINE ORIENTATION

There is no intrinsic reason why the raster on this conventional horizontal screen should consist of horizontal lines. The raster could be just as effectively "written" with vertical strokes. But this would result in a larger number of shorter lines—and a significant increase in the amount of time "wasted" by the need to return the electron beam to the starting edge before each line is traced. The horizontal-horizontal configuration minimizes the number of retrace strokes, allowing more time to scan the "active" lines as a percentage of the fixed refresh interval. The electron beam can scan at a slower rate, increasing the luminance of the display because more power is being delivered per unit area. The instantaneous data rate is also lower, which reduces the required bandwidth of the interface and monitor circuits and the readout rate of the display memory.

All of these benefits accrue to a vertically oriented display provided the raster lines are also scanned in a vertical direction (i.e., by turning a conventional monitor on its side). Such displays can be readily adapted to the generation of images, but they would require major restructuring of the text-oriented system architectures which could make maximum use of the vertical format. In most commercially available vertical-monitor systems, therefore, the raster lines are still scanned horizontally, from top to bottom.

The demands of this configuration on monitor performance can be impressive. One vertically oriented system, for example, scans (and retraces) 800 short raster lines at a full-frame refresh rate of 60 Hz. The horizontal-scan interval is only 20 microseconds, of which 25% is taken up by the retrace stroke. In order to display up to 8,000 characters on the screen, pulse rise/fall times have been reduced to 4 nanoseconds, compared to a conventional 20 nanoseconds. To provide this response, monitor circuits have been designed with a 100-MHz bandwidth—five to ten times the normal requirement.

A square raster centered on a horizontally oriented screen would nominally represent a midpoint between the horizontal and vertical configurations. The raster lines are shorter, as in the case of a vertical display. The number of lines remains the same as those of a horizontal display. But these comparisons are misleading. Customary practice is to "squeeze in" the sides of the raster without changing the horizontal-raster timing relationships. There is no increase, therefore, in the percentage of time taken up by the retrace strokes. In fact, the shorter lines mean that the scanning speed is actually reduced, increasing the luminance and reducing the required monitor bandwidth. We will be using the centered-square configuration as our model raster in the following discussions on display size and resolution.

SCREEN SIZE

CRT monitors are available with nominal screen diagonals ranging from an inch to over 25 inches. The selection of an appropriate monitor screen size becomes, therefore, another fundamental decision which the systems designer must make. Screen size affects the interaction with the operator, the perceived resolution of the display, the required bandwidth of the monitor and interface circuits, and ultimately the size (and cost) of the display memory. In the case of display memory, for example, there is no value in storing data for more pixels than can be displayed—or discerned—on the monitor screen.

Internally, a monitor CRT is a projection-type display device. The amount of information which can be theoretically projected onto the CRT faceplate remains constant, independent of screen size. The principal advantage to be gained by increasing the size is a broader spatial distribution of the display detail. Conversely, small screen sizes tend to compact the image elements, with a likelihood of overlapping and loss of information when a lower limit is exceeded (see below).

The "human factors" which should be considered in the selection of an appropriate screen size are summarized in the next chapter. Most of these point toward the use of the smallest size that will allow the required information to be clearly "read" by the user. Small-screen luminances are generally higher, and the screen comes closer to matching the operator's field of maximum visual acuity. Small-screen monitors also offer advantages in terms of economy, ease of packaging, and extended cathode life due to the lower electron-beam current required for adequate display luminance. On the negative side, phosphor life may be significantly lower if the electron-beam density is elevated. With the same electron-beam current in both cases, the useful life of a 9-inch monitor may be less than a fifth as long as that of a 20-inch monitor.

Figure 9–1 indicates the maximum raster display areas obtainable on a range of monitor sizes. Monitor specification sheets often give "pic-

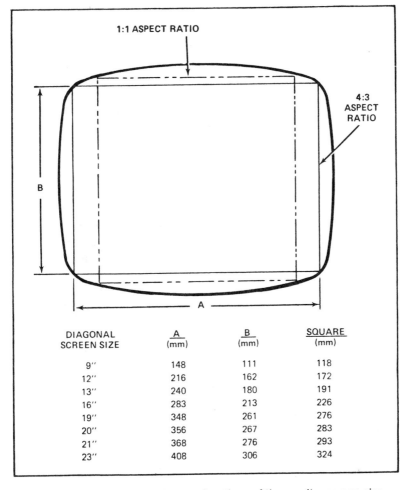

DIAGONAL SCREEN SIZE	A (mm)	B (mm)	SQUARE (mm)
9"	148	111	118
12"	216	162	172
13"	240	180	191
16"	283	213	226
19"	348	261	276
20"	356	267	283
21"	368	276	293
23"	408	306	324

Figure 9–1. Raster dimensions as functions of the monitor screen size.

ture" (i.e., television) dimensions which must be adjusted downward when, as is usually the case, all four corners of a graphics image must be clearly visible. The millimeter values given in Figure 9-1 are, on average, 10% less than the usual specification-sheet dimensions. The square-raster values take advantage of the slightly oval shape of most monitor bezels and are 6% higher than the vertical dimensions for 4:3 rasters.

DISPLAY RESOLUTION

Throughout the previous chapters, "resolution" has been defined by the number of pixels stored in display memory and transmitted to the monitor during each frame-refresh cycle. The bandwidth of the interface, for example, must be capable of preserving the "system" resolution established by the number of pixel-to-pixel signal transitions which could occur while each raster line is scanned. The same bandwidth considerations apply to the monitor circuits which process the display signal and drive the electron gun (or guns) of the monitor CRT. It is entirely possible, however, that a severe degradation in the system resolution can occur at the final display stage—if individual pixels can no longer be readily perceived by the operator.

Display resolution is determined almost entirely by dimensional mathematics. A square raster with 512 raster lines and 512 pixels per line contains a total of 262,144 pixels. Each pixel area is, in effect, a square with sides measuring approximately 0.002 of the raster height or width. When displayed on a 19-inch monitor, the pixels would measure 0.54 millimeter on each side. The same pixels on a 13-inch monitor would have side dimensions of only 0.37 millimeter.

The pixel images on the display screen are not, however, square. Instead, they are formed by an electron beam with, at best, a circular or slightly oval shape (depending on the position of the beam relative to the center of the screen). Moreover, the luminance generated by the beam has a Gaussian distribution, as shown in Figure 9-2. It is inevitable, then, that a certain amount of overlapping between pixel images will occur, especially if a further requirement is that each pixel area is to be "filled" with display luminance.

Overlapping is a benefit when images consist of solid areas or subtly changing intensities or colors. Figure 9-3 illustrates how a column of pixels can produce a relatively smooth luminous output across a group of raster lines. But the Gaussian spread of the electron beam creates major problems when sharp image transitions are required—as in the extreme case when graphic elements are to be separated by a single

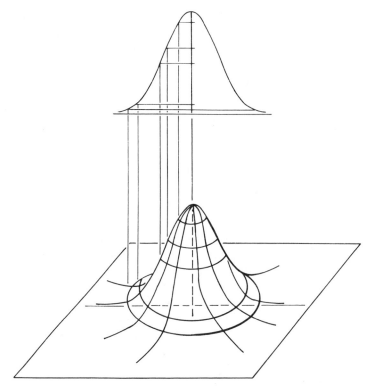

Figure 9-2. Gaussian distribution of electron-beam spot luminance. (Source: Reference 1)

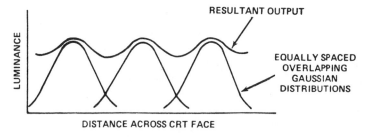

Figure 9-3. Effect of overlapping raster lines or pixel images. (Source: Reference 1)

pixel width. The Gaussian "skirts" of the pixels on each side would raise the luminance in the intervening area, reducing the contrast between image and background.

The loss of contrast from this effect is given a numerical value by the "modulation transfer function"—the ratio between maximum small-area (pixel, raster line) and large-area contrasts. If there is no loss of contrast due to overlapping, the MTF is 1.0, 100%, or zero dB. A 50% contrast loss (16 dB) is normally considered to be the limit for adequate monitor performance. Larger losses in contrast would have the effect of reducing the display resolution because individual pixels would be difficult to distinguish—even on close inspection.

The MTF can be improved, of course, by reducing the spot size of the electron beam. But this lowers the overall luminance of the display and may make the raster lines *too* distinguishable. A compromise is therefore required. Spot sizes, measured at the diameter of 50% maximum luminance, are generally set to approximately the same dimension as the raster-line spacing—which would be on the order of 0.5 and 0.3 millimeter for the 19-inch and 13-inch monitors described above. Smaller monitors would require correspondingly smaller spot sizes to maintain an equivalent MTF, and this eventually sets one of the lower limits on the extent to which the screen size can be reduced and still produce a crisp, high-resolution display. With 0.2 millimeters as a practical lower limit on spot size, the minimum square-raster dimensions for a 512-by-512 display would be on the order of 100 millimeters. For a 1024-by-1024 display, the minimum would be 200 millimeters—requiring at least a 13-inch monitor.

Display Filters

Contributing to the MTF loss—and the potential loss of display resolution—are the diffusing effects of secondary-electron emissions within the phosphor layer and the "halation" caused by reflections within the glass faceplate. Figure 9-4 shows how halation rings may form around each pixel location, again reducing the effective display contrast.

Fortunately, most of the steps taken to minimize the contrast-reducing effects of reflected ambient light—such as "etching" the faceplate or adding a filter—also lower the amount of contrast loss due to halation. Etching acts by diffusing the light at the glass-air interface. Normal practice is to bond a treated glass plate directly to the front surface of the CRT. The diffusing layer reduces the amount of light reflected back toward the phosphor. The displayed image is also slightly

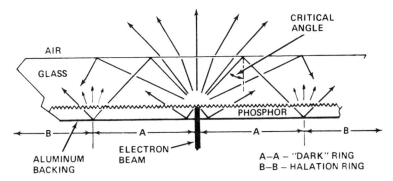

Figure 9-4. Halation ring formed by reflections within glass faceplate. (Source: Reference 1)

diffused, so etching represents a trade-off between two negative effects.

Filters, either laminated to the faceplate or mounted separately, act by simply absorbing a fraction of the light—both wanted and unwanted. Luminance generated by halation tends to leave the surface at an oblique angle and therefore follows a longer path through the filter layer. The same would be true of oblique ambient light. In addition, reflected ambient light must pass through the filter twice and is consequently attenuated twice as much as light emitted by the phosphor layer. But again a trade-off is involved. Filters reduce the display luminance and can also affect the display resolution.

A variety of filtering materials and processes are commercially available, often combined with such anti-reflection measures as vacuum-deposited optical coatings. Polarizing layers have proved particularly effective. In one instance, the "filter" is actually an assembly of miniature louvres which shade the screen from overhead light sources.

COLOR RESOLUTION

The preceding paragraphs provide general guidelines on the effects that screen size, spot size, halation, and ambient light have on display resolution. In the case of aperture-mask color monitors, however, another major factor must be taken into account: the "pitch" or distance between the aperture-mask holes or slots.

In principle, the resolution of a color monitor should equal that of the aperture openings (i.e., one pixel per aperture). Experience indicates, however, that significant improvements in the appearance of the display occur as the bandwidth of the monitor is increased far beyond the theoretical pixel-density limit set by the number of aperture openings. Other factors are at work, therefore, which need to be examined.

There is, for example, no synchronization (or registration) between the pixel locations and aperture-mask pattern. To avoid "missing" or low-luminance pixels it becomes necessary to increase the spot size so that at least two aperture openings are being continuously scanned. The result may be an electron-beam spot which is two or three times as large as the nominal pixel area.

The size of the aperture-mask pitch and the extent to which it potentially affects resolution are both functions of the type of color CRT. Four distinctly different types are now in use. The classical configuration is the delta-delta construction shown in Figure 9–5. The aperture holes in the metal mask form delta-shaped equilateral triangles, resulting in an interlaced pattern with offset holes in both the horizontal and vertical dimensions. The three electron guns are also mounted in a delta cluster. Ideally, the three beams coverge and crossover at the

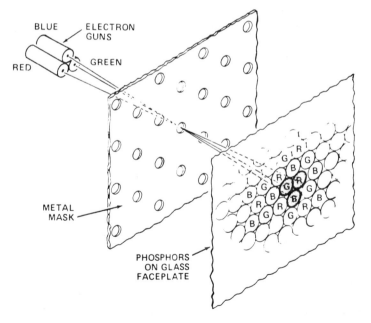

Figure 9–5. Delta-delta color CRT. Electron guns and aperture mask both have a delta configuration.

plane of the aperture mask. The geometry is arranged so that each beam impinges on one of three colored-phosphor dots and is "shadowed" from the other two. The result is a cluster of primary-color dots with a perceived color established at normal viewing distances by the relative amplitudes of the three electron-beam currents (see Appendix III). Less than 20% of the beam electrons pass through the holes; the balance are trapped by the metal mask. Very high beam currents are therefore required.

The pitch of a standard-resolution delta mask ranges from 0.66 millimeter for large-screen CRT's (over 20 inches) to 0.42 millimeter for miniature CRT's (less than 5 inches). At mid-range, the distance from hole to hole is approximately 0.60 millimeter. Interlacing reduces the vertical distance between rows of holes to only half the pitch dimension. In terms of spot size, however, the controlling factor is the horizontal column-to-column gap which equals the pitch times the cosine of 30° (0.7), or approximately 0.4 millimeters for an average monitor. The nominal spot size for the converging beams must therefore cover a diameter approaching 1.0 millimeter in order to assure full-luminance pixels.

One way to reduce the spot size would be to specify a "high-resolution" color monitor with four times the aperture density of a conventional monitor. The pitch of a high-resolution mask is approximately 0.31 millimeter, which reduces the horizontal column-to-column distance to only 0.22 millimeter. The spot size can thus be reduced to less than 0.5 millimeter—a value approaching that of a monochrome display—although the designer may choose, instead, to maintain a larger spot size—covering four or five aperture openings—to reduce the moiré effects which can occur when repetitive graphic-image patterns "beat" with the spatial frequency of the holes in the metal mask.

The high-resolution apertures have even smaller diameters than those of a conventional aperture mask. Even higher beam currents are therefore required to maintain display luminance. Convergence of the three beams must also be more precise.

Convergence problems created by the delta-delta arrangement can be reduced in turn, by using a precision in-line (PIL) electron-gun assembly instead of the conventional delta guns. Figure 9–6 shows the geometry of this PIL-delta configuration as it applies to both standard and high-resolution monitors. The beams from the three in-line guns are "self-converging," eliminating the need for complex convergence circuits and adjustment procedures. The dot pattern produced by the converging beams is also different—forming a slightly elongated oval. The pitch of the aperture mask remains exactly the same, however, so

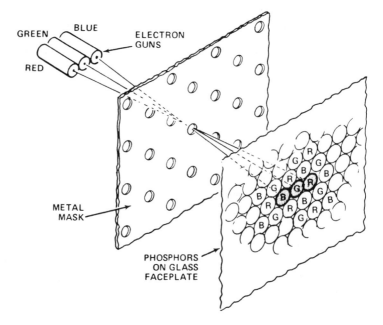

Figure 9–6. PIL-delta color CRT. In-line electron guns are combined with delta-type aperture mask.

there are no changes in the color resolution or the required spot diameters.

The in-line gun arrangement was first perfected for a different type of color CRT—fabricated with a slotted metal mask and vertical phosphor stripes on the CRT faceplate. Figure 9–7 shows this configuration. The bridges between slots are required to give the mask structural stability, but are sufficiently small so that resolution in the vertical direction is theoretically unaffected. By contrast, the horizontal pitch is on the order of 0.7 to 1.0 millimeter, requiring very large spot sizes to avoid blanked-out pixels. Counterbalancing this negative attribute are the high luminances which can be achieved at moderate beam currents. The slotted mask traps less than half of the beam electrons, compared to the 80% blocked by a delta mask.

Similar advantages and disadvantages apply to the proprietary design illustrated in Figure 9–8. The mask consists of stretched, end-supported metal strips, producing truly infinite vertical resolution. The horizontal pitch approaches 1.0 millimeter. The strips require the use of a cylindrical CRT faceplate. Another feature of the design is the "single-gun" structure with a single large-diameter focusing "lens" for all three electron beams.

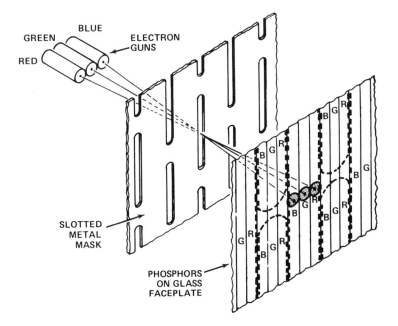

Figure 9-7. In-line electron guns combined with slotted aperture mask and vertical phosphor stripes.

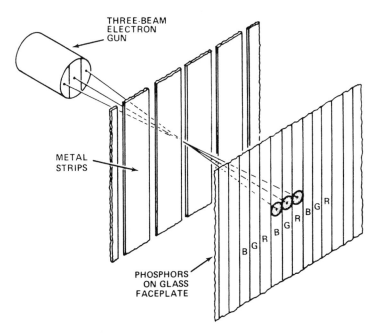

Figure 9-8. Single-lens, three-beam electron gun with a metal-strip mask and vertical phosphor stripes.

Color-Signal Resolution

Reviewing these details, we can see that every type of aperture mask requires a spot size that is much larger than the theoretical dimensions of the pixels being displayed. How, then, can the eye perceive individual pixels? How can we explain, in fact, the definite improvement in display appearance that occurs when the monitor bandwidth is increased to support a pixel density that exceeds even the aperture-opening density?

The answer lies in the human visual system. The nerve structure behind the retina serves to "sharpen" images far beyond the limits set by the eye's optical apparatus. Moreover, the processed data is transmitted immediately to the brain and stored separately from the images that precede and follow the current image. In effect, then, the Gaussian spread of the electron-beam spot is narrowed by the eye to a much smaller-diameter dot.

Moreover, only one pixel color or intensity is on a display at a time—never two simultaneous colors, side by side. The next pixel center is a measurable distance from the first, occurs at a later time, and is "stored" as a separate image. No overlapping in the conventional sense occurs, therefore, and the perceived resolution can at least approximate the resolution (bandwidth) of the color signal itself.

There is, however, an upper limit established by the speed of the eye-brain system. Empirical evidence indicates that at bandwidths above 70 megahertz, further improvements become marginal. Individual viewers and viewing conditions would affect the absolute limit—probably in the neighborhood of 100 megahertz.

All of this assumes, of course, that the "resolution" of the color signal has been preserved by the monitor amplification circuits. Figure 9-9 is a generalized block diagram of a monochrome monitor. An RGB monitor is essentially three such monitors with shared synchronization circuits and CRT. All processing of the three color signals is performed in parallel, from the input connectors to the three CRT gun assemblies. Clearly the critical factor is the bandwidth of the amplifier or amplifiers which increase each display signal to the CRT-drive level, typically 10 to 50 volts. From the discussion in Chapter 8, this bandwidth should be on the order of 20 MHz or more for most graphics applications.

A variety of ways are used to define this monitor specification. In addition to bandwidth, the manufacturer may state the minimum rise and fall times at the electron-gun interface—typically 20 to 40 nanoseconds—or the number of pixels which can be displayed along each raster line.

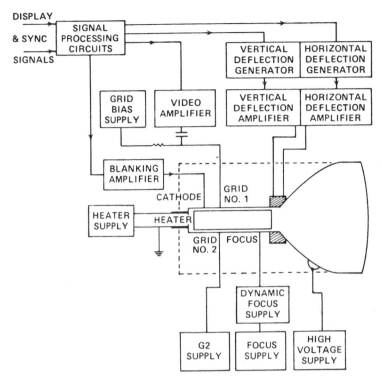

Figure 9-9. Basic block diagram, monochrome-monitor signal processing circuits.

Equivalent specifications are rarely given for monitors designed to process the encoded-color signals described in Chapter 8 and Appendix II. All of the color-encoding standards start with the requirement that the color information must be compressed within the limits imposed by the established broadcast channels. In the case of the NTSC standard, for example, the color information is used to modulate two subcarrier signals, one with a bandwidth of 1.3 MHz, the other with a bandwidth of 0.5 MHz. Most commercial monitors process the combined signal to produce two derived signals with equal bandwidths on the order of 1.0 MHz.

The effect is both to spread a lower maximum number of pixels along the raster line and to "soften" the color transitions between pixels. Vertical resolution is limited by the number of lines per frame dictated by the color-encoding standard. In practical terms the maximum pixel-by-pixel color resolution of a color-encoded raster—of any size or aspect ratio—would be 150-horizontal by 480-vertical pixels.

MONITOR ENHANCEMENTS

Both the CRT and the graphics-display CRT monitor are still evolving as commercial products. A variety of monitor enhancements should be evaluated, therefore, before a selection is made.

Many of these innovations relate to reliability and device life. The use of impregnated cathodes is an example. Every CRT will eventually "burn out," just like any other electron tube. Figure 9–10 illustrates how a reserve supply of barium compound can continuously refresh the surface of a porous tungsten cathode, allowing the CRT to be driven at very high current densities and still give thousands of hours of service.

Other enhancements relate more directly to performance and should be considered within the context of a specific application. The conventional CRT electron gun, for example, "crosses over" the electron beam to give the focusing elements a point source. A parallel-flow design increases the number of electrons directed at the CRT faceplate without a corresponding increase in the cathode "loading factor." Small spot sizes are somewhat more difficult to achieve, so the technique represents a trade-off between luminance and resolution.

Similar trade-offs apply to the choice of electrostatic or electromagnetic focusing and deflection. Figure 9–11 indicates that an all-electrostatic design would be preferred for systems requiring very fast scanning rates and modest resolution (spot size). An all-magnetic design reverses this order. Most raster-scan graphics monitors consequently use an electrostatic-focus, electromagnetic-deflection combination which represents a compromise between resolution and speed.

Manufacturers may also incorporate special circuitry into the design

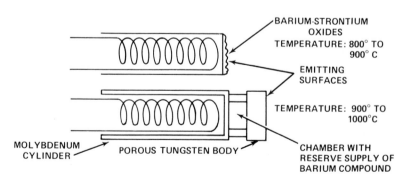

Figure 9–10. Conventional cathode compared with extended-life cathode. (Source: Reference 1)

FOCUS-DEFLECTION COMBINATIONS

DEFLECTION	FOCUS	CHARACTERISTICS	APPLICATION	RESOLUTION
ELECTROSTATIC	ELECTROSTATIC	HIGH SPEED MODERATE RESOLUTION	OSCILLOSCOPE	450 TO 500
MAGNETIC	ELECTROSTATIC	MODERATE TO HIGH RESOLUTION	TELEVISION COMPUTER GRAPHICS	700 TO 900
MAGNETIC	MAGNETIC	HIGHEST RESOLUTION	PROJECTION RECORDING	1600 TO 2000
ELECTROSTATIC	MAGENTIC	- -	NOT GENERALLY EMPLOYED	

Figure 9-11. Electrostatic and electromagnetic deflection/focus trade-offs. (Source: Reference 1)

of the monitor itself. One example is a "beam-current feedback" circuit which maintains the black level of the display (see Glossary) at a constant value despite CRT aging and component drift. The CRT beam current is sampled during each vertical retrace. Feedback adjustments are then made to the dc level of the display-signal amplifier to correct for any detected error.

CRT monitors are analog devices, subject to all the uncertainties which affect the performance of such devices. Enhancements like the beam-current feedback circuit help to make the monitor a stable dependable system component in the otherwise digital environment.

10

The Human Interface

We can assume that every computer system conceived by the human brain serves a human purpose—however abstract or indirect. In the case of a computer-based raster graphics system, the human interactions are immediate and direct. The principal purpose of a graphics system is to communicate information to a human observer. A secondary purpose, which may be equally important in the context of the application, is to facilitate the observer's response to the displayed information. The characteristics of the human "machine" become, therefore, major considerations in the design of a raster graphics system. In fact, because we can do so little to modify these characteristics, they are among the most important of all the factors which the system designer must take into account.

Nearly all of the major concerns addressed by this Handbook—the need for increased resolution, the avoidance of flicker, the benefits conveyed by color and animation—have little to do with information-processing technology. Instead, they relate directly to the way the human eye and brain "see." There would be, as a matter of fact, no reason for computer-based graphics if it weren't for the unique nature of the eye as a sensing organ.

In data-processing terms, the eye is a parallel input device. By contrast, the ear and mouth are serial input/output devices. If we glance at strange surroundings for a few seconds, then close our eyes, it might take a half hour to describe verbally what we have seen. Moreover, any listener would have to laboriously remember what we have said to reconstruct the scene as a mental image. A printed alphanumeric record—on paper or on a monitor screen—is an analog of the serial mouth-ear communication link. Yet we are forced to use our parallel-input eyes to enter the information. We must also remember what we have read in order to correlate the facts and establish interrelationships that would be clearly evident if we were able to "input" all of the information simultaneously.

A graphics representation does this for us. It returns our eyes to a parallel mode. But the effectiveness of the graphics display depends on the degree to which the graphics system designer takes advantage of the human eye's capabilities—and works within its limitations. In a very direct sense, then, the design of a raster graphics system must start with the design of the eye itself.

STRUCTURE OF THE EYE

Figure 10-1 shows a horizontal cross section of the human eye. The cornea acts as a highly transparent shield, with a refractive index of 1.376 (compared to the 1.00 refractive index of air). Directly behind the cornea, in the anterior chamber, is the aqueous. The aqueous supplies oxygen and other nutrients to the lens and is the vehicle for transporting waste away from the lens and cornea. The aqueous performs one other important function. It maintains an appropriate pressure within the eyeball. Without the accurate maintenance of pressure, cornea and lens fail to function properly. If too much pressure builds up, for example, glaucoma can result.

The iris contains muscles which control the opening to the lens. When a large amount of light reaches the lens, the muscles contract, narrowing the opening. When a small amount of light reaches the lens, the muscles dilate, broadening the opening to the eye. This activity

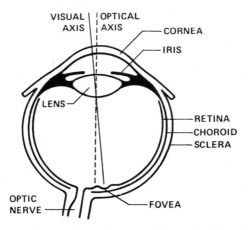

Figure 10-1. Horizontal cross-sectional view of the right eye.

helps to maintain the amount of light reaching the retina at a constant level.

In some animals focusing is accomplished by moving the retina nearer to or farther from the lens. In the human eye the refracting power of the lens is varied. The lens focuses the image on the retina by thickening or thinning its structure, depending on the closeness of the object.

In order for us to see nearby objects clearly (within 20 feet), three actions must occur. First the two eyes must "converge" on the object by turning slightly inward. For objects beyond 20 feet the sight lines are so nearly parallel that convergence is not necessary. The eyes must also constrict slightly, and the lens must thicken in order to alter the focal length. These three simultaneous actions are called "accommodation."

There is a limitation to the nearness an object can be and still be accommodated. This limit is known as the "near point" and varies in distance with age. (The "far point" is infinity.) At three years of age it is approximately 3 inches from the eye. At 40 years the distance has doubled to 6 inches. At 60 years it has extended to 16 inches.

The near point is of prime concern in the design of a graphics system in which the operator must manually interact with the screen. The screen must be near enough to be comfortably reached by an instrument held in the hand but far enough to be beyond the near point. While a distance of 10 to 12 inches from the operator's eyes to the screen would be appropriate for most people, a good many older operators would have difficulty.

A minimum of 16 to 18 inches should allow comfortable viewing by most operators. But the designer must also keep in mind the maximum arm reach of the shortest person. Again, comfort would dictate a reach in the range of 16 to 18 inches.

The retina (Figure 10-1) is the part of the eye that converts light energy to chemical energy. The retina is an extremely complex organ made up of 10 layers of cells. These layers can be broken down into four groups. The first two groups, the ganglion cells and the bipolar cells, are highly transparent, allowing light to pass through them. Light passes until it reaches the rods and cones where it is absorbed. It is here that the photochemical process takes place. Light that is not filtered out by the rods and cones is absorbed by the pigment epithelium.

The chemical energy produced by the rods and cones is transmitted to the bipolar cells. The bipolar cells in turn connect to the ganglion cells which contain the optic fibers. The optic fibers carry the signal to the brain. Considering that there are approximately 6 million cones and 120 million rods in the retina and only one million optic fibers, an extensive amount of "data processing" is accomplished within the eye—before the information is processed by the brain.

COLOR DETECTION

Color can greatly influence what we see. It can create moods, call our attention to specific details, and help us to view complex information in an orderly manner. But how do we see color?

There are several theories that have been proposed to answer that question. The most widely accepted view is based on two experimentally established facts:

1. The cones, concentrated in a small area of the retina called the "fovea," only 0.25 millimeter in diameter, are the receptors for color. Rods, which make up the bulk of the cells in the peripheral areas of the retina, can sense only gray-scale intensity.
2. From the hues red, green and blue, all colors can be derived.

Based on these two facts, an assumption is made that there are three types of cones, each containing a different pigment which chemically responds to red, green or blue light frequencies. An object's color is perceived by the degree to which each of the three types of cones is excited by the light entering the eye. The method used by a color-CRT monitor to generate a full range of hues and saturations—by modulating the intensity of red, green, and blue phosphors—directly matches, therefore, the way our eye and brain register the sensation we call "color." Fuller descriptions of these relationships are given in Chapter 2 and Appendix III.

EYE MOVEMENTS

Movement of the eye occurs for three reasons:

- Voluntary
- Reflex—from visual stimuli
- Reflex—from non-visual stimuli

Before discussing the types of eye movement, let's first briefly examine how the eye moves. Cranial nerves send electrical impulses down motor nerves to six muscles controlling the movement of the eye. These six muscles are arranged so that they provide movement to the eye in every possible direction: upward, downward, to each side, and in all four oblique directions.

The cranial nerves are stimulated to action by one of the three reasons listed above. Voluntary movement occurs when we make a point to look at a certain thing or in a certain direction. For example, in reading this book we voluntarily direct our eyes to the page and to each word. (Some involuntary actions can also take place at the same time.) A quite different type of voluntary movement occurs when our eyes are following a moving object. When a person is scanning a static image, such as this page, the eyes move in a short, jerky manner. The movements, called "saccades," last 1/30 to 1/50 of a second with intervening pauses of 1/3 to 1/5 of a second. It is during the pauses that we actually read. When a person is watching a moving object, the eyes move smoothly if the object itself is moving below a threshold rate of approximately 30 degrees per second. If the object moves at a more rapid rate, the eye reverts to the saccade mode.

In reflex eye movement caused by visual stimuli, the eye moves involuntarily to an object. There can be several causes for this. A moving object in a field of non-moving objects will cause the eyes to focus on the moving object. A brightly colored or high-luminance object against a dull or dark background will have the same result. Advertisers have made use of this knowledge for years, directing a reader's eyes across an advertisement in a predetermined pattern. (This will be covered later in the chapter when we discuss graphics composition.)

VISUAL ACUITY

The "resolution" of a graphics system has been frequently used to qualify its performance. Briefly, we have concluded that the greater the number of horizontal lines and pixels per line, the "better" the resolution. However, as we study the eye it becomes clear that what we are saying in part is that the closer together the lines and pixels are, the less able we are to discern between them.

There is a definite, measurable separation distance below which two lines or spots will merge in our eyes into one line or spot. This distance is ultimately based on the physical spacing between cones within the fovea area of the retina.

"Acuity"—the ability to distinguish details—is a function, therefore, of both the focusing ability and spatial structure of the eye. Acuity varies widely, therefore, from person to person, and under different viewing conditions. Acuity decreases, for example, with decreased brightness and contrast.

The limited visual acuity of the human eye—on the order of one-half to one minute of arc—actually works for us in a number of cases. When viewing raster-scanned images, it allows us to merge hundreds of thousands of pixels into one, smoothly shaded image. It permits us to see a stair-stepped diagonal line on a monitor as a smooth, straight line. In hardcopy images it allows us to integrate thousands of multicolored dots into a single color.

VISUAL RETENTION

Another subject that has been frequently discussed throughout this Handbook is "flicker." The image displayed by a raster-scan monitor must be refreshed at a rate above a threshold level to avoid an annoying, fatiguing on-off flicker.

The factors that establish this "critical flicker frequency" are complex and only partly understood. They involve both the chemistry of the receptor cells and the neuron architecture of the retina. For our purposes, however, two experimentally derived facts are of paramount importance. The first is that the critical fusion frequency or "flicker threshold" is a function of the luminance of the image. As noted in Chapter 2, the higher the luminance of the image, the higher the threshold frequency. The second fact is that flicker is also an area phenomenon. Interlaced raster lines can appear flicker-free, even though individual lines are flickering.

FIELD OF VISION

As rods and cones progress in distance from the fovea, the space between them becomes greater. In our discussion on resolution above, the point was made that the distance between receptive cells determines the limit of visual acuity. It follows then, that the further from the fovea that an image is received, the less acute our perception becomes. The principal purpose of this "peripheral vision" is simply to notify us of unusual movements or light sources on which we should focus our attention.

It is evident from Figure 10-1 that we can focus on just a small spot at any given moment. Everything else in our field of vision is a blur. And the farther from the center of focus, the more blurred the image becomes.

This information should be considered when designing an interactive graphics system. In applications in which the operator must manually interact directly with the monitor screen (e.g., with a lightpen) or where the screen must be very close for other reasons, such as viewing fine detail, the effective field of view will be very small —independent of the size of the screen. The implication is that there is a limit to any advantage gained by a larger screen. Moreover, the number of lines and pixels per inch increases as the screen becomes smaller, enhancing the visual resolution. The lower total light output from the smaller surface also reduces the flicker threshold.

If, however, the application dictates the use of a large-screen monitor, it is important to keep in mind that images away from the concentration point of the operator will not be easily seen. Images at the borders of the monitor may be easily missed, particularly if the operator's attention is concentrated at the center of the screen. One solution is to move the monitor further from the eye—substituting a joystick, for example, instead of a lightpen for operator interactions.

VIEWING DISTANCE

Of course, in instances where the monitor is used solely as an output device, there is no strict limitation of any kind on the viewing distance. Yet certain guidelines should be followed, particularly if the monitor is to be viewed for long periods of time, such as in proofreading or drafting applications. If the letters and other graphic elements are large enough, they can be read at any reasonable distance. But most individuals are more comfortable when the reading material is within an arm-length distance.

On the other hand, in applications where we would like to view the entire screen in a single glance, such as in process-control monitoring, the screen should be far enough away to allow good visual acuity over the entire surface.

VIEWING ANGLE

As the viewing position progresses further from the monitor, the angle at which the surface is viewed becomes more critical. When the operator is viewing the monitor from a nearby position, a simple movement of the head will narrow the angle. When viewing is from a greater distance, the operator may have to walk several feet to obtain a more direct view.

Objectionable distortions begin to take place at horizontal angles beyond 30°. At 45° the distortion may become critical in applications where line direction and relative spacing must be observed. Beyond 45°, distortion is objectionable in any application. Consideration must also be given to the vertical angle at which the operator views the monitor. Generally any angle beyond 30° above the horizontal plane of the operator's eyes will cause viewing discomfort.

GRAPHICS COMPOSITION

The designer (and user) of a graphics system should be concerned not only with the content of the information displayed but also with its form. By following simple graphics-composition techniques, the ability of the viewer to perceive and understand the displayed information can be significantly enhanced. Composition techniques can be used, for example, to direct the viewer's eyes from one point on the monitor screen to another. They can also be employed to separate elements on a screen, or to call the viewer's attention to certain elements of information.

Earlier in this chapter we discussed how the eye moves and what causes us to focus our attention on certain visual details. If we relate these facts to graphics displays we can establish a few basic rules about composition. Without other influence, a person with a Western cultural background will automatically start at the upper left of the screen, move to the right and progress in a clockwise direction. This is particularly true if the screen is filled with text or if it has several small illustrations of equal "weight."

Weight in this context is the relative impact an element has on the eye. Size, brightness, and color all contribute to an image's weight or impact. In Figure 10–2a the elements are of equal size and brightness, so the eye goes immediately to the upper left element. In Figure 10–2b the eye travels to the upper box. In Figure 10–2c it shifts to the lower right box. In Figure 10–2d, the eye will generally start at the large box at the top and then move immediately to the smaller but "heavier" box in the lower left corner.

The rule, then, is to give the greatest weight to the element to be seen first, with lower degrees of weight to the elements that should be viewed next. The movement can be assisted by keeping in mind the direction the eye would automatically take if not prompted by the graphics design.

DO'S AND DON'TS OF GRAPHICS COMPOSITION

Crowding. It is not necessary to fill the entire screen with information. Save information for the next image. A screen crowded with information tires the viewer just by its appearance. It also makes it difficult to

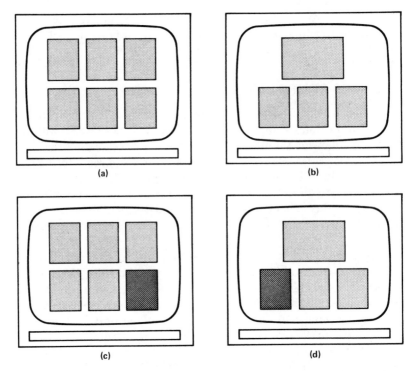

Figure 10-2. Use of graphical "weighting" to guide the viewer's attention. (Source: Reference 4)

follow the intended pathway for the eyes. If there is too much information on a screen, the eyes have difficulty sorting it out and the viewer
feels confused.

"Black space" on the other hand can work for the graphics designer.
It has as much significance as text or illustrations. It provides a contrast to them and can be used to give the eyes direction of movement
and rest. One final word about crowding. Do not crowd the text
around the illustration. Give it breathing room. This sets it off and
gives it greater importance.

Balance. Balance is giving each element of the image its proper
weight and size so that, together, all the elements form a pleasing appearance. It is, of course, highly subjective.

Partitioning. When dividing the screen into separate partitions for
multiple images, do not use identically equal parts. For example, if the
screen is to be divided into two parts, make one side bigger than the
other. Precise uniformity tends to give the image an overall dull feel-

ing. This can be counteracted by "unbalancing" each half but this is strictly a second choice.

Text. If the image contains a great deal of text it is advisable to break the text into several short paragraphs. Space between paragraphs, or indented paragraphs, are also helpful. A large block of text repels the viewer. The length of the lines in the text should also be considered. A general rule of thumb is that a line should not contain more than 60 characters. If the type is so small that more characters will fit on the screen, use either wider margins or multiple columns.

"Leading"—the vertical distance between successive lines—is another aspect that should be carefully considered. If the lines are too close, they interfere with each other and the text is difficult to read. If the lines are too far apart, the text requires excessive space and the lines again become more difficult to read. Generally a vertical distance of slightly more than the height of a small letter is an acceptable compromise.

A decision must also be made on whether to use all capital letters, upper and lower case, or all lower case. If there are more than just a few words, use upper and lower case titles. All capitals can be imposing, but very difficult to read.

Type Style. Type styles can be divided into two categories: serif and sans-serif (without serif). Serifs are fine lines that finish off the main strokes of letters. In general, serif letters provide greater contrast to each other and are therefore easier to read. They also generate more display luminance and therefore have greater weight. Most magazines, newspapers and books which require a great deal of reading use serif type styles. Sans-serif styles are of relatively recent origin and are, in general, evenly weighted. Due to the lack of contrast they are somewhat more difficult to read than serif letters. However, they are considered to be "stronger" and more "technical." The important points to remember about the use of type are that the selected type style should provide good readability and that once a style is chosen, it should be used consistently throughout a graphics-display project.

Shapes. When using shapes, make them perfect. Do not make a block almost square. Make it truly square. If two lines are meant to be parallel, make them truly parallel. Nothing can cause an illustration to appear more unprofessional than "untrue" shapes.

Graphs and Charts. Graphs and charts can take a variety of forms. Their principal functions are to *relate* and *compare* data, indicating trends, for example, as a function of time or some other variable. Of the basic types of charts, the line graph provides the feeling of a trend more rapidly and accurately than any type of bar chart. A horizontal bar chart is, in fact, relatively difficult to read with any degree of accuracy.

Color. Color is an excellent attention-getter. A small spot of color on a bland background will immediately draw the viewer's attention to it, no matter how small the spot may be. A bright color against soft colors has the same effect. A colored heading, for example, can lead the eye into a block of text. Color can also help to give direction to the eye, moving it in the desired direction.

By varying background colors, color can be used to separate image elements. Color can also provide a converse effect, helping to integrate separate images.

Color "codes" permit the viewer to relate certain shades to certain meanings throughout a series of graphs, helping the viewer to "read" the graphs more quickly and easily, with greater understanding.

Color can invoke certain attitudes and feelings—depending in part on cultural conditioning. Red and orange are generally viewed as warm "foreground" colors, blue as a cool "background" color. Green and yellow seem to be indifferent.

Color combinations take on different hues and meaning. When red, a foreground color, is used with blue, a background color, maximum depth is achieved. Gray alongside red will appear greenish. Alongside green it will appear reddish. Green appears cool when surrounded by yellow but warm when surrounded by blue.

To make colors stand out best, they should be placed against white—except for yellow, which can barely be seen. Only a few colors, such as yellow or white, stand out well against black.

FATIGUE

Eye fatigue is a serious problem in situations where the viewer must stare constantly at a monitor screen. The eye must continuously accommodate for the close-in vision.

Low resolution and visible flicker will rapidly bring on fatigue. It is absolutely imperative that a high resolution, no-flicker monitor be used in applications calling for constant viewing. Anything less will seriously curtail the effectiveness of the operator.

There are several other ways to avoid eye fatigue. The location of the monitor is an important factor. If the distance from the viewer is too great, the operator will have difficulty focusing on the image details; too near, and the eye movement necessary to scan the screen will cause fatigue.

The angle of the monitor to the axis of the eye is also an important factor. As noted earlier, the vertical viewing angle should not exceed 30 degrees above the horizontal plane of the eye under any conditions. For continuous viewing the angle should be horizontal or downward. The horizontal angle from the axis of the eye should also be kept as near to zero as possible.

Eye fatigue can be reduced by putting graphics composition techniques to work:

- Give the eye a clear pathway to follow. Do not make it wander over the screen, wondering where to go next.
- Allow ample breathing room between elements. Do not make the eye work to separate them.
- Exercise care in color combinations. Some combinations will make the eye work very hard while others are quite harmonious. Clashing colors are excellent when used to draw our attention but are difficult to look at for any length of time.

Ambient light can have a direct effect on fatigue. Too much lighting can wash out the image and cause strain. A room that is too dark can cause a severe contrast between the dark room and bright screen, increasing eye strain. Sharp glare of any kind should be avoided.

In a number of applications, such as process control, continuous monitoring of the screen may be necessary in order to guard against potentially dangerous conditions. The operator can be relieved of this arduous task by providing an audible signal to attract his attention. This has the double benefit of freeing the operator for other assignments. Visual signals may also be given, but they should not be out of the range of a 30° cone subtended on the eye. If flashing signals are used, no other flashing lights should be on or near the screen. A dark background should be used to help the signal light to stand out.

MANUAL CONTROLS

The hand is the primary "interactive device" at the human interface. It is the hand (or fingers) that passes the brain impulses to the computer input via a keyboard, joystick, or digitizer tablet.

Finger movement provides the most dexterous movement of the hand/arm system. The fingers, however, provide the least strength and are least able to move distances. The arm, of course, is very strong and has the greatest sweep of movement but is the least dexterous.

Interactive controls can be designed so that strength and sweep-of-movement are not factors. Precise movement is an inherent need when a cursor must be positioned to within a pixel distance. It stands to reason, therefore, to design the controls for finger manipulation. To achieve this goal it may be necessary to provide hand rests so that only fingers move when manipulating a joystick or other input device.

Consideration should also be given to the movement ratio of the joystick to the cursor on the monitor. A tradeoff between speed and accuracy must usually be made. If speed and accuracy are both critical, but not required simultaneously, a method for changing the ratio may be worthwhile.

POSITION AND LOCATION OF CONTROLS

Keyboards, joysticks, and digitizer tablets must be located within easy reach of the operator seated at a console. The operator should not be required to stretch his arms or shift his gaze from the monitor. To facilitate the accuracy of cursor movement, the elbow should be allowed to bend in a restful position, putting little or no strain on the arm.

The keyboard should be placed directly in front of the monitor so that the operator can view the screen while he works the keyboard. Ideally, it should be placed at standard typewriter height.

If the operator is forced to stretch for the joystick, perhaps causing him to view the screen at an angle, accuracy will be severely impaired. He will also tire quickly. Single-hand controls should be movable whenever possible to allow use by both right- and left-handed persons.

Keyboards and keypads should resemble typewriter and adding machine keyboards as closely as possible. The designer should take advantage, too, of other learned factors. Our culture has conditioned us to accept red as the color implying danger or "stop." Green implies "go," yellow, "caution." It can only cause confusion and create errors to attempt to override these and other natural impulses. With a joystick, the instinct would be to associate forward movement with "up," backward, with "down."

The operator is an integral part of an interactive graphics system—contributing directly to its efficiency, reliability, and accuracy. The entire system design should reflect this fact.

References

1. Tannas, Lawrence E., Jr. *Flat-Panel Displays*. New York: Van Nostrand Reinhold Co., 1984.
2. Sherr, Sol. *Electronic Displays*. New York: John Wiley & Sons, Inc., 1979.
3. SIGGRAPH, *Status Report of the Graphic Standards Planning Committee*. Computer Graphics, Volume 13, Number 3, Association for Computing Machinery, New York, 1979.
4. Van Deusen, Edmund. *Computer Videographics: Color, Composition, Typography*, CC Exchange, P.O. Box 1251, Laguna Beach, CA, 1981.
5. Kelly, K. L. Color Designations for Lights. *Journal of the Optical Society of America 33:*627–632 (1943).
6. MacAdam, D. L. Maximum Attainable Luminance Efficiency of Various Chromaticities. *Journal of the Optical Society of America* **49:**120 (1950).
7. MacAdam, D. L. Visual Sensitivities to Color Differences in Daylight. *Journal of the Optical Society of America* **32:**247 (1942).

Appendix I
Glossary of Terms

Accommodation—Adjustment of the focus and binocular angle of the eyes for a given viewing distance.

Achromatic Region—The area of a chromaticity diagram in which acceptable "white" reference points can be located.

Acknowledgement—Output to the operator of a logical input device indicating that a trigger has fired.

Adaptation—Adjustment of the pupil aperture and light-sensing sensitivity of the eye-brain system to a given ambient luminance level.

Angstrom Unit—A wavelength measure equal to one ten-billionth of a meter. Ten angstrom units equal one nanometer.

Alychne—In color diagrams, the straight line which represents hypothetical colors of zero luminance.

Aspect Ratio—The ratio of width to height of a display surface. The standard television aspect ratio is 4:3.

Aspects of Primitives—Ways in which the appearance of a graphic primitive can vary. In GKS, aspects are controlled either directly by primitive attributes, or indirectly through a bundle table. Primitives inside segments have aspects controlled through the segment containing them, e.g., highlighting.

Attribute—A particular property that applies to a display element (primitive) or a segment. Examples: highlighting, character height.

Auto Balance—A system for detecting and automatically adjusting for errors in color alignment in the white, gray, and black areas of a display.

Automatic Brightness Control—A system for controlling the brightness of a display as a function of the ambient light.

Automatic Pedestal Control—A system which adjusts the pedestal height of a composite display signal as a function of the input or any other specified parameter.

Back Porch—The portion of a composite display signal which lies between the trailing edges of a horizontal sync pulse and the corresponding blanking pulse.

Barrel Distortion—A distortion that makes a displayed image appear to bulge outward on all four sides.

Beam—A concentrated, unidirectional flow of electrons or other energy.

Beam-Current Feedback—A system which maintains a constant black level by sampling the electron-beam current during each vertical retrace and adjusting the dc level of the display-signal amplifier to correct for any error.

Black Body—A radiator of uniform temperature whose radiant flux in all parts of the spectrum is the maximum obtainable from any radiator at the same temperature, and which absorbs all radiant energy that impinges on it.

Black-Body Locus—On a CIE diagram, the location of the colors produced by a black body as the temperature increases from approximately 1,000°K to infinity.

Black Compression—The reduction in gain at those levels corresponding to dark areas in a display as compared to the gain at the mid-range light level. Also called black saturation.

Black Level—The display-signal level corresponding to a specified limit for black peaks.

Black Negative—A display signal in which the polarity of the voltage corresponding to black is negative with respect to the voltage which corresponds to white.

Black Peak—The maximum excursion of the display signal in the black direction.

Blanking—The process of decreasing (or increasing) the display-signal level so that no visible retrace will appear on the display screen.

Blanking Level—The level of a composite display signal which separates the range containing display information from the range containing synchronizing information. Also called the pedestal level, or blacker-than-black.

Blanking Signal—A sequence of recurrent blanking pulses related in time to the scanning process.

Bleeding White—A condition in which white display areas appear to flow irregularly into black areas.

Blooming—Regions of a CRT display where brightness is excessive due to an enlargement of the spot size and halation of the phosphor surface.

Breezeway—The portion of the back porch between the trailing edge of the sync pulse and the start of the color burst.

Bridging Amplifier—An amplifier for bridging an electrical circuit without introducing any apparent change in the performance of the circuit.

Brightness—A psycho-physiological attribute of visual perception in which a source appears to emit or reflect more or less light. Its psycho-physical, photometric equivalent is luminance.

Bundle Index—In GKS, an index into a bundle table for a particular output primitive. It defines the workstation-dependent aspects of the primitive.

Bundle Table—A workstation-dependent table associated with a particular type of primitive. Entries in the table specify all the workstation-dependent aspects of the primitive. In GKS, bundle tables exist for the following primitives: polyline, polymarker, text and fill area.

Candle Power—Luminous intensity expressed in candelas.

CCIR—Abbreviation for Consultative Committee, International Radio. Used to identify an international standard for composite monochrome display signals.

Cell Array—A GKS primitive consisting of a rectangular grid of equal-size rectangular cells, each having a single color. The cells do not necessarily map one-to-one with pixels.

CIE—Abbreviation for the Commission Internationale de l'Eclairage, formerly referred to as the International Commission on Illumination (ICI).

Charge-Coupled Device (CCD)—A self-scanning semiconductor array that utilizes MOS technology, surface storage, and information transfer by digital shift register techniques.

Choice Device—A GKS logical input device providing a non-negative integer defining one of a set of alternatives.

Chroma—A dimension of the Munsell color system which corresponds most closely to saturation.

Chroma Control—The control on a color monitor which regulates the saturation of colors.

Chroma Detector—Detects the absence of chrominance information at the input of a color encoder. The chroma detector automatically deletes the color burst from the color-encoder output when the absence of chrominance is detected.

Chrominance—The colormetric difference (dominant wavelength and purity) between any color and a reference "white" of equal luminance. In three-dimensional CIE color space, chrominance is a vector which lies in a plane of constant luminance.

Chrominance Primary—One of the two encoded-color primaries which determine the hue and saturation of a displayed color.

Chrominance Signal—That portion of an encoded-color display signal which contains the color information.

Chromaticity—The color quality of light which is defined by its dominant wavelength and purity (see Chrominance).

Chromaticity Coefficient—The ratio of any one of the chromaticity values of a three-component color to the sum of the three values (also called chromaticity or trichromatic coordinate).

Chromaticity Diagrams—Any plane diagram formed by plotting one of the three chromaticity coefficients against another. All chromaticity diagrams can be translated from one to another, provided that four points on the plane are identified for both diagrams.

Chromaticity Value—The scalar value of any one component of a three-component color (also called a tristimulus value). The unit value of each component is the amount of that component added to the other two components to produce a reference "white."

Chromatopsia—An abnormal state of vision in which colorless objects appear in color.

Clamping—A process that establishes a fixed reference level at the beginning of each raster line.

Clipping—In computer graphics, removing parts of display elements that lie outside a given boundary, usually a window or viewpoint.

Clipping—In television, the shearing off of the peaks of a signal. For a display signal, this may affect either the white or black peaks. For a composite display signal, the sync pulses may also be affected.

Coarse Chrominance Primary—The color-encoded chrominance primary transmitted in a narrower bandwidth.

Color Burst—A burst of chrominance subcarrier on the back porch of a composite color-encoded signal.

Color-Coordinate Transformation—The computation of the chromaticity values of a color in terms of one set of primaries from those of the same color in another set of primaries.

Color Contamination—An error of color rendition due to incomplete separation of the color components of a display.

Color Contrast—The ratio of the luminance values of two colors.

Color Data—The programmed values which determine the amplitudes of the signal which drive a color display or recording device.

Color-Difference Signal—An encoded-color value which, when added to the luminance signal, produces a signal representative of one of the chromaticity values of the transmitted color.

Color Dilution—A reduction in the saturation (purity) of a color by the addition of white light.

Color Encoder—A device which produces an encoded-color signal from separate red, green, and blue color inputs.

Color Edging—Extraneous colors appearing at the edges of colored images.

Color Fringing—Spurious colors introduced into a display by field-to-field changes in the position of displayed images.

Color-Mixture Data—Synonymous with chromaticity values, the preferred term.

Color Purity—A psycho-physical measurement of the degree to which a color is free of white light. Its psycho-physiological equivalent is saturation. The term is also used to define the absence of color contamination in the operation of a three-color CRT display.

Color Saturation—A psycho-physiological measurement of the degree to which a color appears to be free of white light.

Color Table—A workstation-dependent table in which the entries specify the values of the red, green, and blue intensities defining a particular color.

Color Temperature—The temperature to which a black body must be heated to produce a color matching that of the source.

Color Threshold—The luminance level below which color is no longer discernible. The level varies for different colors.

Color Triangle—Typically an equilateral triangle with apexes representing red, green and blue primaries. Sometimes called a Maxwell triangle. A non-equilateral triangle can also be drawn on a CIE chromaticity diagram to represent the range of chromaticities obtainable as additive mixtures of any three primaries.

Colorimeter—A device for comparing and specifying colors.

Colorimetric Purity—The relative luminances of the spectrum and "white" components of a color (see Color Purity and Excitation Purity).

Complementary Color—A color which, when combined with another color, produces a reference "white" (black, gray, or white).

Complementary Wavelength—The wavelength of a single-frequency light which produces a reference "white" (black, gray, or white) when combined with a sample color.

Comb Filter—A multiple-bandpass filter. Used to preserve the luminance component of an encoded-color display signal.

Composite Color Signal—A color display signal which includes blanking and synchronizing signals and color burst.

Composite Color Sync—A signal which includes all the sync signals, plus the color-burst reference signal in its proper time relationship.

Composite Display Signal—A blanked display signal combined with all of the appropriate synchronizing signals.

Contrast—The ratio between the maximum and minimum luminance values of a display.

Contrast Control—A manual gain control for a display monitor. It affects both luminance and contrast.

Convergence—The intersection of the three electron beams of an aperture-mask color CRT tube at the plane of the aperture mask.

Coordinate Graphics—Computer graphics in which display images are generated from display commands and coordinate data.

Correlated Color Temperature—On a CIE diagram, the closest point on the black-body locus, as measured in the direction of least perceptible color difference.

Critical Flicker Frequency—The minimum number of alterations per second of two different visual stimuli (luminance, hue, or saturation) which will produce a constant effect, as if from a single invariable stimulus.

Current Position—The Core System values that define the current drawing location in world coordinates. It is set to the origin of the world coordinate system at Core System initialization.

Cyan—The hue sensation evoked by radiations with a dominant wavelength of approximately 494 nanometers. The complement of cyan is red.

dB (Decibel)—A measure of the ratio of two signals. The dB value is $20 \times \log_{10}$ of a voltage or current ratio or $10 \times \log_{10}$ of a power ratio.

DC Restoration—The re-establishment of the dc and low-frequency components of a display signal which have been suppressed by ac coupling. The amount of restoration is usually established by sampling the display signal at a time when its level represents a known luminance value.

Decoder—Circuitry which transforms an encoded-color signal into separate red, green, and blue signals.

Device Coordinate (DC)—A coordinate expressed in a coordinate system that is device-dependent. In GKS, DC units are meters on a device capable of producing a precisely scaled image. Appropriate workstation-dependent units otherwise apply.

Device Coordinate System—A device-dependent coordinate system whose coordinates are typically in integer units (e.g., raster lines and pixels).

Device Driver—The device-dependent part of a host-computer graphics software package. The device driver generates a device-dependent output and handles all device-dependent interactions with the host-computer software and hardware.

Device Space—The space defined by the addressable points of a display device.

Dichromatic Vision—A form of defective color vision in which all colors can be matched by a mixture of only two stimuli. The spectrum is seen as two regions of different hues, plus a colorless band.

Display Device—A device (for example, refresh display, storage tube display, or plotter) on which display images can be represented.

Display Element—A basic graphic element or primitive that can be used to construct a display image. Examples: polyline, polymarker, text.

Display Image—A collection of display elements or segments that are represented together at any one time on a display surface.

Display Space—That portion of the device space corresponding to the area available for displaying images. In GKS, display space is also used to refer to the working space of an input device such as a digitizer.

Display Surface—In a display device, the medium on which display images appear.

Dominant Wavelength—The wavelength of a light of a single frequency which matches a given color when combined with an appropriate amount of a reference "white" light.

Echo—The immediate notification to the operator of the current value provided by an input device.

Efficiency—In display applications, the ratio of luminance flux to the power supplied to a radiant source. It is expressed as lumens per watt.

Electrostatic Focusing—A method of focusing the CRT electron beam by application of electrostatic potentials to one or more focusing elements.

Equal-Energy Source—A hypothetical light source for which the time rate of energy emission per unit of wavelength is constant throughout the visual spectrum.

Equalizing Pulses—Pulses at twice the line frequency occurring just before and just after the vertical synchronizing pulses.

Escape—A facility within a device-independent software system which is the only access to implementation-dependent support functions.

Excitation Purity—On a CIE chromaticity diagram, the ratio of the sample-color and spectrum-color distances from the reference "white" color, as measured along the dominant-wavelength vector. For non-spectrum colors, the denominator is the distance to the purple boundary.

Fade—The gradual lowering of a signal amplitude.

Fader—A control or group of controls for effecting fade-in and fade-out of display signals.

Fechner's Law—The intensity of a sensory response is generally proportional to the logarithm of the stimulus intensity. The luminosity system of measurement serves to linearize this effect for visual stimuli.

Feedback—Output indicating to the operator the application program's interpretation of a logical input value.

Field—One of the two or more equal parts into which a display frame is divided in an interlaced scanning system.

Field Frequency—The number of fields displayed per second. The United States standard is 60 fields / second. The European standard is 50 fields / second. Also called field-repetition rate.

Field Period—The time interval equal to the reciprocal of the field frequency.

Fill Area—A GKS primitive consisting of a polygon (closed boundary) which may be hollow or may be filled with a uniform color, a pattern, or a hatch style.

Fill-Area Bundle Table—A table associating specific values for all workstation-dependent aspects of a fill-area primitive with a fill-area bundle index. In GKS, this table contains entries consisting of interior style, style index, and color index.

Filter—In optics, a transparent material characterized by selective absorption of light according to wavelength. In electronics, a circuit component which selectively absorbs ac energy according to frequency.

Fine Chrominance Primary—The chrominance primary transmitted with a maximum bandwidth.

Flicker—A perceived rapid periodic change. Flicker disappears when the frequency of the stimulus change exceeds a rate called the critical flicker frequency.

Flyback—The shorter of the two time intervals which comprise a sawtooth wave. In raster scanning, the retrace interval.

Focusing—The process of controlling the convergence of a single electron beam.

Focus Control—A manual adjustment for bringing the electron beam of a CRT to a minimum-size spot.

Foot-Candle—A unit of illumination equal to the illumination which occurs when uniformly distributed luminous flux is impinging on an area at a rate of one lumen per square foot.

Footlambert—A unit of luminance equal to the uniform luminance of a perfectly diffusing surface emitting or reflecting luminous flux at the rate of one lumen per square foot.

Fovea—A small (less than a degree of visual angle) ellipse-shaped depression in the central region of the retina. Represents the area of sharpest color-sensing vision.

Frame—The total amount of instantaneous information (as perceived by the viewer) presented by a display. In two-field interlaced raster scanning, a frame is the time interval between the vertical retrace at the start of the first field and the end of the second field.

Frame Buffer—A separate or selected portion of a display memory which contains a full frame of display data.

Frame Frequency—The number of frames displayed per second. The United States standard is 30 frames/second. The European standard is 25 frames/second.

Frame Period—A time interval equal to the reciprocal of the frame frequency.

Frequency Interlace—Interleaving of the chrominance and luminance sidebands of a color-encoded signal to minimize interference effects.

Front Porch—The portion of a composite display signal which lies between the leading edges of a horizontal blanking pulse and the corresponding sync pulse.

Gain—An increase in voltage or power, usually expressed in dB.

Gamma—The power exponent used to approximate the curve of display-luminance output versus signal-input amplitude.

Gamma Correction—An exponential variation in the signal input to provide a linear transfer function from signal source to display output.

Generalized Drawing Primitive (GDP)—In GKS, a display element (primitive) used to address special geometric workstation capabilities such as curve drawing.

Genlock—A circuit used to lock the frequency of an internal sync generator to an external source.

GKS Level—Two values in the range 0 to 2 and a to c which together define the set of functional capabilities provided by a specific GKS implementation.

GKS Metafile (GKSM)—A sequential file that can be written or read by GKS; used for transmittal and long-term storage of graphical information.

Glitches—A form of low-frequency interference appearing as a narrow horizontal bar moving vertically on a raster-scan display.

Graphic Primitive—See Display Element.

Grassmann's Law—The sum (or mixture) of two colors can be matched by summing the primary-color components of each color.

Gray Scale—Variations in the luminance value of "white" light, from black to white. Shades of gray are defined as gray-scale graduations that differ by the square root of 2.

Hidden-Line Removal—In three-dimensional, wire-frame graphics, the process of eliminating lines which would be hidden if the represented object were opaque.

Hidden-Surface Removal—In three-dimensional graphics, the process of eliminating the representation of surfaces which would be obscured by opaque foreground surfaces if photographed by a hypothetical camera.

Highlighting—A device-independent attribute that emphasizes a segment by modifying its visual attributes.

Horizontal Hold Control—Varies the free-running frequency of the horizontal deflection oscillator.

Horizontal Resolution—In raster-scan graphics systems, the number of discernable signal transitions along a raster line, or the number of display-memory addresses representing pixels along the horizontal axis of the display. In video systems, the number of vertical test-pattern lines which can be reproduced by a camera and monitor.

Horizontal Retrace—Return of the electron beam to the left margin of the CRT screen at the start of each raster line.

Hue—A psycho-physiological term corresponding to the psycho-physical term of dominant (or complementary) wavelength. White, gray, and black may be considered as colors, but not as hues.

ICI—An abbreviation for the International Commission on Illumination (see CIE).

"I" Signal—The wideband color-signal component produced by modulating the color subcarrier at a phase of -57° removed from the burst reference phase. Also called the "in-phase" signal. The signal reproduces a range of colors from orange to cyan.

Iconoscope—A camera tube in which a high-velocity electron beam scans a photoactive mosaic which has an electrical-storage capability.

Illuminance—The density of luminance flux impinging on a surface. It is the quotient of the flux divided by the "apparent" or projected area of the surface.

Illuminants—A series of reference "whites" defined by their spectral distributions.

Image—A displayed view of one or more objects or parts of objects.

Image Transformation—A Core System segment attribute which permits the image defined by a segment to appear in varying sizes, orientations, and/or positions on the view surface.

Implementation Mandatory—Describes a property that must be realized identically, by all implementations of a graphics standard.

Input Class—A set of input devices that are logically equivalent with respect to their functions. In GKS, the input classes are: Locator, Stroke, Valuator, Choice, Pick, and String.

Input Level—The peak-to-peak voltage of a composite display signal.

Intensity—See Luminous Intensity. Also a non-technical synonym for both luminance and brightness.

Interlaced Scanning—A raster-scanning process in which the raster lines which compose two or more "fields" are interleaved to form a single "frame."

Ion Spot—An area on the display surface of a CRT which is darker than the surrounding area due to a loss of sensitivity caused by negative-ion bombardment.

Ion Trap—An arrangement of magnetic fields and apertures which allows the passage of electrons but obstructs the passage of ions.

Jitter—Instability of a signal in amplitude and/or phase.

Keystone Distortion—The keystone-shaped raster produced by scanning a plane which is not normal to the average direction of the beam.

Lambert—A unit of luminance equal to the uniform luminance of a perfectly diffusing surface emitting or reflecting light at the rate of one lumen per square centimeter.

Leading Edge—The waveform of a pulse as it rises or falls from 10 to 90 percent of its total amplitude.

Light—Radiant energy capable of stimulating the retina in the human eye.

Line Amplifier—An amplifier that feeds a display-signal transmission line. Also called a program amplifier.

Line Frequency—The number of horizontal scan lines per second, including both the visible raster lines and those that occur during the vertical-retrace intervals.

Linearity—The degree to which changes in the input to a system produce directly proportional changes in the output.

Linearity Control—Maintains a constant scanning speed as each raster line is traced.

Locator Device—A GKS logical input device providing a position in world coordinates and a normalization transformation number.

Logical Input Device—A logical input device is an abstraction of one or more physical devices, which delivers logical input values to the program (see Input Class).

Logical Input Value—A value delivered by a logical input device.

Loop Through—A method for driving a series of monitors with bridged coaxial-line connections. Also called looping.

Loss—A reduction in signal level or strength, usually expressed in dB.

Low-Frequency Distortion—Distortion effects which occur at frequencies below the line frequency.

Luminance—Luminous intensity reflected or emitted by a surface in a given direction per unit of apparent area. Measured in nits.

Luminance Signal—The portion of a color-encoded display signal which contains luminance information.

Lumen—The unit of luminous flux or rate of luminous energy flow. It is equal to the flux radiating through a unit solid angle (steradian) from a uniform point source of one candela.

Luminosity Function—The ratio of the photometric quantity at a given wavelength to a corresponding radiometric quantity in standard units (lumens per watt).

Luminosity Coefficient—The chromaticity-value multiplier for each component of a three-component color which will result in a three-product sum equal to the luminance of the color.

Luminous Efficiency—The ratio of luminous flux to radiant flux. It is expressed in lumens per watt of radiant flux. (The term "efficiency" or "display efficiency" is based on the power supplied to the source rather than the radiant flux from the source.)

Luminous Flux—The time rate of luminous energy flow, measured by its capacity to evoke a visual sensation. It is expressed in lumens.

Luminous Intensity—The luminous flux radiated by a point source. It is expressed in candela.

Lux—The international unit of illumination. One lux equals one lumen per square meter.

Magenta—The hue attribute evoked by a wavelength combination which is the approximate complement of 515 nanometers. It is the complement of green.

Magnetic Focusing—A method of focusing an electron beam by the action of a magnetic field.

Marker—A glyph with a specified appearance, which is used to identify a particular location.

Maxwell Triangle—A color diagram in the form of an equilateral triangle, with the primaries represented at the vertices.

Measure—A value associated with a logical input device together with a mapping from the value delivered by a physical device. The logical input value delivered by a logical input device is the current value of the measure.

Modeling System—A high-level system for defining objects in world coordinates.

Modulation Transfer Function—The ratio of maximum attainable contrasts between adjoining small display areas (e.g., pixels) and large areas. Nominally expressed as percent or dB.

Moire—A spurious display pattern resulting from interference beats between two sets of periodic or spaced occurrences.

Monochrome—Any combination of colors of the same hue, but of different saturations and luminances.

Monochrome Signal—A waveform that controls the luminance (and saturation, if the color has a hue) of a monochrome display. The term may also refer to the luminance-signal portion of a color-encoded display signal.

Munsell Color System—A color-definition system based on uniform color scales representing two of three variables: hue, value, and chroma. Value corresponds to luminance; chroma corresponds to saturation.

Negative Image—A monochrome display signal with a polarity opposite to the normal polarity (i.e., white and black areas are reversed).

Negative Modulation—A form of modulation in which an increase in transmitted power corresponds to a decrease in display luminance.

New Frame Action—The elimination of all temporary information from a display and the rewriting of all visible retained information. On a hardcopy device, the recording medium is advanced to an unrecorded area.

NDC Space—A finite region within a normalized-device-coordinate (NDC) system. It defines the maximum region usable by an application program.

NDC System—A device-independent two-dimensional or three-dimensional Cartesian coordinate system based on normalized-device-coordinate (NDC) values in the range 0 to 1.

Normalization Transformation—A transformation that maps the boundary and interior of a window to the boundary and interior of a viewport. In GKS, this transformation maps positions in world coordinates to normalized device coordinates.

Normalized Device Coordinates (NDC)—A coordinate specified in a device-independent intermediate coordinate system (see NDC System).

Notch Filter—A filter designed to reject a very narrow band of frequencies.

NTSC—Abbreviation for the National Television System Committee. Used to identify the color-encoding method adopted by the committee in 1953. The NTSC standard was the first monochrome-compatible, simultaneous color system used for public broadcasting.

Object—A conceptual graphical unit in an application program. Objects are described in world coordinates in terms of primitive functions and attributes.

Operating Space—See Display Space.

Operator—Person manipulating physical input devices so as to change the measures of logical input devices and cause their triggers to fire.

Orthicon—A camera tube in which a low-velocity electron beam scans a photoactive mosaic which has an electrical storage capability.

Ostwald Color System—A color-definition system based on color charts. The theoretical variables are hue, full color content, white content and black content. Hues are indicated by an arbitrary set of hue numbers.

Output Primitive—See Display Element.

Pairing—A faulty interlace scan during which alternate raster lines overlap each other, reducing the effective vertical resolution of the display.

PAL—Abbreviation for Phase Alternation (or Alternating) Line, a color-encoding system in which one of the subcarrier phases derived from the color burst is inverted in phase from one line to the next in order to minimize errors in hue which may occur during color transmission.

Patches—Portions of solid-object surfaces, as calculated and displayed by three-dimensional graphics software. Patch definitions often form the basis of shading algorithms.

Peak Power—Corresponds in amplitude to synchronizing peaks when a display signal has been negatively modulated.

Peak Power Output—The output power averaged over a carrier cycle at the maximum amplitude which can occur under any combination of signals transmitted.

Peak-to-Peak—The amplitude difference between the most positive and most negative excursions of an electrical signal.

Peak Pulse Amplitude—The maximum absolute peak value of a pulse, excluding unwanted excursions such as spikes.

Pedestal Level—The level of a composite display signal which divides the display-signal amplitudes from the sync-signal amplitudes (see Blanking Level).

Phosphor—A substance capable of luminescence when excited by an energy source (e.g., electromagnetic waves, accelerated electrons, an electrical field).

Photocathode—An electrode that emits electrons when subjected to electromagnetic radiation in and near the visible spectrum.

Photoconductivity—Changes in the electrical conductivity of a material as the result of absorption of photons.

Photoelectric Emission—The emission of electrons by certain materials upon exposure to electromagnetic radiation in and near the visible spectrum.

Photometer—Any optical device which uses a comparison technique to measure luminous intensity, luminance, or illumination. An equality-of-brightness photometer is based on simultaneous comparison of adjoining visual areas; a flicker photometer compares successive stimuli in the same visual area.

Photopic Vision—The eye-brain response to luminance levels sufficient to permit the full discrimination of colors. Also called daylight vision, as contrasted to twilight or scotopic vision.

Pick Device—A GKS logical input device that provides the pick identifier attached to a selected (picked) primitive and the associated segment name.

Pick Identifier—A number attached to individual primitives within a segment and returned by a pick device. The same pick identifier can be assigned to different primitives.

Picture—See Display Image.

Picture Element—The smallest segment of a raster line which can be discretely controlled by the display system. Also called a pixel, pel, or pixcell.

Pin-Cushion Distortion—A distortion that makes a displayed image appear to bulge inward on all four sides.

Pixel—See Picture Element.

Polarity—The potential of a portion of the display signal representing a dark area relative to the potential representing a light area. Polarity is stated as "black negative" or "black positive."

Polyline—A GKS and core primitive consisting of a set of connected lines.

Polyline Bundle Table—A table associating specific values for all workstation-dependent aspects of a polyline primitive with a polyline bundle index. In GKS, the table contains entries consisting of linetype, linewidth scale factor, and color index.

Polymarker—A GKS and core output primitive consisting of a set of locations, each to be indicated by a marker.

Polymarker Bundle Table—A table associating specific values for all workstation-dependent aspects of a polymarker primitive with a polymarker bundle index. In GKS, the table contains entries consisting of marker type, marker size, scale factor, and color index.

Portable Programs—Software that is both host-computer and display-device independent.

Positive Modulation—A form of modulation in which an increase in transmitted power corresponds to an increase in display luminance.

Primaries—Colors of constant chromaticity which are mixed to produce or specify other colors.

Primitive—A graphic element (e.g., a line or a text string) having a specific appearance. Primitive attributes determine certain aspects of this appearance.

Primitive Attribute—A general characteristic of a display primitive, such as color, intensity, linestyle, or linewidth. Primitive attribute values are selected by the application in a workstation-independent manner, but can have workstation-dependent effects.

Prompt—Output to the operator indicating that a specific logical input device is available.

Purity—(See Color Purity, Colorimetric Purity, and Excitation Purity.)

Purity Coil—An electromagnetic device placed about the neck of a delta-type color CRT to control the angles at which the three beams approach the aperture mask.

Purkinje Effect—The decrease in luminosity of reds and oranges relative to blues and greens as luminance is reduced. The effect is associated with the change in relative sensitivies during the transition from the photopic to scotopic states.

Purple Boundary—Straight line drawn between the ends of the spectrum locus on the CIE chromaticity diagram.

"Q" Signal—The narrowband signal produced by modulating the color sub-carrier at a phase − 147° removed from the burst reference phase. Also called the "quadrature" signal. The signal reproduces a range of colors from purple to yellow-green.

RF Pattern—A term used to describe a fine herringbone pattern in a picture which is caused by a high-frequency interference.

Radiance—The electromagnetic flux radiated per unit solid angle (steradian) per unit of projected area of the source. Measured as watts per steradian per square meter.

Radiant Flux—The time rate of radiant-energy flow.

Raster—A predetermined pattern of scanning lines which provides substantially uniform coverage of a display area.

Raster Graphics—Computer graphics in which a display image is composed of an array of pixels arranged in rows and columns.

Reference Black Level—The display-signal level corresponding to a specified maximum limit for black peaks.

Reference Stimulus—An alternate term for "primary" in a multi-component color measurement system. Also used to identify the reference color in color comparisons.

Reference White Level—The display-signal level corresponding to a specified maximum limit for white peaks.

Relative Luminosity—The ratio value of the luminosity at a particular wavelength to the value at the wavelength of maximum luminosity (555 nanometers for photopic vision).

Resolution—The number of addressable, controllable display or picture elements, or the number of hypothetical coordinate locations which can be used to position graphic elements on a display surface.

Retained Segment—A named Core System segment that has associated retained-segment dynamic attributes which may be modified.

Retrace Interval—The time period during which the direction of sweep is reversed and no information is displayed. Also called return interval.

Return Trace—The path of a scanning spot during the retrace interval.

Roll—A loss of vertical synchronization which causes the displayed image to move up or down.

Rolloff—A gradual decrease in a signal level.

Rotation—Turning all or part of a display image about an axis.

Saturation—A psycho-physiological perception of the degree to which a color is undiluted with white light. Its psycho-physical equivalent is called purity.

Scaling—Enlarging or reducing all or part of a display image by multiplying the coordinates of display elements by a constant value. For different scaling in two orthogonal directions, two constant values are required.

Scanning—The process of successively addressing points on a display surface, either randomly or in a fixed pattern (as in raster scanning).

Scanning Linearity—The uniformity of the scanning speed during the tracing of a raster line.

Scanning Lines—The total number of lines scanned in one direction during a frame interval, including those which are blanked during the vertical retrace. Calculated by dividing the line frequency by the frame frequency.

Scotopic Vision—The eye-brain response to luminance levels below that required for the full discrimination of colors. Also called twilight or night vision, as contrasted to photopic or daylight vision.

SECAM—Abbreviation for Systéme Electronique Couleur Avec Mémoire (or Sequential Color with Memory). A color-encoding system in which the red and blue color-difference information is transmitted on alternate lines, requiring a one-line "memory" in order to decode for green.

Segment—An ordered collection of primitives defining an image on the display surface.

Segment—A collection of display elements that can be manipulated as a unit.

Segment Attributes—Attributes that apply only to segments. In GKS, segment attributes are visibility, highlighting, detectability, segment priority, and segment transformation.

Segment Priority—A segment attribute used to determine which of several overlapping segments takes precedence for graphic output and input.

Segment Transformation—A transformation which causes the display elements defined by a segment to appear with varying position (translation), size (scale), and/or orientation (rotation) on the display surface.

Setup—The ratio of the difference between black level and blanking level to the difference between reference white level and blanking level, expressed in percent or IRE units.

Shades of Gray—A division of the gray scale from black to white into a series of discrete luminance shades with a square-root-of-2 difference between successive shades.

Shading—An unintentional large-area brightness gradient in a display. Also used to describe graphics software algorithms that establish the appearance of solid-object surfaces.

Shift—See Translation.

Signal-to-Noise Ratio—The ratio of the peak level of a display signal to the level of any noise on the signal. Usually expressed in dB.

Snow—A display condition produced by random noise on a display signal, usually indicative of a weak signal.

Spectrum Locus—The points representing fully saturated spectrum colors on a CIE chromaticity chart.

Standard Illuminant—One of several reference "white" colors specified in such a way that its energy distribution is reproducible.

Standard Observer—A hypothetical observer with a visual response mechanism possessing the colormetric properties defined by the 1931 CIE tables of distribution coefficients and chromaticity coefficients of the equal-energy spectrum.

Steradian—A unit solid angle, defined as the solid angle subtended by an area r^2 on the surface of a sphere with radius r.

Streaking—A display condition in which objects appear to extend horizontally beyond their normal boundaries.

String Device—A GKS logical input device providing a character string (text) as its result.

Stroke Device—A GKS logical input device providing a sequence of world coordinate positions and a normalization transformation number.

Switcher-Fader—A control mechanism which permits two or more display signals to be selectively fed into a distribution system. The "fader" control permits gradual transition from one signal to another.

Sync—A contraction of synchronous or synchronization.

Sync Compression—A reduction in the amplitude of the sync signal with respect to the display signal.

Sync Generator—A device for generating a synchronizing signal.

Sync Level—The level of the peaks of the synchronizing signal.

Sync Signal—A signal that synchronizes the scanning operation of a raster-scan monitor. May also include a phase reference for an encoded-color monitor.

Synchronous Demodulation—The process of separately detecting the I and Q sidebands of an encoder-color subcarrier system.

Tearing—A display condition in which groups of horizontal lines are displaced in an irregular manner.

Telecine—A camera system designed specifically to raster-scan 35mm slides and motion picture film.

Television Broadcast Band—The frequencies extending from 54 to 890 MHz which are assignable to television broadcast stations.

Television Channels (U.S.)—A band of frequencies 6 MHz wide in the television broadcast band and designated either by number or by the limiting frequencies.

Temporary Segment—A nameless Core System segment having no segment attributes. The image defined by a temporary segment remains visible only as long as information is added to the display.

Text—A GKS output primitive consisting of a character string.

Text Bundle Table—A table associating specific values for all workstation-dependent aspects of a text primitive with a text bundle index. In GKS, this table contains entries consisting of text font and precision, character expansion factor, character spacing, and color index.

Text Font and Precision—An aspect of text primitives in GKS. Font and precision together determine the shape of the characters being output on a particular workstation. In addition, precision describes the fidelity with which other text aspects match those requested by an application program.

Trace Interval—The time during which a visible raster line is scanned.

Translation—The application of a constant displacement to the position of all or part of a display image.

Trichromatic Coefficient—See Chromaticity Coefficient.

Trigger—A physical input device or set of devices which an operator can use to indicate significant moments in time.

Tristimulus Value—See Chromaticity Value and Color Data.

Two-and-a-Half Dimensions—The effect produced by two-dimensional viewing software when overlapping objects are given a display priority.

Valuator Device—A GKS logical input device providing a real number.

Vertical Hold Control—A manual control which varies the free-running period of the vertical deflection oscillator.

Vertical Resolution—In raster-scan graphics systems, the number of visible raster lines displayed by a monitor, or the number of display-memory addresses representing pixels along the vertical axis of the display. In video systems, the number of horizontal test-pattern lines which can be reproduced by a camera and monitor (typically equal to 70 percent of the displayed raster lines).

Vertical Retrace—The return of the electron beam to the top of the CRT screen at the start of each field or frame interval.

Video Amplifier—A wideband amplifier used for processing raster-scan display signals.

Video Band—The frequency band used to transmit a composite video signal.

Video Signal (Non-Composite)—A signal containing display information and horizontal and vertical blanking (see Composite Display Signal).

View Surface—A Core System two-dimensional logical output surface. Images on a view surface are recreated on a physical output surface (e.g., a display screen) in a device-dependent way by the device driver for that output device.

Viewing Operation—An operation that maps positions in world coordinates to positions in normalized device coordinates. It also specifies the portion of the world coordinate space that is to be displayed.

Viewing Transformation—See Normalization Transformation.

Viewport—An application-program-specified part of NDC space.

View Surface—See Display Surface.

Visual Acuity—The capacity of the eyes to resolve small details in the discrimination of form. The threshold separation of two small spots is one measure of acuity. Nominal value for visual acuity is one minute of arc.

Webber's Law—The approximate luminance-difference threshold is a constant fraction of the luminance value over a wide range.

White—The common usage word for high-luminance achromatic colors.

White Compression—Amplitude compression of the signal levels corresponding to white regions of a display.

White Level—The display signal level corresponding to a specified maximum limit for white peaks.

White Peak—The maximum excursion of a display signal in the white direction.

White Peak Clipping—Limiting the amplitude of the display signal to a preselected maximum white level.

Wideband Axis—The phase of the chrominance component for which a wider transmission bandwidth is provided.

Window—A predefined part of a world-coordinate space.

Window/Viewport Transformation—See Normalization Transformation.

Workstation—In GKS, an abstract graphical workstation which serves as the logical interface through which the application program controls physical devices.

Workstation Mandatory—A property that must be realized identically on all workstations of a standard implementation.

Workstation Transformation—A transformation that maps the boundary and interior of a workstation window into the boundary and interior of a workstation viewport without changing the aspect ratio of the window. In GKS, this transformation maps positions in normalized device coordinates to device coordinates. In order to preserve the aspect ratio, the interior of the workstation window may not map to the whole of the workstation viewport.

Workstation Viewport—A portion of display space currently selected for output of graphics.

Workstation Window—A rectangular region within the NDC system, which is represented on a display space.

World Coordinate System—A device-independent three-dimensional Cartesian coordinate system in which two- and three-dimensional objects are described to a viewing system.

Y Signal—The component of a color-encoded display signal representing luminance information. The signal produces a black-and-white image on a standard monochrome monitor. It is made up by combining specified fractions of the red (0.30), green (0.59), and blue (0.11) color signals.

Zero Subcarrier Chromaticity—The chromaticity which is to be displayed when the chrominance subcarrier amplitude is zero.

Zoom—To enlarge or reduce, on a continuously variable scale, the size of a displayed image.

Appendix II
Display-Signal
Standards

Display-signal standards assure compatibility between signal-information sources and display or recording devices.

The principal standards applying to both television and graphics systems have been established by the Electronic Industries Association (EIA). They nominally apply to monochrome display systems, but the same standards are widely used to establish the characteristics of each of the three color-input signals which drive a non-encoded (e.g., RGB) color monitor.

There are three basic standards for encoded-color display signals: NTSC, PAL, and SECAM. These are described briefly at the end of this section, with special emphasis on the NTSC standard which applies to all government-regulated broadcast color systems in the United States.

EIA RS-170 STANDARD

(The following paragraphs are edited excerpts from EIA RS-170, which provides performance standards for monochrome display systems. The waveform drawing is derived from EIA RS-170A, a tentative standard for color display systems.)

These standards are intended to apply only to locally generated signals where control can be exercised over display quality.

Impedance

Impedance is defined as the complex ratio of voltage to current in a two-terminal network, expressed in ohms.

The standard load impedance of the source shall have a value of 75 ohms ± 5% over the frequency range of 0 to 4.5 MHz and shall be connected for single-ended operation. The internal impedance of the source shall be 75 ohms ± 10% at those frequencies where the impedance of the output condenser (if used) may be neglected. The time constant of the internal impedance combined with the standard load impedance shall be 0.1 second or greater.

Direct Current in Output

The open circuit dc voltage of the display source shall not exceed 2 volts. The short-circuit dc current shall not exceed 2 milliamperes. These dc values are presumed to be independent of the output signal.

Polarity

Polarity is defined as the sense of the potential of a portion of the signal representing a dark area of an image relative to the potential of a portion of the signal representing a light area. Polarity is stated as "black-negative" or "black-positive." The standard polarity of the output of the source shall be black-negative.

Composite Display Signal

Display Signal—The signal resulting from the scanning process.

Sync Signal—The signal employed for the synchronization of scanning.

Sync Level—The level of the peaks of the sync signal.

Blanking Level—That level of a composite display signal which separates the range containing display information from the range containing synchronizing information.

Black Peak—A peak excursion of the display signal in the black direction.

White Peak—A peak excursion of the display signal in the white direction.

Reference White Level—The display signal level corresponding to a specified maximum limit for white peaks.

Reference Black Level—The display signal level corresponding to a specified maximum limit for black peaks.

Setup—The ratio between reference black level and reference white level, both measured from blanking level. It is usually expressed in percent.

Composite Display Signal—The signal which results from combining a blanked display signal with the sync signal.

Blanked Display Signal—The signal resulting from blanking a display signal.

Level—Signal amplitude measured in accordance with specified techniques, or a specified position on an amplitude scale applied to a signal waveform.

It shall be standard that the display signal as measured from blanking level to reference white level across the standard load impedance of the source be 1.0 ± 0.05 volt.

It shall be standard that the synchronizing signal as measured across the standard load impedance of the source be 40 ± 5% of the display signal.

It shall be standard that throughout a given transmission the synchronizing signal be maintained constant within ± 4% as measured across the standard load impedance of the source. This variation may take place on a long-time basis only and not during successive cycles. The allowable amplitude variation over one frame should be considerably smaller.

The amplitude of blanking level referred to the ac axis of the signal at the source output shall not vary more than ± 5% of the sync signal amplitude during one field. The ac axis of the signal shall be determined by averaging the signals over one field. The sync amplitude is designated in IRE units in Figure A2-1. It shall be standard that the minimum setup be 7.5 ± 2.5%.

Geometric Distortion

Geometric distortion is defined as any aberration which causes the reproduced image to be geometrically dissimilar to the perspective plane projection of the original image.

It shall be standard that no image element be displaced from its true position referred to the original by more than 2% of the display height. It is desirable that the distortion be held as much below this minimum standard as conditions permit. The instantaneous apparent scanning velocity, since it is a measure of the magnification of the system, shall vary from the mean velocity in a gradual fashion.

Resolving Power

The resolving power of a display system or a portion thereof is a measure of its ability to delineate detail. It is expressed in terms of the

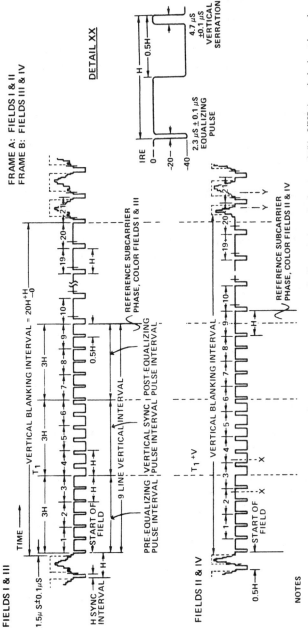

Figure A2-1a. RS-170 waveforms, composite display signal, 1 of 2. (Source: EIA)

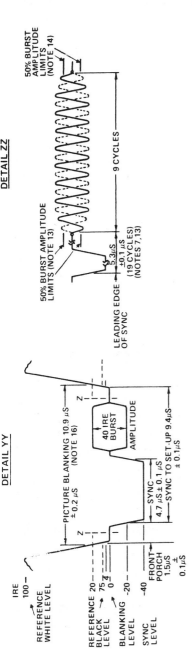

DETAIL ZZ

DETAIL YY

50% BURST AMPLITUDE LIMITS (NOTE 14)

50% BURST AMPLITUDE LIMITS (NOTE 13)

9 CYCLES

5.3μS ±0.1 μS (19 CYCLES) (NOTES 7,13)

LEADING EDGE OF SYNC

IRE 100 —

REFERENCE WHITE LEVEL

PICTURE BLANKING 10.9 μS ±0.2 μS (NOTE 16)

40 IRE BURST

AMPLITUDE

REFERENCE BLACK LEVEL 20
75
0

BLANKING LEVEL -20

-40

SYNC LEVEL

FRONT PORCH 1.5μS ± 0.1μS

SYNC 4.7 μS ± 0.1 μS

SYNC TO SET-UP 9.4μS ± 0.1μS

7. The zero-crossings of reference subcarrier shall be nominally coincident with the 50% point of the leading edges of all horizontal sync pulses. For those cases where the relationship between sync and subcarrier is critical for program integration, the tolerance on this coincidence is ± 40° of reference subcarrier.

8. All rise times and fall times unless otherwise specified are to be 0.14 μS ± 0.02 μS measured from 10% to 90% amplitude points. All pulse widths are measured at 50% amplitude points, unless otherwise specified.

9. Tolerance on sync level, reference black level (set-up) and peak to peak burst amplitude shall be ± 2 IRE units.

10. The interval beginning with line 17 and extending through line 20 of each field may be used for test, cue and control signals.

11. Extraneous synchronous signals during blanking intervals, including residual subcarrier, shall not exceed 1 IRE unit. Extraneous non-synchronous signals during blanking intervals shall not exceed 0.5 IRE unit. All special purpose signals (VITS, VIR, etc.) when added to the vertical blanking interval are excepted. Overshoot on all pulses during sync and blanking, vertical and horizontal, shall not exceed 2 IRE units.

12. Burst envelope rise time is 0.3 μS + 0.2 μS − 0.1 μS measured between the 10% and 90% amplitude points. Burst is not present during the nine line vertical interval.

13. The start of burst is defined by the zero-crossing (positive or negative slope) that precedes the first half cycle of subcarrier that is 50% or greater of the burst amplitude. Its position is nominally 19 cycles of subcarrier from the 50% amplitude point of leading edge of sync. (see Detail ZZ)

14. The end of burst is defined by the zero-crossing (positive or negative slope) that follows the last half cycle of subcarrier that is 50% or greater of the burst amplitude.

15. Monochrome signals shall be in accordance with this drawing except that burst is omitted, and fields III and IV are identical to fields I and II respectively.

16. Occasionally, measurement of picture blanking at 20 IRE units is not possible because of image content as verified on a monitor.

Figure A2–1b. RS-170 waveforms, composite display signal, 2 of 2. (Source: EIA)

number of lines resolved on a test chart. For a number of lines N (normally alternate black and white lines) the width of each line is $1/N$ times the picture height.

It shall be standard that the resolving power of the overall system be at least 350 lines in the vertical direction and 400 lines in the horizontal direction, both measurements to be made near the center of the display.

Aspect Ratio

Aspect ratio is defined as the ratio of the frame width to the frame height. "Frame" is defined as the total area scanned while the display signal is not blanked.

The standard aspect ratio of a frame shall be 4:3 on condition that the horizontal blanking interval be 17.5% of the line period and the vertical blanking interval be 7.5% of the frame period. No specific tolerances are assigned to this ratio but it is understood that the tolerance allowed for geometric distortion will provide adequate limits for permissible variation in the aspect ratio.

Sync Signal Tolerance

It shall be standard that the synchronizing signal waveform conform with Figure A2-2.

It shall be standard that the time of occurrence of the leading edge of any horizontal pulse "N" of any group of twenty horizontal pulses not differ from "NH" by more than 0.001H where "H" is the average interval between the leading edges of horizontal pulses as determined by an averaging process carried out over a period of not less than 20 or more than 100 lines.

It shall be standard that the rate of change of the frequency of recurrence of the leading edges of the horizontal sync pulses appearing in the source output be not greater than 0.15 per cent per second, the frequency to be determined by an averaging process carried out over a period of not less than 20 or more than 100 lines, such lines not to include any portion of the vertical blanking signal.

It shall be standard that the frequency of horizontal and vertical scanning pulses not vary from the values established by the standards of frame frequency and number or scanning lines by more than ± 1% regardless of variations in frequency of the power source supplying the system.

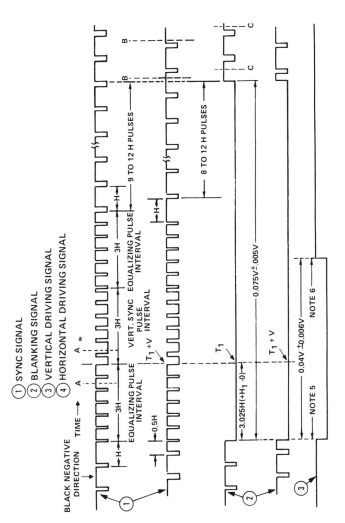

All signal amplitudes shall be adjustable over the range from 3.5 to 4.5 volts across a load impedance of 75 ohms ± 5%. Negative signal polarity shall be available for all pulses. Source impedance for all output circuits shall be 75 ohms ± 10%.

Figure A2–2a. RS-170 waveforms, composite sync-signal generator, 1 of 2. (Source: EIA)

NOTES:

1. H = time from start of one line to start of next line.

2. V = time from start of one field to start of next field.

3. Leading and trailing edges of vertical driving and vertical blanking signals should be complete in less than 0.1H.

4. All tolerances and limits shown in this drawing are permissible only for long time variations.

5. Timing adjustment, if any shall include this condition.

6. The vertical driving pulse duration shall be 0.04V, ± 0.006V. The horizontal driving pulse duration shall be 0.1H, ± 0.005H.

7. The time relationship and waveform of the blanking and sync signals shall be such that their addition will result in a standard RETMA signal. The time relationship shall be adjustable in order to satisfy this relationship for the condition where the blanking signal is delayed with respect to the sync signal over the range from 0.0H to 0.05H.

8. The standard RETMA values of frequency and rate of change of frequency for the horizontal components of the sync signal at the output of the picture line amplified shall also apply to the horizontal components of the output signals from the recommended sync generator.

9. All rise and decay times shall be measured between 0.1 and 0.9 amplitude reference lines.

10. The time of occurrence of the leading edge of any horizontal pulse "N" of any group of twenty horizontal pulses appearing on any of the output signals from a standard sync generator shall not differ from "NH" by more than 0.0008H where H is the average interval between the leading edges of the pulses as determined by an averaging process carried out over a period of not less than 20 nor more than 100 lines.

11. Equalizing pulse area shall be between 0.45 and 0.5 of the area of a horizontal sync pulse.

12. The overshoot on any of the pulses shall not exceed 5%.

13. The output level of the blanking signal and the sync signal shall not vary more than ±3% under the following conditions:

    A. The a.c. voltage supplying the sync generator shall be in the range between 110V and 120V and must not vary more than ±5V during test.

    B. A period of 5 hours continuous operation shall be considered adequate for this measurement, after suitable warm-up.

    C. The room ambient shall be in the range between 20 deg. and 40 deg. C. and shall not change more than 10 deg. C. during this test.

14. Adjustment shall be possible between minimum and maximum limits so that aspect ratio can be set to the normal value.

Figure A2-2b. RS-170 waveforms, composite sync-signal generator, 2 of 2. (Source: EIA)

EIA RS-330 STANDARD

(The following paragraphs are edited excerpts from EIA RS-330, which provides performance standards for high-performance raster-scan systems.)

It shall be standard that the blanked picture signal with setup (non-composite), as measured from blanking level to reference white level across the standard load impedance of the source, be 0.714 ± 0.1 volt (100 IRE units).

It shall be standard that the synchronizing signal as measured across the standard load impedance of the source be 0.286 ± 0.05 volts (nominally 40 IRE units).

It shall be standard that the setup be 7.5 ± 5 IRE units (2.5% to 12.5% of the blanked display signal).

Resolving Power

Resolution—A measure of the ability to delineate display detail.

Limiting Resolution—A measure of resolution usually expressed in terms of the maximum number of lines per display height discriminated on a camera test chart. Note: For a number of lines N (alternate black and white lines) with width of each line is $1/N$ times the picture height.

Resolution Response—The ratio of (1) the peak-to-peak signal amplitude, given by a test pattern consisting of alternate black and white bars of equal width corresponding to a specified line number to (2) the peak-to-peak signal amplitude, given by large area blacks and large area whites having the same luminance as the black and white bars in the test pattern.

Line Number—In measuring resolution, the ratio of the frame height to the width of each bar of a test pattern composed of alternate equal-width black and white bars, as projected on the frame.

It shall be standard that the limiting resolution of the source be at least 350 lines in the vertical direction and 600 lines in the horizontal direction, both measurements to be made using resolution wedges near the center of the display.

Sync Signal Tolerance

It shall be standard that the synchronizing signal waveform at the output of the source conform with Figure A2–3.

It shall be standard that the time of occurrence of the leading edge of

NOTES:

1. $\beta = 0.714 \pm .1$ volts (100 IRE Units).

2. $\alpha = 0.286$ (40 IRE Units) nominal.

3. Sync to total signal ratio $\left(\dfrac{\alpha}{\beta + \alpha}\right) = (28.6 \pm 5)\,\%$.

4. Blanking = 7.5 ± 5 IRE Units (2.5% to 12.5% of β).

5. Horizontal rise times measured from 10% to 90% amplitudes shall be less than $0.3\ \mu S$.

6. Overshoot on horizontal blanking signal shall not exceed 0.02β at beginning of front porch and 0.05β at end of back porch.

7. Overshoot on sync signal shall not exceed 0.05β.

8. T_0 = start of vertical sync pulse.

9. T_1 = start of vertical blanking.

10. $T_1 = T_0 \, {}^{+\,0}_{-\,250}\ \mu S$.

11. A — vertical sync pulse = $150 \pm 50\ \mu S$ measured between 90% amplitude points.

12. Rise and fall times of vertical blanking and vertical sync pulse, measured from 10% to 90% amplitudes, shall be less than $5\ \mu S$.

13. Tilt on vertical sync pulse shall be less than 0.1α.

14. If horizontal information is provided during the vertical sync pulse it must be at 2H rate and as shown in the optional vertical blanking interval waveform.

15. B — vertical serration = $4.5 \pm .5\ \mu S$ measured between the 90% amplitude points. Rise times measured from 10% to 90% amplitudes shall be less than $0.3\ \mu S$.

16. If equalizing pulses are used in the vertical blanking interval waveform they shall be 6 in number preceding the vertical sync pulse and be at 2H rate.

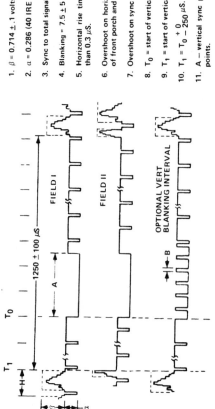

Figure A2-3. RS-330 waveforms, high-performance system. (Source: EIA)

any horizontal pulse "N" of any group of twenty horizontal pulses not differ from "NH" by more than 0.001H where "H" is the average interval between the leading edges of horizontal pulses, as determined by an averaging process carried out over a period of not less than 20 or more than 100 lines. It shall be standard that the frequency of horizontal and vertical scanning pulses not vary from the values established by the standards of frame frequency and number of scanning lines by more than $\pm$ 1% regardless of variations in frequency of the power source supplying the system.

EIA RS-343 STANDARD

(The following paragraphs are edited excerpts from EIA RS-343, which provides performance standards for high-resolution monochrome display systems.)

This standard is written to encompass equipment which operates in the range from 675 to 1023 scanning lines with a field rate of 60 Hz, interlaced 2:1. It is understood that special requirements may require different line numbers. It is recommended that one of the following be considered to satisfy particular requirements: 675, 729, 875, 945, or 1023 lines. The tolerance on any line number in this specification shall be $\pm$ 1%. (See Figure 8–8b, Chapter 8.)

Composite Display Signal

It shall be standard that the blanked display signal with setup (non-composite), as measured from blanking level to reference white level across the standard load impedance of the source, be 0.714 $\pm$ 0.1 volt (100 IRE units).

It shall be standard that the synchronizing signal as measured across the standard load impedance of the source be 0.286 $\pm$ 0.05 volts (nominally 40 IRE units).

It shall be standard that the setup be 7.5 $\pm$ 5 IRE units (2.5% to 12.5% of the blanked display signal).

Resolving Power

Resolution—A measure of the ability to delineate display detail.

Limiting Resolution—A measure of resolution usually expressed in terms of the maximum number of lines per picture height discriminated on a camera test chart. For a number of lines N (alternate black and white lines) the width of each line is 1/N times the picture height.

Resolution Response—The ratio of (1) the peak-to-peak signal amplitude, given by a test pattern consisting of alternate black and white bars of equal width corresponding to a specified line number to (2) the peak-to-peak signal amplitude given by large area blacks and large area whites having the same luminance as the black and white bars in the test pattern.

Line Number—In measuring resolution, the ratio of the frame height to the width of each bar of a test pattern composed of alternate equal-width black and white bars, as projected on the frame.

Aspect Ratio

Aspect ratio is defined as the ratio of the frame width to the frame height. "Frame" is defined as the total area which is scanned while the picture signal is not blanked. The standard aspect ratio of a frame shall be 4:3 or 1:1. No specific tolerances are assigned to this ratio but it is understood that the tolerance allowed for geometric distortion will provide adequate limits for permissible variation in the aspect ratio.

Sync Signal Tolerance

It shall be standard that the synchronizing signal waveform at the output of the source conform with Figure A2-4.

It shall be a minimum standard that the time of occurrence of the leading edge of any horizontal pulse "N" of any group of twenty horizontal pulses not differ from "NH" by more than 0.001H where "H" is the average interval between the leading edges of horizontal pulses as determined by an averaging process carried out over a period of not less than 4% or more than 20% of the total number of scan lines.

It shall be standard that the rate of change of the frequency of recurrence of the leading edges of the horizontal sync pulses appearing in the source output be not greater than 0.15% per second, the frequency to be determined by an averaging process carried out over a period of not less than 4% or more than 20% of the total number of scan lines, such lines not to include any portion of the vertical blanking signal.

It shall be standard that the frequency of horizontal and vertical scanning pulses not vary from the values established by the standards of frame frequency and number of scanning lines by more than ± 0.5%.

COLOR-ENCODING STANDARDS

The first monochrome-compatible standard for color-encoded display signals was adopted by the National Television System Committee

NOTES:

1. $\beta = 0.714 \pm 0.1$ volts (100 IRE Unit).

2. $\alpha = 0.286$ (40 IRE Units) nominal.

3. Sync to total signal ratio $\left(\dfrac{\alpha}{\beta + \alpha}\right) = 28.6 \pm 5\%$.

4. Blanking = 7.5 ± 5 IRE Units (2.5% to 12.5% of β).

5. Horizontal Rise Times measured from 10% to 90% amplitudes shall be less than $0.1\ \mu S$.

6. Overshoot on horizontal blanking signal shall not exceed $0.02\ \beta$ at beginning of front porch and $0.05\ \beta$ at end of back porch.

7. Overshoot on sync signal shall not exceed $0.05\ \beta$.

8. T_0 = start of vertical sync pulse.

9. T_1 = start of vertical blanking.

10. $T_1 = T_0\ {}^{+0}_{-250}\ \mu S$

11. A — vertical sync pulse = $125 \pm 50\ \mu S$ measured between 90% amplitude points.

12. Rise and fall times of vertical blanking and vertical sync pulse, measured from 10% to 90% amplitudes, shall be less than $5\ \mu S$.

13. Tilt on vertical sync pulse shall be less than 0.1α.

14. If horizontal information is provided during the vertical sync pulse it must be at 2H frequency and as shown in the optional vertical blanking interval waveform.

15. B — vertical serration = $2 \pm .5\ \mu S$ measured between the 90% amplitude points. Rise time measured from 10% to 90% amplitudes shall be less than $0.1\ \mu S$.

16. If equalizing pulses are used in the vertical blanking interval waveforms they shall be 6 in number preceding and following the vertical sync pulse, be at 2H frequency and half the width of H sync pulse.

17. It is recommended that for proper interlace the time duration between the leading edge of vertical sync and the leading edge of horizontal sync be a multiple of H/2.

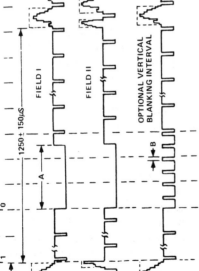
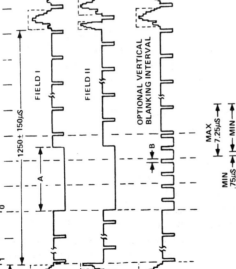

Figure A2–4. RS-343 waveforms, high-resolution systems. (Source: EIA)

(NTSC) in 1953 and applies to all government-regulated broadcast television systems in the United States and a number of other countries (see Chapter 8). Two other color-encoding standards were subsequently developed. The first of these was the SECAM (Systéme Electronique Couleur Avec Mémoire) system originated by Henri de France; the second was the PAL (Phase Alternation Line) system devised by Telefunken.

The basic principle underlying all three color-encoding standards is the merging of two separate image transmissions, a wideband signal carrying luminance information and a narrower-bandwidth chrominance signal. The latter is added to the luminance signal in the form of a modulated subcarrier.

The three primary-color signals are gamma-corrected, as signified by a "prime" notation (′). The luminance signal is then generated as the sum of three color-signal fractions, established by their relative contributions to the luminance of a standard "white" (see Appendix III). The chrominance component is obtained by first subtracting the luminance signal from the color signals to obtain color-difference values: red-minus-luminance, green-minus-luminance, and blue-minus-luminance. Because the luminance is also transmitted as a sum of color fractions, only two of these color-difference signals (or their derivatives) must be transmitted to provide a full definition of all three primary colors.

In the NTSC system, the color-difference signals are weighted, matrixed and filtered to produce a wideband orange-cyan I (in-phase) signal and a narrowband magenta-green Q (quadrature) signal. The two are then used to modulate two 3.58-MHz subcarrier signals which are 90° out of phase with each other. The modulated subcarriers are also -57° and -147° removed from the phase of a subcarrier reference burst which accompanies each horizontal sync pulse (Figure A2–1 and A2–5).

The I and Q bandwidths and representative colors take advantage of the fact that the human eye-brain system can perceive only a limited amount of color in small details and is also relatively limited in its ability to resolve magenta and green details compared to those with orange and cyan colors. The Q-signal bandwidth is therefore kept to 0.5MHz. The I-signal bandwidth is nearly three times as large (1.3MHz), but only the lower sideband components outside the double-sideband Q signal are retained.

When the two subcarrier signals are combined, the resulting phase is a direct analog of the hue, while the amplitude of the combined signal is an indirect measure of the saturation. Thus, a zero subcarrier

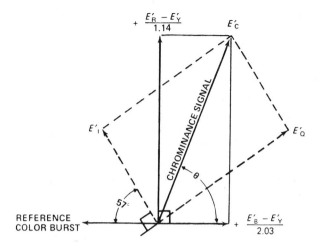

Figure A2-5. Chrominance phasor diagram, NTSC color-encoding standard.

amplitude corresponds to zero saturation, resulting in a monochrome black-and-white image controlled entirely by the magnitude of the luminance signal.

Figures A2-6, A2-7 and A2-8 summarize the frequencies, line rates, and other display-signal characteristics established by the NTSC stan-

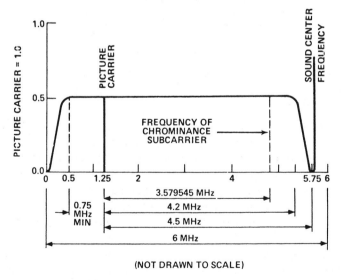

(NOT DRAWN TO SCALE)

Figure A2-6. Amplitude characteristic, NTSC color-encoding standard. Vertical scale is the relative maximum radiated field strength.

NTSC LUMINANCE-MODULATION STANDARDS

Method of luminance modulation	AM, vestigial sideband
Maximum modulating frequency	4.2 MHz
Attenuated sideband	Lower
Width of flat portion of attenuated sideband	0.75 MHz
Width of attenuation slope, fully transmitted sideband	0.3 MHz
Width of attenuation slope, attenuated sideband	0.5 MHz
Polarity of modulation	Negative
Maximum amplitude of modulation envelope	Peak of sync (100%)
Peak-white level	12.5% ± 2.5%
Black level*	74.375% (max), 66.25% (min)
Blanking level	75% ± 2.5%
Setup*	6.25% (max), 3.125% (min)
Peak-sync level	100%
Amplitude characteristic	See Figure A2-5
Transfer characteristic	**
Transfer gradient (gamma)	2.2
Luminance in terms of primary colors	$E_{Y'} = 0.30E_{R'} + 0.59E_{G'} + 0.11E_{B'}$

*The black level is stated indirectly in terms of the setup amplitude, which is standardized as 7.5 percent ± 2.5 percent of the video range from the blanking level to the reference-white level. The maximum and minimum values of black level and setup are the equivalent values in terms of 100% = maximum amplitude of modulation envelope (peak of sync). The maximum setup coincides with the minimum black level.

**The form of the transfer characteristic is not precisely specified. The standard states that the primary-color signals may be respectively of the form $E_R{}^{1/2.2}$, $E_G{}^{1/2.2}$, and $E_B{}^{1/2.2}$, although other forms may be used with advances in the state of the art.

Figure A2-7. Luminance-modulation specifications, NTSC color-encoding standard.

dard. All of these have been carefully selected to reduce the interference, for example, between the audio and video signals, and to facilitate the separation of the luminance and chrominance components. One result is a field rate that differs slightly from the 60-Hz standard for monochrome signals. The difference has been made purposely small, however, so that monochrome receivers and monitors can maintain synchronization even though a color-encoded signal is being received.

Equivalent considerations resulted in a chrominance subcarrier frequency of 4.43 MHz for the PAL and SECAM standards, both of which are designed for systems that operate at 625 lines per frame and 50 frames per second. Both are also designed to avoid the color distor-

NTSC CHROMINANCE-MODULATION STANDARDS

Chrominance-subcarrier frequency and tolerance	3.579545 + 0.000010 MHz
Maximum rate of change of subcarrier frequency	0.1 Hz per sec
Definition of luminance signal	$E_{Y'} = 0.30\ E_{R'} + 0.59\ E_{G'} + 0.11\ E_{B'}$
Definition of Q (quadrature) signal	$E_{Q'} = 0.41\ (E_{B'} - E_{Y'}) + 0.48\ (E_{R'} - E_{Y'})$
Definition of I (inphase) chrominance signal	$E_{I'} = -0.27\ (E_{B'} - E_{Y'}) + 0.74\ (E_{R'} - E_{Y'})$
Phase reference of chrominance signals to color-synchronizing signal	See Figure A2-6
Bandwidth of $E_{Q'}$	Less than 2 dB down at 400 kHz Less than 6 dB down at 500 kHz At least 6 dB down at 600 kHz
Bandwidth of $E_{I'}$	Less than 2 dB down at 1.3 MHz At least 20 dB down at 3.6 MHz
Subcarrier phase tolerance*	±10 electrical degrees
Subcarrier amplitude tolerance**	±20%
Tolerance in time of occurrence of corresponding items in $E_{Y'}$, $E_{Q'}$, and $E_{I'}$	0.05 μsec
Transfer gradient (gamma)	2.2
Transfer characteristic	***
Reference chromaticity of zero subcarrier****	Illuminant C(x=0.310, y=0.316)
Assumed monitor primaries	Red: x=0.67, y=0.33 Green: x=0.21, y=0.71 Blue: x=0.14, y=0.08
Assumed monitor color gamut	See Figure A3-9b
Line-scanning frequency in terms of chrominance subcarrier	3.579545 × 2/455 = 15,734.264 Hz
Field-scanning frequency in terms of chrominance subcarrier	3.579545 × 2/455 × 2/525 = 59.94 Hz
Definition of color picture signal	$E_M = E_{Y'} + E_{Q'}\ (\sin \omega t + 33°) + E_{I'}\ (\cos \omega t + 33°)$ where $\omega = 2\pi\ 3.579545$ radians/sec

*These tolerances apply to subcarrier when reproducing saturated primaries and their complements, at 75% of full amplitude. Closer tolerances may prove to be practicable with advance in the art.

**The ratios of subcarrier amplitudes to luminance amplitudes shall fall within 0.8 and 1.2% of the nominal values.

***The transfer characteristic is not stated specifically. However, one method, given as an example, involves gamma correction of the primary-color signals individually, each to a gradient of 1/2.2.

****The standards state that reproduction based on this reference chromaticity is assumed in the choice of other transmission standards. However, the white chosen for zero subcarrier at the transmitter is at the discretion of the operator.

Figure A2-8. Chrominance-modulation specifications, NTSC color-encoding standard.

tions which can occur during transmission with the NTSC system. In the case of SECAM, for example, only one color value, red or blue, is transmitted with the luminance signal at any instant. Alternate raster lines carry information on luminance and red. These are immediately followed by lines with information on luminance and blue. Two successive raster lines are required, therefore, to obtain the information required to generate a correct green signal (the total amount of color information is also reduced by half). This means that one of the lines must be stored in a memory device (e.g., a delay line) so that full color decoding can be accomplished.

In the PAL system both red and green subcarrier components are transmitted simultaneously, but phase (hue) distortions are minimized by reversing the red-information phase on successive lines. Any phase errors are therefore cancelled by an opposite-direction error on the next line. Again, however, as in the case of the SECAM standard, vertical color resolution is somewhat reduced.

Appendix III
Color Programming

Raster graphics colors are generated by altering the relative intensities of the three monitor "primaries"—typically red, green, and blue. Color programming is the process of calculating the three RGB values which will produce a selected color on the CRT screen when the data is read out of the graphics-system display memory or lookup table (Chapter 7).

Even trained artists find it difficult to anticipate the hue and saturation of a color mixture. There are "colors within colors" which can alter the outcome in unpredictable ways. Color programming must deal with this difficulty on an exaggerated scale. Except for the three single-primary RGB hues, every color on the monitor screen is a mixture of at least two other colors.

The sheer number of programmable colors can also be both a benefit and a burden. With just four bits per primary, up to 4,096 different hues and saturations can be programmed—making it impractical to identify, record, or communicate individual colors with such devices as color chips or by descriptive phrases such as "reddish yellow" or "sky blue." Yet numerical color-data specifications can also be of limited value. Monitor primaries vary depending on the monitor make or model. The same is certain to be true of other display or recording devices added to the system. And even in the case of a single-monitor system, the relative strengths of the primaries will change every time the unit is realigned to a warmer or cooler "white." There is no guarantee, therefore, that color data programmed for one system configuration will result in identical or even similar colors when processed by another system or at another time.

Fortunately, specifiers of color in a variety of other industries, such as textiles, floor coverings, and protective coatings, have faced similar problems for a number of decades. The result has been the development of a highly refined color-specification system which is completely independent of the specific primaries and alignment "white" of a display device. Moreover, the mathematics of the CIE (Commission Internationale de l'Eclairage) system are uniquely adaptable to raster graphics. Linear equations can be used to convert CIE color specifications directly to RGB color-data values. Similar equations permit the system designer, programmer, or operator to predict the exact colors that will be produced by color data stored in the display memory or loaded into a lookup table. Moreover, by using the CIE system as a universal standard, previously defined colors can be "color matched" on any other display or recording device by simply changing the constants in the two sets of transformation equations.

HIS VERSUS DLP

The following pages describe the CIE system and its application to raster graphics. First, however, it is necessary to define with more precision the differences between the subjective sensation of color and its objective measurement. In Chapter 2 it was noted that the psycho-physiological characteristics of a color are its hue (the "color" of the color), intensity (its "brightness"), and saturation (the degree to which it is "undiluted" by white). It was also mentioned that the measurable, psycho-physical counterparts of these HIS values are the DLP parameters called dominant wavelength, luminance, and purity.

Differences between the luminance of a color and its perceived intensity can be dramatic, depending as they do on the adaptation of the eye-brain system to changes in the surrounding luminance. Differences between the other two sets of terms are more subtle. Thus, the perceived hue of a color appears to shift slightly with changes in saturation, even though the dominant wavelength remains constant. The perceptions of hue and saturation also change with the luminance level; in fact, nearly all sense of color is lost when the luminance is very high or very low.

Attention to the distinction between the HIS and DLP terms has been consistently inconsistent throughout this Handbook. Luminance has always been used to define the luminous output of a display because the perceived intensity is so dependent on external factors. At the same time, "hue" and "saturation" have become so embedded in raster graphics terminology that technical license has been taken with their use—except toward the end of this section where equations are given for calculating the purity of a color as a function of its CIE dominant-wavelength vector. It should be understood, however, that whenever hue and saturation are given scalar values, it is dominant wavelength and purity which are being measured.

HIS VERSUS RGB

HIS values correspond to the intuitive way the human eye-brain system perceives and describes color. A light source or reflective surface has a color which can be named, a brightness which can be judged relative to its surroundings, and a "quality" which can be described by such terms as vivid, pastel, or tinted.

In human engineering terms, the ideal color-reproduction system would allow colors to be selected and manipulated on the basis of their HIS values. Television monitors and receivers are among the few devices which come close to this ideal. Encoded-color television signals have components (carrier amplitude, subcarrier amplitude, and subcarrier phase) which can be equated with display intensity, saturation, and hue. The HIS variables can also be adjusted by the television viewer to accommodate personal color preferences or to correct for transmission errors. Within the television display unit, however, the HIS characteristics are immediately "decoded" to the same three-primary system (e.g., RGB) which characterizes most color-reproduction hardware devices.

In principle, the colors generated by a raster graphics system could be programmed in either HIS or RGB terms. Both methods are supported, in fact, by the Core software standard described in Chapter 4. But in reality most hardware color-reproduction devices require a three-primary signal input. This means that even though the colors are system-defined in HIS values, an HIS-to-RGB transformation must take place before the values are output to the display or recording device. Typical transformation equations for this purpose are given in Figures A3–20a and A3–20b. Unless stated otherwise, however, the assumption will be that all color data is to be programmed in RGB values or their equivalent.

There is, of course, no intrinsic reason why color-reproduction hardware must be restricted to primary-color inputs. Why not, for example, drive an HIS television monitor with color-programmed HIS values? The answer is that the present broadcast-imposed television color-

encoding conventions severely limit the color-information bandwidth-
—on the order of 1 MHz compared to the 20–30 MHz for each of the
three signal inputs to a high-performance RGB monitor. A further
answer is that raster graphics color monitors designed for wideband,
three-signal HIS inputs will become available when and if the demand
warrants their commercial development.

RGB VERSUS CMY

Economic constraints generally limit the display memory of a raster
graphics system to the size needed to support the principal display
device—which we can assume is an RGB monitor with a particular set
of CIE-defined primaries aligned to a specific CIE-defined "white."
Color data programmed for this device must serve, therefore, as the information source for all other display and recording devices attached
to the system, including hardcopy equipment or non-emissive displays
which produce subtractive-color images based on the CMY primary-
complements: cyan, magenta, and yellow.

Two methods can be used to make the conversion from RGB to
CMY color-data values. (Exempted from this discussion are color-
transparency, color-negative, and instant-print systems which automatically make the conversion as part of the photographic process.)
The first is to take advantage of the fact that each CMY color is essentially a filter for its complementary primary. A yellow subtractive image, for example, is a "negative" of its blue color-data counterpart.
CMY values can be derived at the device interface, therefore, by simply
subtracting the RGB amplitudes from their full-scale values (e.g., if the
full scale of blue is unity, the yellow signal would equal 1.0 minus the
blue color-data values).

The major problem associated with this RGB-to-CMY conversion
method is that there is rarely an exact spectrographic match between
the primaries of the RGB display and the "minus-primary" complementary colors of the subtractive display or recording device. The
resulting color distortions may or may not be acceptable, depending on
the application.

The second conversion method eliminates the distortion but at the
cost of increased computational complexity at the device interface. The
CIE-to-RGB conversion equations given later in this section are derived from general-purpose transformation procedures which can also
be applied to the RGB-to-CMY conversion. Using the CIE system as

an intermediary, the chromaticities of the CMY "primaries" can be calculated in RGB terms and new constants developed for the color-transformation equations. The RGB-to-CMY equations can then be solved "on the fly" by microprocessor or analog circuits—taking into account the fact that negative data will result whenever the specified color is outside the "gamut" of the subtractive-color device.

Similar options apply when a single display memory programmed for primaries $R_1G_1B_1$ must serve as the data source for other devices with different primaries such as $R_2G_2B_2$. If color distortions are acceptable, the data can be used without change. Again, however, the device interface can include $R_1G_1B_1$-to-$R_2G_2B_2$ transformation circuits to obtain exactly the same colors as those displayed by the original monitor (within the limits established by the relative gamuts of the two devices).

GAMMA CORRECTION

All of these color transformations are based on Grassmann's Law which states that because luminance values are linear, the component luminances of any two multi-component colors can be simply added together algebraically (or subtracted) to obtain the component luminances of the resulting "mixed" color.

The transformation equations presuppose, however, that there is a linear relationship between the color data stored in the display memory and the luminances of the three primary colors displayed on the monitor screen. It is imperative, therefore, that provisions be made to correct for the "gamma" non-linearities introduced by the monitor CRT (Chapter 8). Figure A3-1 shows the effect of gamma on the data-to-luminance transfer function for each primary, using the standard value of 2.2 for the gamma power factor. For example, with all variables expressed as fractions of full scale, a color-data value of 0.400 will generate a primary-color luminance level of only 0.133. Increasing the color-data value by 50% to 0.600 has the effect of raising the luminance 144% to 0.325.

The most expedient ways to apply the $E^{1/2.2}$ gamma corrections to the three color-input signals are to specify a monitor with internal gamma-correction circuitry or to add external analog correction circuits to the monitor interface. The only other option would be to gamma-correct the color-data values for each primary before they are stored in the display memory, but this would tend to "compress" the program-

COLOR-DATA VALUE	PRIMARY SIGNAL*	DISPLAY LUMINANCE*
0000	.000	.000
0001	.067	.003
0010	.133	.012
0011	.200	.029
0100	.267	.055
0101	.333	.087
0110	.400	.133
0111	.467	.187
1000	.533	.250
1001	.600	.325
1010	.667	.410
1011	.733	.505
1100	.800	.612
1101	.867	.731
1110	.933	.858
1111	1.000	1.000

*Fractions of full scale, uncorrected gamma

Figure A3-1. Effect of monitor "gamma" non-linearity on display luminance as a function of 4-bit color-data values.

mable high-luminance color components and limit the number of low-luminance components.

COLOR TRIANGLES

The equilateral or "Maxwell" triangle serves as a convenient device for graphically representing three-primary color systems. Any three colors can act as primaries so long as no combination of two of the colors can be used to create the third. To abstract our discussion we will start with the colors D, E, and F.

Figure A3-2 lists the color parameters we can derive from Maxwell triangles with these three colors at the vertices. Figure A3-3a shows two such triangles. The area of each triangle represents the gamut of colors which can be produced by various combinations of the chosen primaries. The sizes of the two triangles represent the relative luminance levels of the colors which can be formed. The contributions of each primary to a sample color are "full scale" at the respective vertices and drop to zero at the opposite faces.

When a sample color is placed at point C in both triangles, the relative contributions of the three primaries are defined by the areas D, E, and F. However, since the triangles are equilateral, we can just as

Display Primaries	D, E, F
Chromaticity Values	D, E, F
Chromaticity Values of Color C	D_C, E_C, F_C
Total Chromaticity of C	$T_C = D_C + E_C + F_C$
Chromaticity Coefficients of C	$d_C = \dfrac{D_C}{T_C}$
	$e_C = \dfrac{E_C}{T_C}$
	$f_C = \dfrac{F_C}{T_C}$
	$\therefore d_C + e_C + f_C = 1$
Alignment "White"	W
Aligned Chromaticity Values	$D_W = 1$
	$E_W = 1$
	$F_W = 1$
	$\therefore D_W = E_W = F_W$

Figure A3-2. Terms and symbols for color triangle DEF aligned to a specified illuminant W.

easily apply these "chromaticity value" designations to the height vectors drawn perpendicularly from point C to each of the sides, as shown in Figure A3-3b. Because C is at the same location in both triangles, the relative values of D, E, and F are the same. In absolute terms, however, we can see that D_2, for example, represents a higher chromaticity value than D_1 because all of the contributing luminances depicted by the larger triangle are greater than those of the smaller triangle.

No matter where the color C is placed within the triangles, the sum of the chromaticity values will always equal a total value T—the height of each triangle—as illustrated in Figure A3-3c. T is therefore representative of both the total chromaticity value of the color C and its luminance (the sum of the luminance contributions made by each primary). Again, T_2 is larger than T_1 because of the higher luminance levels signified by the larger triangle. If, however, we divide the color C chromaticity values D, E, and F for each triangle by their respective T's, we arrive at chromaticity coefficients—d, e, and f—which are exactly the same for both triangles (Figure A3-3d). We have, in effect, eliminated luminance as a variable and concentrated our definition of the color C to just its "chromaticity." We have also gained the convenience of chromaticity measurements in which the three components always add up to unity ($d + e + f = 1$).

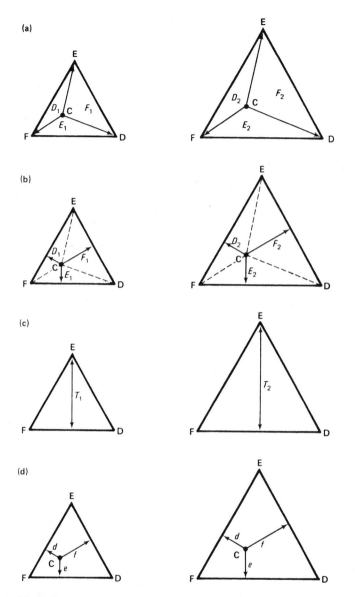

Figure A3–3. Color triangles representing two different full-scale DEF luminance levels.

Translating these terms to color programming, chromaticity values equate with the color data stored in the display memory or loaded into a lookup table. Total chromaticity equates with the sum of the color-data values for a given pixel. Chromaticity coefficients define the hue and saturation of a pixel, independent of its intensity.

ALIGNMENT TO "WHITE"

The equilateral-triangle convention implies that the luminances of the three primaries at the vertices are equal. We could, for example, give each full-scale primary an absolute luminance value, such as 20 nits. This would adversely affect, however, the point within the triangle where the three primaries combine to form "white." Equal luminances would place the white point close to one vertex and far from the other two.

The shape of the luminosity-function curve in Chapter 2 makes it clear that when a "balanced" white light is separated into its component colors, the luminance values of the various colors are far from equal. The same inequalities would apply when the colors are recombined to form white. Only small luminances of blue and red, for example, would be required to balance a high-luminance green. In effect, blue and red have much more "weight" than green; it takes more radiant power to "raise" them to a particular luminance level. (We will be encountering this concept of color "weight" again when we discuss the mixing of colors and the relative sensitivities of the eye-brain system to small color differences.)

To bring the color triangle into "alignment" so that important parameters such as saturation can be readily visualized and measured, a convention has been adopted to *start* with the white point at the centroid, as shown in Figure A3–4. The three chromaticity values D_w, E_w,

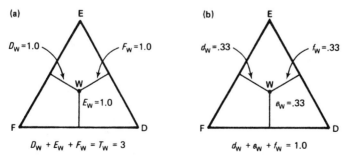

Figure A3–4. "Alignment" of color triangle DEF to illuminant W.

F_w are then given arbitrary values of 1.0 for a specified luminance level (size of triangle). Higher or lower white luminances—including dark grays—would have D_w, E_w, F_w values which vary widely from 1.0. But the values for the three primaries would, in every case, remain equal to each other. The same would be true, of course, for the chromaticity coefficients d_w, e_w, f_w which, independent of luminance, would remain constant at 0.33.

The numerical value used to convert a primary's white-point luminance to a chromaticity value of 1.0 is known as its "luminosity coefficient" and can serve as a conversion factor to determine the luminance corresponding to any other chromaticity value—for the specified primary. Each of the three primaries is, in effect, measured on a different chromaticity scale—uniquely defined for each combination of primaries and white point.

Exactly the same type of arbitrary scaling takes place when a three-primary color CRT monitor is aligned to a reference white. The monitor amplifier circuits are adjusted so that equal color-input signals (separate or encoded) will always display a white, gray, or black image. Less blue and red is required to produce the desired white, so again—as in the case of a white-aligned color triangle—full-scale blue and red monitor luminances will always be much lower than the full-scale green luminance.

CARTESIAN COLOR COORDINATES

It is the similarity between white-aligned color triangles and white-aligned CRT monitors which makes color-definition methods such as the CIE system so adaptable to raster graphics color programming. It would be an advantage, however, if the principles of the color triangle could be expressed in the more familiar form of rectangular Cartesian coordinates.

One way to achieve this objective would be to create a three-dimensional color space with right-angle Cartesian coordinates representing the chromaticity values of the three white-aligned primaries. The endpoint of a color vector drawn from the origin would establish the magnitude of the three chromaticity values, D, E, and F. Chromaticity coefficients could be graphically plotted by calculating the intersection of the color vector and the plane of an equilateral color triangle connecting equal points along the three coordinate axes. If the triangle is at the 1.0 points, as shown in Figure A3–5a, the three coefficients could also be measured directly along the coordinate axes. The value of e, for example, would increase from nearly zero when the

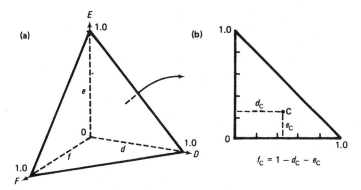

Figure A3-5. Projection of color-space triangle to a two dimensional, Cartesian-coordinate triangle.

color-vector intersection point is near the base of the triangle to approximately 1.0 when the point is close to the vertex located along the E-coordinate line.

Color-vector notations of this type provide the convenience of Cartesian coordinates but still require the processing of three coordinate values. Reduction to a two-dimensional, graph-paper representation takes one more step—a projection of the unit-value color triangle onto one of the planes formed by two coordinate axes. Figure A3-5b indicates a projection of this type onto the D-E plane. The resulting "chromaticity diagram" plots e_c (of color C) as a function of d_c. But both coefficients are also functions of a "third-dimension" requirement: all three chromaticity coefficients, including the missing f_c, must add up to 1.0.

THE CIE COLOR-DEFINITION SYSTEM

Chromaticity diagrams derived from conventional color triangles have three basic limitations, all of which are addressed by the CIE color-definition system:

- Individual diagrams are limited to a single set of primaries and alignment white. They must be reconstructed, therefore, every time the alignment or primaries are changed.
- Colors defined by the diagrams are restricted to those that lie within the color triangles. Few if any of the more vivid, saturated colors would normally be represented—for reasons given below.
- The diagrams indicate only the chromaticity coefficients. The

chromaticity (color data) values would be in the same proportion, but there is no indication of their magnitude. Thus, even if the luminosity coefficients used during the white alignment were known, there is no way to convert the chromaticity-diagram information into luminance values.

The CIE members, meeting in England in 1931, set as their goal the development of a universal two-dimensional chromaticity diagram on which any set of primaries would be plotted and aligned to any reference white. Further objectives were that all of the fully saturated spectral colors would be included on the diagram, and a way would be found to provide luminance information without complicating the two-dimensional simplicity of the chromaticity diagram.

The task of defining saturated colors is complicated by the nature of primaries and their complements. The complement of every primary color is, by definition, a combination of the other two primaries. Stated another way, all three primaries are half-complements of each other. Any additive mixture of primaries will always have, therefore, an unsaturated effect. Moreover, nearly all color-reproduction devices, including CRT monitors, start with primaries which are already partially unsaturated by other "hidden" colors. And even if pure laser beams are used, "cross-talk" between the color-sensing cones in the human eye reduces the perceived saturation of primary mixtures.

The classical colorimetric method for matching and defining highly saturated color samples has been to add one or more primary colors to the sample to desaturate it to within the bounds of the reference primaries. The primary values added to the sample are then treated as negative quantities, resulting in negative chromaticity coefficients that lie outside the conventional chromaticity diagram. Following this procedure and assuming that the D, E, and F primaries are generally red, green, and blue, the locus of fully saturated spectrum colors might be the dashed line shown in Figure A3–6a.

Starting with color-matching data accumulated by independent research groups, the CIE defined three hypothetical "supersaturated" primaries—red X, green Y, and blue Z—which would form a color triangle completely enclosing the spectrum locus and therefore all physically realizable colors (Figure A3–6b). Going a step further, the CIE group decided that the spectrum energy distribution of the Y primary should match the values of the photopic luminosity-function curve (which peaks in the green region). It was also decided that the X and Z primaries should lie on the alychne, the line of hypothetical colors formed when the subtractive color-matching process is carried to its theoretical, zero-luminance limit.

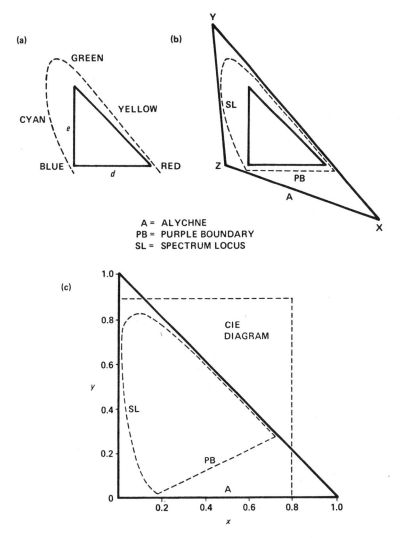

Figure A3–6. Conceptual stages in the development of the CIE chromaticity diagram. (Source: Reference 4)

The combined effect of these decisions was to give the Y chromaticity value a unique dual significance. It not only contributes to the total chromaticity of a color but also represents its luminance—measured in any real or arbitrary units. The only requirement is that the same units must then be used to scale the X and Z chromaticity values for the color and the equivalent values for all other colors being compared or mixed with the first color.

A final decision by the CIE was to align the hypothetical XYZ color triangle with a hypothetical equal-energy "white" (equal radiant energy at each wavelength across the visible spectrum). The data was then transformed to a standard chromaticity-diagram format, as shown in Figure A3-6c.

The CIE chromaticity diagram has now served as a universal color-specification device for a half century. Only two cautions should be expressed. The luminosity-function curve used to define the Y primary has been in use since 1924 and has been found to be slightly in error at the blue end of the spectrum. In addition, the original 1931 CIE diagram was based on observations with 2° visual fields. A revised diagram based on observations with 10° fields was adopted in 1964 and would theoretically be more appropriate for raster graphics applications. The changes are very minor, however, and we can expect that the 1931 diagram will continue to serve as the principal colorimetric standard for the foreseeable future.

COLOR "WEIGHTS"

Figure A3-7 shows the location of representative colors on the CIE diagram. The vividness of the colors ranges from zero saturation at the center to full saturation along the spectrum locus and the purple boundary joining the blue and red spectrum endpoints. The curved lines separating the color areas reflect the slight change in perceived hue which occurs with changes in saturation.

Most of the upper half of the diagram is occupied by a few greenish hues. The remainder is crowded with hues dominated by the "weightier" blue and red primaries. Figure A3-8, which is essentially a restatement of the lumens-per-watt spectrum curve presented in Chapter 2, again emphasizes the qualitative differences between the primaries. If we invert the data to watts per lumen, we can see that relatively low luminances of blue and red represent much higher radiance power levels compared to equal luminances of green. One lumen of green, for example, would be generated by pixels radiating 2 or 3 milliwatts of power. It would take 5 to 10 milliwatts to generate a lumen of red, 10 to 20 milliwatts for a lumen of blue.

The y chromaticity coefficients for the three primaries reflect these differences and also help the color programmer to avoid intuitive errors. It might be assumed, for example, that equal luminances of the red and green primaries would generate a mid-range yellow on the monitor screen. Yet experiment would indicate a strong shift toward orange.

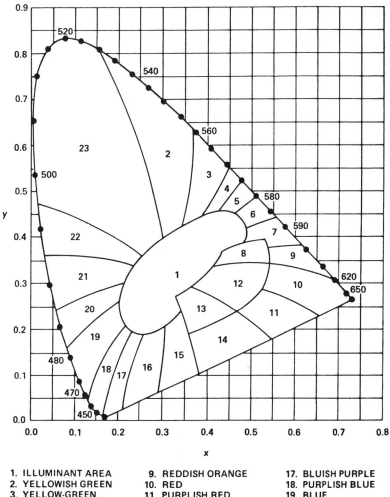

1. ILLUMINANT AREA
2. YELLOWISH GREEN
3. YELLOW-GREEN
4. GREENISH YELLOW
5. YELLOW
6. YELLOWISH ORANGE
7. ORANGE
8. ORANGE PINK

9. REDDISH ORANGE
10. RED
11. PURPLISH RED
12. PINK
13. PURPLISH PINK
14. RED PURPLE
15. REDDISH PURPLE
16. PURPLE

17. BLUISH PURPLE
18. PURPLISH BLUE
19. BLUE
20. GREENISH BLUE
21. BLUE-GREEN
22. BLUISH GREEN
23. GREEN

Figure A3-7. Perception of hues within the boundaries of "real" colors on the CIE chromaticity diagram. (Source: Reference 5)

The reason for this "red shift" can be deduced from the CIE coefficients. The green primary has a relatively high y coefficient, which means that its chromaticity value Y_G is a large fraction of its total chromaticity, T_G. The red primary has a much lower y, signifying that

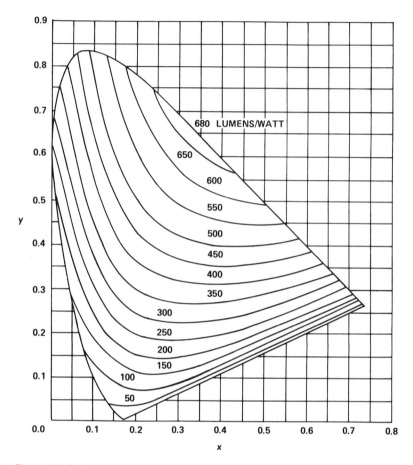

Figure A3-8. Luminous efficiency (lumens per watt of radiated power) plotted on CIE chromaticity diagram. (Source: Reference 6)

Y_R is a smaller fraction of T_R. We have stated, however, that luminances Y_G and Y_R are equal. T_R must therefore be much larger than T_G. In words, the luminances may be the same, but the *total* chromaticity of the red is significantly greater than that of the green. Returning to intuition, we can guess that the mixture would be weighted toward the higher-chromaticity red—which corresponds with the experimental results.

A general rule can be derived from this example: For colors of equal luminance, total chromaticities will always be inversely proportional to the respective y coefficients. Luminances will be proportional to the y coefficients only when the total chromaticities are equal. (The white alignment of a color monitor compensates for these different primary "weights." Thus equal red and green *color-data values* would indeed produce a mid-range yellow.)

CIE-RGB CONVERSION EQUATIONS

CIE color specifications normally take the form of CIE-diagram coefficients and a luminance value $(x, y. Y)$. If the luminance is not specified, Y can be given any arbitrary value such as 1 or 10.

Conversions between CIE specifications and color-programming data can be viewed as simple transformations from one three-dimensional system to another. A given color can be defined in terms of either the hypothetical XYZ primaries of the CIE system or the real RGB primaries of a color CRT monitor. Color triangles are used for both definitions—the CIE diagram for the XYZ primaries and a triangle drawn on the CIE diagram for the RGB primaries.

A basic rule of plane geometry is that coordinate transformations from one set of triangular coordinates to another can be accomplished with simple linear equations provided that four points have been defined in both coordinate systems. Three of these points would obviously be the vertices of the RGB triangle superimposed on the CIE diagram—plotted on the basis of the red-green-blue CIE specifications supplied by the color-CRT manufacturer. The fourth reference point would be the "white" used to align the monitor at the factory or in the field.

RGB primaries can vary over a wide range. Figure A3-9a lists the

		CIE Chromaticity Coefficients	
		x	y
CIE Spectrum Primaries	Red	0.735	0.265
	Green	0.274	0.717
	Blue	0.167	0.009
NTSC Standard Primaries	Red	0.670	0.330
	Green	0.210	0.710
	Blue	0.140	0.080
Graphics-Monitor Primaries	Red	0.628	0.346
	Green	0.268	0.588
	Blue	0.150	0.070

Note: CIE chromaticity coefficient $z = 1 - x - y$.

Figure A3-9a. CIE chromaticity coefficients for representative RGB primaries.

CIE coefficients for three distinctly different sets of primaries. The first consists of the three spectrum colors which were used to establish the specifications for the CIE diagram. The second set represents the NTSC standard primaries established in 1953. The third is a representative set of present-day monitor primaries. The color triangles formed by these primaries are shown graphically in Figure A3–9b. The smaller

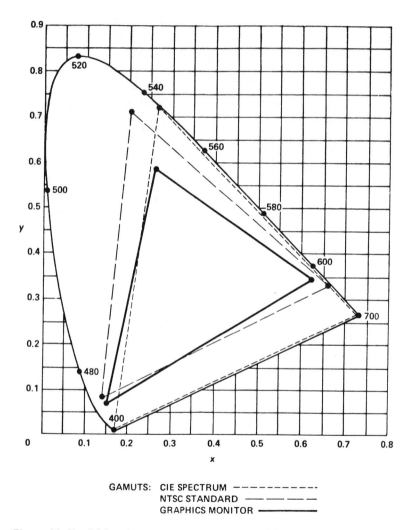

Figure A3–9b. RGB color triangles formed by plotting the primaries listed in Figure A3–9a.

gamut of the graphics monitor reflects a trade-off based on the availability of new phosphors with higher luminance and longer life.

Alignment whites can also vary over a broad range. CIE coefficients and chromaticity values for a variety of standard illuminants and color temperatures are listed in Figure A3–10a and plotted on the CIE diagram in Figure A3–10b. Illuminant A approximates the "warm" color of a gas-filled tungsten lamp. Illuminant B represents the color of sunlight at noon. Illuminant C is the color of an overcast sky at midday and is the alignment white dictated by the NTSC color-encoding standard. Most monitors are now factory-aligned to Illuminant D_{6500}, a somewhat greener white which represents "average daylight" with a color temperature of approximately 6500°K.

The dashed lines in Figure A3–10b indicate directions of color change which will be least discernable to the human eye and are used to "correlate" the color temperatures of sources which do not coincide

Standard "Whites"	CIE Chromaticity Coefficients		CIE Chromaticity Values		
	x_W	y_W	X_W	Y_W	Z_W
Equal-Energy White	0.333	0.333	1.000	1.000	1.000
Illuminant A	0.448	0.408	1.099	1.000	0.356
Illuminant B	0.349	0.352	0.991	1.000	0.853
Illuminant C	0.310	0.316	0.981	1.000	1.182
Illuminant D_{5500}	0.332	0.348	0.957	1.000	0.921
Illuminant D_{6500}	0.313	0.329	0.950	1.000	1.089
Illuminant D_{7500}	0.299	0.315	0.949	1.000	1.225
Color Temperatures °K					
3,000°	0.437	0.404	1.082	1.000	.394
4,000°	0.380	0.377	1.008	1.000	.645
5,000°	0.345	0.352	.980	1.000	.861
6,000°	0.322	0.332	.970	1.000	1.042
7,000°	0.306	0.317	.965	1.000	1.189
8,000°	0.295	0.305	.967	1.000	1.312
9,000°	0.287	0.296	.970	1.000	1.409
10,000°	0.281	0.288	.976	1.000	1.497
20,000°	0.257	0.258	.996	1.000	1.880
40,000°	0.247	0.245	1.008	1.000	2.074

Note: CIE chromaticity coefficient $z = 1 - x - y$.

Figure A3–10a. CIE chromaticity coefficients and chromaticity values for standard illuminants and a range of selected black-body temperatures.

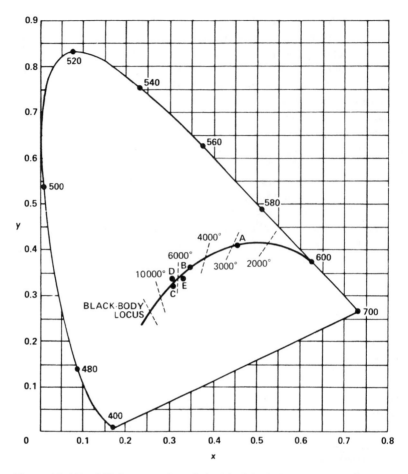

Figure A3–10b. CIE-diagram plot of the black-body locus, correlatèd-temperature lines, and illuminants A, B, C, D6500 (D) and equal-energy white (E).

with the black-body locus—a curved line that defines the color of a theoretical black body as it is heated from a temperature of approximately 1,000°K to infinity.

Figures A3–11, A3–12, and A3–13 give the procedures and equations for calculating the color-programming transformations, starting with specification-sheet values for the RGB primaries and a specified alignment white. Both transformations, CIE-to-RGB and RGB-to-CIE, require calculations in which each of the three primaries is defined in terms of the other system's three primaries. A total of nine conversion factors must be computed, therefore, for each of the two

Given: (1) CIE chromaticity coefficient specifications for RGB-monitor primaries.

Red Primary: x_R, y_R, z_R
Green Primary: x_G, y_G, z_G
Blue Primary: x_B, y_B, z_B

(2) CIE chromaticity values for a selected "white."

From Figure A3-10: X_W, Y_W, Z_W

CIE-to-RGB transformation determinant

$$k_D = x_R (y_G z_B - y_B z_G) + x_G (y_B z_R - y_R z_B) + x_B (y_R z_G - y_G z_R)$$

CIE-to-RGB transformation constants

$$k_1 = \frac{y_G z_B - y_B z_G}{k_D} \qquad k_2 = \frac{x_B z_G - x_G z_B}{k_D} \qquad k_3 = \frac{x_G y_B - x_B y_G}{k_D}$$

$$k_4 = \frac{y_B z_R - y_R z_B}{k_D} \qquad k_5 = \frac{x_R z_B - x_B z_R}{k_D} \qquad k_6 = \frac{x_B y_R - x_R y_B}{k_D}$$

$$k_7 = \frac{y_R z_G - y_G z_R}{k_D} \qquad k_8 = \frac{x_G z_R - x_R z_G}{k_D} \qquad k_9 = \frac{x_R y_G - x_G y_R}{k_D}$$

Equations for calculating the total CIE chromaticities of RGB primaries aligned to W

$$T_R = k_1 X_W + k_2 Y_W + k_3 Z_W$$
$$T_G = k_4 X_W + k_5 Y_W + k_6 Z_W$$
$$T_B = k_7 X_W + k_8 Y_W + k_9 Z_W$$

Example:
The following total CIE chromaticities would apply to the graphics-monitor RGB primaries described in Figure A3-9 when aligned to Illuminant D_{6500}:

$$T_R = 0.759$$
$$T_G = 1.115$$
$$T_B = 1.166$$

The aligned RGB primaries would make the following fractional contributions to the luminosity of W at any gray-scale level:

$$Y_R = y_R T_R = (0.346)(0.759) = 0.26$$
$$Y_G = y_G T_G = (0.588)(1.115) = 0.66$$
$$Y_B = y_B T_B = (0.070)(1.166) = \underline{0.08}$$
$$1.00$$

Figure A3-11. Procedures and equations for calculating the conversion factors for a monitor with specified RGB primaries and alignment "white." (Source: Reference 4)

Given: A color C with CIE specification (x_C, y_C, Y_C).

Equations for calculating a full set of CIE chromaticity values for C

$$X_C = \left(\frac{x_C}{y_C}\right)Y_C \qquad Y_C = Y_C \qquad Z_C = \left(\frac{1 - x_C - y_C}{y_C}\right)Y_C$$

Equations for converting CIE chromaticity values to RGB color-data values, using monitor conversion factors defined in Figure A3-11

$$R_C = \left(\frac{k_1}{T_R}\right)X_C + \left(\frac{k_2}{T_R}\right)Y_C + \left(\frac{k_3}{T_R}\right)Z_C$$

$$G_C = \left(\frac{k_4}{T_G}\right)X_C + \left(\frac{k_5}{T_G}\right)Y_C + \left(\frac{k_6}{T_G}\right)Z_C$$

$$B_C = \left(\frac{k_7}{T_B}\right)X_C + \left(\frac{k_8}{T_B}\right)Y_C + \left(\frac{k_9}{T_B}\right)Z_C$$

Example:

The following CIE-to-RGB conversion factors would apply to the monitor described in Figure A3-11:

$$R_C = (2.750)X_C + (-1.149)Y_C + (-0.426)Z_C$$

$$G_C = (-1.118)X_C + (2.026)Y_C + (0.033)Z_C$$

$$B_C = (0.138)X_C + (-0.333)Y_C + (1.104)Z_C$$

For example, given an "orange" color with CIE specification (0.5, 0.4, 10.0), the following may be calculated:

CIE Chromaticity Values	Color-Data Values
$X_C = 12.50$	$R_C = 21.82$
$Y_C = 10.00$	$G_C = 6.36$
$Z_C = 2.50$	$B_C = 1.16$

Note: Calculations assume a linear (gamma-corrected) data-to-luminance transfer function. If Y_C is not specified, use any convenient scalar value, such as 1.0 or 10.0. If color-data values correspond to display-signal amplitudes which exceed the monitor-input maximum, reduce color-data values in proportion so that all signals are equal to or less than specified maximum.

Figure A3–12. Procedure for converting a CIE color specification to RGB color-data values.

transformation procedures. Once these have been determined, however, they remain constant for the lifetime of the system and can be applied to any color generated by the monitor.

GRAY-SCALE LUMINANCES

One of the intermediate steps in the calculation of the transformation factors is the determination of the total chromaticity values of the RGB primaries when they are aligned to a selected white. The example in Figure A3-11 has been extended to indicate how these three values can

Given: A color C defined by color-data values R_C, G_C, B_C.

Equations for converting RGB color-data values to CIE chromaticity values, using monitor conversion factors defined in Figure A3-11

$$X_C = (x_R T_R)R_C + (x_G T_G)G_C + (x_B T_B)B_C$$

$$Y_C = (y_R T_R)R_C + (y_G T_G)G_C + (y_B T_B)B_C$$

$$Z_C = (z_R T_R)R_C + (z_G T_G)G_C + (z_B T_B)B_C$$

Equations for converting CIE chromaticity values to CIE coefficients

$$X_C + Y_C + Z_C = T_C$$

$$x_C = \frac{X_C}{T_C}$$

$$y_C = \frac{Y_C}{T_C}$$

$$z_C = \frac{Z_C}{T_C}$$

Example:
The following RGB-to-CIE conversion factors would apply to the monitor described in Figure A3-11:

$$X_C = (0.476)R_C + (0.299)G_C + (0.175)B_C$$

$$Y_C = (0.262)R_C + (0.656)G_C + (0.082)B_C$$

$$Z_C = (0.020)R_C + (0.161)G_C + (0.909)B_C$$

For example, given RGB color-data values of R_C = 0.5, G_C = 12.0, B_C = 18.0, the following may be calculated:

CIE Chromaticity Values	CIE Chromaticity Coefficients
X_C = 6.98	x_C = 0.20
Y_C = 9.48	y_C = 0.27
Z_C = 18.30	z_C = 0.53

The conventional CIE specification (x, y, Y) for this "greenish-blue" color would be (0.20, 0.27, 9.48).

Note: Calculations assume a linear (gamma-corrected) data-to-luminance transfer function.

Figure A3–13. Procedure for converting RGB color-data values to a CIE color specification.

then be used to determine the relative luminance contributions of the three primaries when they are combined to form any gray-scale value—from black to full-scale white.

The luminance contributions are directly proportional to the luminosity coefficients established by the alignment procedure. They can be used, therefore, to calculate the luminances of the primaries when other colors are formed (provided the absolute luminance of the alignment white is also known).

A more important application would be to establish the magnitude of the color fractions which should be combined in a summing circuit to produce a "natural looking" monochrome display signal (Chapter 8, Figure 8-13). The NTSC color-encoding standard—based on the original NTSC primaries and alignment to Illuminant C—sets the percentages at 30% red, 59% green, and 11% blue. The Figure A3-11 example indicates that the corresponding values for a present-day monitor aligned to Illuminate D_{6500} would be 26%, 66% and 8%.

GRAPHICAL CIE-RGB CONVERSIONS

It is also possible to "read" color-data values directly off the CIE diagram, or to "plot" color-data values directly on the diagram, using graphical procedures. The precision of the conversions is considerably lower, but would be adequate for many applications.

The monitor primaries and alignment white are marked on a tissue overlay (Figure A3-14). The resulting RGB triangle will rarely be equilateral and W will almost never be at the centroid. Perpendicular measurements can not be used, therefore, to determine the contributions made by each primary—as in the case of the Maxwell triangles shown in Figure A3-3. Instead, separate scales must be established for each of the three color-data coefficients, r, g, and b ($R + G + B$ divided by R, G, and B).

Figure A3-14a shows how the alignment-white point can be used to determine b (blue-fraction) proportions along the blue-red border. A line extending from G through W represents colors in which the blue-red content is 50% blue, 50% red. Line G-B and its extension represent colors in which the blue-red content is 100% blue, 0% red. (Depending on the shape of the triangle, the extensions of the G-W and G-B lines outside of the triangle may or may not be necessary.)

The next step is to rotate a line originating at R until it intersects the extension of line G-W at a distance that is exactly half the distance from R to the intersection with the extension of G-B. (A zero-center ruler used by commercial artists is a convenient tool for establishing this vector.) The total distance is then divided into ten equal parts and lines drawn from G to the one-tenth intervals. The resulting intersection points along R-B represent corresponding b-coefficient values for colors formed by combining the red and blue primaries.

Equivalent b-coefficient points for green-blue colors are established along line G-B by repeating the above procedure, starting with a line extending from R through W. The b-coefficient divisions along R-B and G-B are then connected (Figure A3-14b) to establish lines of con-

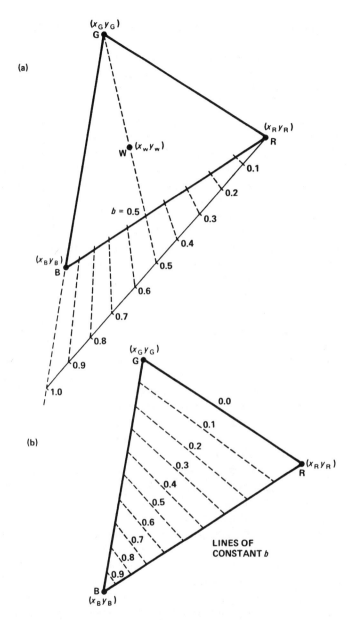

Figure A3-14. Graphical procedure (see text) for directly converting CIE color specifications to RGB color-data values. (Source: Reference 4)

stant *b* ranging from 1.0 at the blue vertex to 0.0 along the opposite side of the triangle.

Exactly the same steps are used to plot lines of constant *g* and *r,* either on the same tissue or with separate tissues superimposed on each other *and* on the CIE diagram.

Conversions from RGB to CIE chromaticity coefficients would be accomplished by adding a color's data values together to obtain a total color-data value. Each color-data value is then divided by the total to obtain a set of color-data coefficients, *r, g, b.* The color is located by interpolating between the lines of constant *r, g,* and *b* on the overlay tissues, and the *x, y* chromaticity coefficients read directly off of the CIE diagram below the tissues.

The conversion from a CIE specification to color-data values is a reverse of this process. A color would be located according to its *x, y* coordinates and the *r, g, b* coefficients read off the tissues. Color-data values can then be calculated by multiplying each coefficient by the total color-data value $(R + G + B)$ which represents the desired luminance of the displayed color.

COLOR COMBINATIONS

As noted earlier, every color generated by a CRT monitor (except for the three primary hues) is a mixture of at least two other colors. There may also be occasions when it is necessary to calculate the result of "mixing" two non-primary colors, as when two separate color images are to be merged on the monitor screen.

The CIE diagram can serve as a convenient vehicle for determining the resultant hue and saturation. Color-data values are converted to CIE terms, the colors are "mixed" either algebraically (Figure A3-15) or graphically (Figure A3-16), and the resulting color mixture, C_M, converted back to color-data values.

Figure A3-16 reinforces the concept that colors have a "weight" determined by both their absolute luminances and their relative *y*-coefficient values. The graphical procedure is identical to that used for determining the center of gravity of a physical system in which two weights are acting at a distance from each other. Notice that the perpendicular line drawn at C_1 is proportional to the total chromaticity of color C_2, while the corresponding line at C_2 is proportional to the total chromaticity of C_1. The distances along the line of color mixtures are, in fact, inversely proportional to the two total-chromaticity values. In colors, as with weights, the shift is always toward the "heavier" component.

Given: Two colors, C_1 and C_2, with CIE specifications (x_{C1}, y_{C1}, Y_{C1}) and (x_{C2}, y_{C2}, Y_{C2}).

Equations for calculating the chromaticity "weights" of C_1 and C_2

$$T_{C1} = \frac{Y_{C1}}{y_{C1}}$$

$$T_{C2} = \frac{Y_{C2}}{y_{C2}}$$

Equations for calculating the CIE specification of color mixture C_M

$$x_M = \frac{x_{C1}T_{C1} + x_{C2}T_{C2}}{T_{C1} + T_{C2}}$$

$$y_M = \frac{y_{C1}T_{C1} + y_{C2}T_{C2}}{T_{C1} + T_{C2}}$$

$$Y_M = y_M(T_{C1} + T_{C2}) = Y_{C1} + Y_{C2}$$

Example:

The following calculations can be used to specify the new color that would result from mixing the two colors defined in Figures A3-12 (0.50, 0.40, 10.00) and A3-13 (0.20, 0.27, 9.48). The "weight" of the first color is (10.0/0.40) = 25.00. The "weight" of the second color is (9.48/0.27) = 35.11.

$$x_M = \frac{(0.50)(25.00) + (0.20)(35.11)}{25.00 + 35.11} = 0.325$$

$$y_M = \frac{(0.40)(25.00) + (0.27)(35.11)}{25.00 + 35.11} = 0.324$$

$$Y_M = (0.324)(25.00 + 35.11) = 19.48$$

The resulting color (0.325, 0.324, 19.48) is a high-luminance "white" produced by combining two nearly complimentary colors.

Figure A3-15. Procedure for calculating the CIE color specification representing a mixture of two CIE-specified colors.

DOMINANT WAVELENGTH

The CIE diagram is based on psycho-physical data—as evidenced by the curved "hue" lines in Figure A3-7 and the straight "dominant-wavelength" lines in Figure A3-17.

The dominant wavelength of a color C is determined by extending a line from W (the alignment "white") through C until it intersects either the spectrum locus or the purple boundary at a point designated as S. If the intersection is with the spectrum locus, the dominant wavelength can be read directly off the CIE diagram, using the wavelength values shown along the locus. In Figure A3-17, for example, C has a dominant wavelength of 540 nanometers.

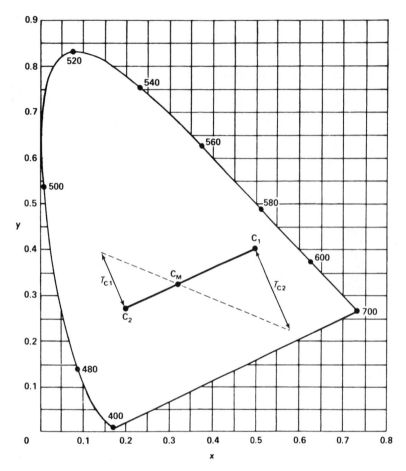

Figure A3-16. Graphical procedure for determining the CIE-diagram location of a mixed color.

If the intersection point is along the purple boundary, as in the case of S_2 in Figure A3-17, the dominant-wavelength vector is extended in the opposite direction until it intersects the spectrum locus. Again, the intersection point establishes a wavelength value, but with a lower-case "c" to indicate that the color is a "complement" of the indicated spectrum color. Colors along the line from W to S_2, for example, would have a complementary dominant wavelength of 560c.

COLOR PURITY

Purity—the psycho-physical equivalent of saturation—can be generally defined as the degree to which a color is "undiluted" by white.

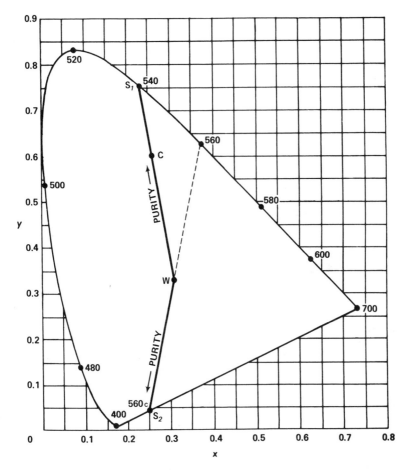

Figure A3–17. Graphical representation of dominant wavelength and excitation purity.

Purity is measured on the CIE diagram as a function of linear distances along a color's dominant-wavelength vector. If the color is at the intersection point with the spectrum locus or purple boundary, it has a purity of 1.0 or 100%. If the color is at W (the alignment "white"), it has a purity of 0.0 or 0%. The purity of any intermediate color C is calculated by dividing the distance W-C by the total length of the dominant-wavelength vector, W-S.

Purity can also be calculated as a function of three sets of chromaticity coefficients. Figure A3–18 provides the *x-y* coordinates for the spectrum colors at 10-nanometer intervals; purple-boundary coordinates lie along a straight line between the spectrum endpoints.

nm	x	y	nm	x	y
410	0.173	0.005	560	0.373	0.625
420	0.171	0.005	570	0.444	0.555
430	0.169	0.007	580	0.513	0.487
440	0.164	0.011	590	0.575	0.424
450	0.157	0.018	600	0.627	0.373
460	0.144	0.030	610	0.666	0.334
470	0.124	0.058	620	0.691	0.308
480	0.091	0.133	630	0.708	0.292
490	0.045	0.295	640	0.719	0.281
500	0.008	0.538	650	0.726	0.274
510	0.014	0.750	660	0.730	0.270
520	0.074	0.834	670	0.732	0.268
530	0.155	0.806	680	0.733	0.267
540	0.230	0.754	690	0.734	0.266
550	0.302	0.692	700	0.735	0.265

Figure A3-18. CIE chromaticity coefficients for the spectrum colors.

Given: (1) A monitor with RGB primaries aligned to a "white" with CIE chromaticity coefficients x_W, y_W, z_W (Figure A3-10).

(2) A color C with CIE chromaticity coefficients x_C, y_C, z_C, and a dominant-wavelength vector which intersects the spectrum locus or purple boundary at x_S, y_S, z_S.

Equations for calculating the excitation purity of C

$$P = \frac{x_C - x_W}{x_S - x_W} \quad \text{or} \quad P = \frac{y_C - y_W}{y_S - y_W}$$

Example:
The "white" chromaticity coefficients for a monitor aligned to D_{6500} are $x_W = 0.313$, $y_W = 0.329$. A color with coefficients of $x_C = 0.260$, $y_C = 0.600$, has a dominant wavelength of 540 nanometers. The spectrum locus at 540 nanometers has coefficients of $x_S = 0.230$, $y_S = 0.754$.

$$P = \frac{(0.260) - (0.313)}{(0.230) - (0.313)} = \frac{0.053}{0.083} = 0.639$$

or

$$P = \frac{(0.600) - (0.329)}{(0.754) - (0.329)} = \frac{0.271}{0.425} = 0.638$$

Of the two optional calculations, the second would be more accurate in this case. If the dominant-wavelength vector is generally horizontal, the first equation should be used.

Figure A3-19. Equations for calculating the excitation purity of a color with a specified dominant wavelength.

Figure A3-10 lists the coordinates for a variety of alignment whites. Assuming that the CIE coefficients of a sample color are also known, the purity of the color can be precisely calculated by using the equations given in Figure A3-19.

The CIE-diagram purity value is identified as "excitation purity" to differentiate it from "colorimetric purity"—a luminance ratio calculated by dividing the colorimeter reading for the spectrum component of a sample color by the reading obtained when "white" has been added to match the sample color. A variety of other definitions and measurement methods for purity or saturation may be encountered (see below). In every case, however, the values tend to increase as colors become more "vivid" and decrease as the shades become pastel or tinted.

HIS-RGB TRANSFORMATIONS

In principle, the CIE diagram could serve as the basis for HIS (hue, intensity, saturation) color programming. A table of spectrum-locus and purple-boundary coefficients could be stored, for example, in computer memory. Color-programmed purities and dominant wavelengths could then be transformed to x-y coordinate values or directly to RGB color-data values for driving a color monitor.

Current practice, however, has been to construct a three-dimensional "color model" for HIS-designated colors. Figures A3-20a and A3-20b list the transformation equations for a typical double-cone color model (Figure A3-20c). Hue is the angular position around the circumferences of the cones with full-scale values of either 1.0 or 360°. It is common, in such cases, to place the primary colors and their complements at angular positions which approximate those of the NTSC vector diagram (Appendix II). Blue serves as the "origin" with an angular value of 0°. Magenta is at 60°, red at 120°, yellow at 180°, green at 240°, and cyan at 300°. The complement of a color is its angular value plus 180°.

No effort is made to compensate for the fact that full-scale (1.0) color-data values for the three primary hues generate significantly different display luminances. Instead, the arbitrary placement of the hues around the circumference is matched by equally arbitrary definitions and calculations for the intensity and saturation characteristics of a color. To simplify the mathematics, both are calculated on the basis of only two of the three color-data values—the largest and smallest.

In reality, of course, all three primary color-data values are needed. The intensity of a mixed-primary color corresponds to the sum of three

Given: R, G, B, each in the range of 0 to 1.0

Set-up equations

M = largest value, R, G, or B
m = least value, R, G, or B

$$r = \frac{M-R}{M-m}$$

$$g = \frac{M-G}{M-m}$$

$$b = \frac{M-B}{M-m}$$

Note: At least one of the r, g, or b values is 0, corresponding to the color with the largest value, and at least one of the r, g, or b values is 1, corresponding to the color with the least value.

Equation for calculating intensity in the range of 0 to 1.0

$$I = \frac{M+m}{2}$$

Equations for calculating saturation in the range of 0 to 1.0

If M = m, S = 0

If I ≤ 0.5, $S = \frac{M-m}{M+m}$

If I > 0.5, $S = \frac{M-m}{2-M-m}$

Equations for calculating hue in the range of 0 to 360
If M = m, H = 0
If R = M, H = 60 (2 + b − g)
If G = M, H = 60 (4 + r − b)
If B = M, H = 60 (6 + g − r)

Figure A3–20a. Equations for converting RGB to HIS color-data values. (Source: Reference 3)

primary-color luminances. Hue is established by the ratio between the two largest primary-color values. The effect of the lowest-magnitude primary is to "dilute" the color—lowering the saturation—by combining with the other two primaries to form white.

Yet the simplified color model does correspond in a general way to the way colors are perceived. Intensity is calculated as the average of the largest and smallest primary values. Saturation is essentially the ratio between the difference and sum of the two values—with the dif-

Given: H in the range of 0 to 360; I and S in the range of 0 to 1.0

Set-up equations

If I $\leq$ 0.5, M = I (1 + S)

If I $>$ 0.5, M = I + S $-$ I(S)

m = 2I $-$ M

Equations for calculating R in the range of 0 to 1.0

If H $<$ 60, R = m + (M$-$m) $\left(\frac{H}{60}\right)$

If H $<$ 180, R = M

If H $<$ 240, R = m + (M$-$m) $\left(\frac{240-H}{60}\right)$

If H $<$ 360, R = m

Equations for calculating G in the range of 0 to 1.0

If H $<$ 120, G = m

If H $<$ 180, G = m + (M$-$m) $\left(\frac{H-120}{60}\right)$

If H $<$ 300, G = M

If H $<$ 360, G = m + (M$-$m) $\left(\frac{360-H}{60}\right)$

Equations for calculating B in the range of 0 to 1.0

If H $<$ 60, B = M

If H $<$ 120, B = m + (M$-$m) $\left(\frac{120-H}{60}\right)$

If H $<$ 240, B = m

If H $<$ 300, B = m + (M$-$m) $\left(\frac{H-240}{60}\right)$

Figure A3-20b. Equations for converting HIS to RGB color-data values. (Source: Reference 3)

ference corresponding to "color content" while the sum corresponds to "color plus white."

The third primary value, which can be at any level between the two extremes, will affect the actual intensity and saturation in a compensating manner. As the third primary increases in magnitude it increases the "brightness" and simultaneously decreases the "whiteness" of the color. The eye-brain system tends to interpret these two effects as opposites, resulting in a constant "lightness" across horizontal planes in the color model.

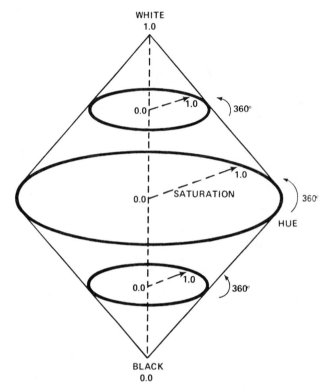

Figure A3–20c. Double-cone color model for HIS-RGB transformation equations listed in Figures A3–20a and A3–20b.

The entire outer surface of the model represents fully saturated colors, as defined by the transformation equations. The surface of the lower cone, for example, consists of m = 0 colors with values of M increasing from 0 to 1. The vividness of the colors reaches a maximum at M = 1, the interface between the two cones. The surface of the upper cone consists of M = 1 colors with values of m increasing from 0 to 1. Vividness decreases until only a desaturated white remains at M = m = 1.

UNIFORM CHROMATICITY SCALES

Color models such as the one shown in Figure A3–20c are highly specific. Colors can be defined with high precision, but only in the context of a given set of primaries and a particular alignment white. There is no convenient way to transform the values to another model or to CIE-diagram values.

This disadvantage is often counterbalanced, however, by the linear relationships which exist between color-model values and the way colors are preceived by the eye-brain system. Such linearities are severely lacking in the CIE diagram, as evidenced by the perceptible-difference ellipses shown in Figure A3–21. Relatively small coordinate-value shifts in hue and saturation (the two axes) can be perceived in the "heavier" blue and red regions of the diagram compared to equivalent

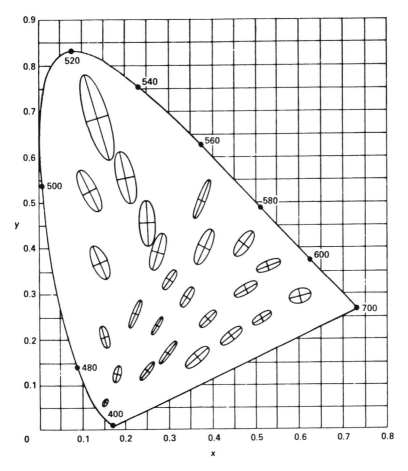

Figure A3-21. Perceptibility of color differences at various hues and saturations. (Source: Reference 7)

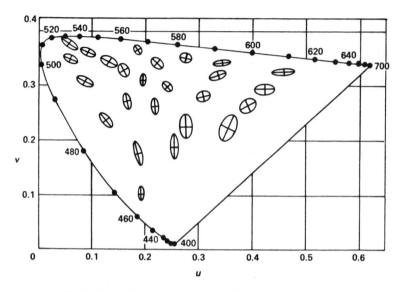

Figure A3–22. Uniform-chromaticity-scale (UCS) diagram, 1960 CIE-UCS transformation equations. (Source: Reference 7)

changes in the green areas. (The ellipse dimensions have been multiplied by a factor of ten to facilitate the comparisons.)

A variety of diagram modifications have been devised to correct for this deficiency. The most widely used is the 1960 UCS (uniform chromaticity scale) diagram shown in Figure A3–22. The effect of the CIE-to-UCS transformation is to "shrink" the green region of the CIE diagram so that changes in the u-v coordinates of the UCS diagram will be more uniformly perceived. Equations for the transformation are as follows:

$$u = \frac{4x}{-2x + 12y + 3} \qquad v = \frac{6y}{-2x + 12y + 3}$$

The 1960 CIE-UCS diagram reduces the differences in the perceptible-difference ellipses, but preserves their elongated shape. Color theorists are therefore shifting to a 1976 CIE-UCS diagram in which the ellipses have a more circular form. The following equations apply to the 1976 version (note the prime marks to distinguish between the two diagrams):

$$u' = \frac{2x}{-x + 6y + 1.5} \qquad v' = \frac{4.5y}{-x + 6y + 1.5}$$

A number of monitor manufacturers are now listing both x-y and u-v coordinate values for the RGB primaries as an aid to system designers and users. All of the principles outlined for CIE-diagram color programming can be extended to include colors defined by UCS coordinates. The only added computations are those represented by the CIE-UCS transformation equations.

Index